BRUCE SCHOENFELD

SIMON & SCHUSTER
NEW YORK LONDON TORONTO SYDNEY TOKYO SINGAPORE

THE LAST SERIOUS THING

A SEASON
AT THE
BULLFIGHTS

SIMON & SCHUSTER
Simon & Schuster Building
Rockefeller Center
1230 Avenue of the Americas
New York, New York 10020

1   3   5   7   9   10   8   6   4   2

Library of Congress Cataloging-in-Publication data
Schoenfeld, Bruce.
The last serious thing : a season at the bullfights / Bruce Schoenfeld
p.   cm.
1.Bullfights—Spain   I.Title.
GV1108.5.S36   1992
791.8'2'0946—dc20
91-40204
CIP

ISBN: 0-671-72748-6

In Memory, N.P.S.

ACKNOWLEDGMENTS

This book would not be a reality, at least in its finished form, without the help and support I received from John Fulton, David Shipley, Michael Bass and Scott Price. Special thanks also to Irene López-Melendo Lannes, Manolo Valverde Ferrer and Ofelia Romero, to Rosa and José Marí at Ibs, to Marie Arana-Ward, Beatrice Chipouras, Joe Distler, Rollene Saal and Jeffrey Zucker, to Ernest Hemingway and James Michener for helping to initiate me into the magical world of the corrida, and to Juan Antonio Ruiz Román for explaining everything, without words.

CONTENTS

ACKNOWLEDGMENTS 6

PART I: THE CITY OF THE BULLS 11
1: A PASSIONATE WELCOME 13
2: THE CEMETERY 18
3: WHAT THE PAPERS SAY 25
4: THE TICKET LINE 34
5: TESTING BULLS 41
6: FIRST OF THE SEASON 50
7: MEETING ESPARTACO 57

PART II: THE FERIA 67
1: CREATING A RIVALRY 69
2: A WEEK OF DISCUSSION 80
3: THE AFICIONADO'S DILEMMA 90
4: THE LATEST HERO 98
5: THE *EXTRANJEROS* 108
6: THE GYPSY WAY 118
7: DEFENDING THE FAITH 127
8: THE TRIUMPH OF ESPARTACO 136
9: WAITING FOR THE MIRACLE 143
10: THE END OF SOMETHING 152
11: THE MORNING AFTER 163

PART III: THIS DANGEROUS SUMMER 167
1: OF ART AND LIFE 169
2: NEWS OF A GORING 179

3: FOLLOWING THE CONTENDERS 189

4: FEARS FOR FULTON 197

5: THIRTY YEARS OF FRUSTRATION 206

6: TO CÓRDOBA AND MADRID 215

7: THE BLOOMING OF THE RIVALRY 222

8: TRANSCENDENCE 232

THE ONLY SERIOUS THING THAT REMAINS IN THE WORLD
IS BULLFIGHTING.

—Federico García Lorca
February 20, 1930

PART ONE

THE CITY

OF THE

BULLS

1

A PASSIONATE
WELCOME

THERE'S an old man with no teeth
in the back seat of the station wagon and he's speaking Spanish with
such a harsh and peculiar accent that I can't understand a word. His
creaky sentences sound almost extraterrestrial. With each burst of sound
I have to hold back the laughter. The laugh will soon be on me, however,
because he's going to give a speech and I'll have to listen to it.

John Fulton, the American bullfighter, is driving the car. He snaps
me back to reality, saying there's a severe fine for not using the seat belt,
so I buckle up. The standard procedure here is to send traffic tickets to
whoever owns the vehicle. There's no flashing siren, just a computer-
printed notice in the mail. You may not have had any idea you were
violating the law. You may not have even been in the country.

"That happened to me," says John. It is not surprising; Fulton's hard
luck over three decades as an American living in Spain is the stuff of
legend.

"What did you do?"

"I paid it. I had been in Florida visiting my mother so I went in and
showed them my passport stamps. They didn't care. It cost seventy
bucks."

Fulton, the old man and I are going to Utrera, forty minutes down
the Ronda highway from the ancient and multifarious city of Sevilla.

There is a dinner and the old man is the honored guest: Manuel Borbujos, retired newspaperman.

He was an opera critic and a war correspondent and a sports reporter, but is best known for writing on bullfights. He says something that sounds like radio static and John translates: "I have done everything a newspaperman can do."

Utrera is just a village but it has produced several bullfighters. A modestly successful matador named Curro Duran lives there and some fans have opened a *peña* in his honor. A peña is a cross between a fan club and a bar; aficionados drink there and eat *tapas* and talk about bullfighting. Often they organize journeys to see their favorite *torero* perform in some distant bullring. On occasion there are guest speakers. Tonight there is Borbujos.

This peña has Curro Duran memorabilia all over its walls, photos and posters and even a painting. Soon Duran arrives. He has wavy black hair and is wearing a black leather jacket and a ratty green sweater. It is not hard to recognize him. He looks embarrassed about standing in a room filled with his own image. Borbujos sees Duran and rushes over and soon is reading to him from a list. Duran isn't saying a word, and I'm thinking maybe he can't understand Borbujos either.

We take seats in the front under the podium. Borbujos is on the dais with Duran and the president of the peña. There are maybe fifty people in the audience on folding chairs, including several print journalists and a local television crew. Borbujos is introduced and begins to talk.

The talk lasts eighty-five minutes and is unintelligible to me. The droning is hypnotically rhythmic, like the crashing of the tide, and I feel exhausted, almost drugged. I pull on my nose and pinch my face to avoid dozing off. And I'm not the only one. I look up at Duran, seated to the left of Borbujos, and see in the matador a portrait of stupefaction. His mouth is open and his eyes are unfocused.

Behind us much of the audience is stepping to the bar for beers and tapas but we are stuck in front. Finally Borbujos reaches a climax. And then he says the only sentences I understand in all the time I know him:

"There have been too many words written about bullfighting already," he declares, suddenly clear as a trumpet. "If I had five pesetas for every bullfighting book out there I would be a rich man today. The last thing we aficionados need is another one."

He is staring directly at me.

■■■

As John Fulton knows better than anyone, the Spanish are notoriously protective of bullfighting and its place in their culture. The idea of an American coming to Sevilla to write a book about the *corrida de toros* strikes many Spaniards as funny, and many others as threatening. Fulton once asked me if, having seen the Sevillano attitude toward bullfighting, I could imagine anything more difficult than a foreigner trying to succeed as a matador. I told him I could: a foreigner trying to succeed as a bullfight critic. He liked the comment so much he repeated it to Borbujos.

V. S. Pritchett called Sevilla the city of the bull. I hadn't been living here long before I knew he wasn't exaggerating. Everybody in Sevilla knows a matador or is related to a bull breeder or lives next door to Juan Belmonte's nephew or has some connection, and usually more than one, to the taurine world. By unscientific reckoning, I figure three-quarters of the bars and restaurants in the city, from some of the finest to the seediest, have bullfight memorabilia on their walls. There are posters advertising fights, called *carteles*, bulls' heads stuffed and mounted, action photos, even the bloody *banderillas* that are artfully placed underneath a bull's hide during the spectacle. It must enable proprietors to save drastically on decorating costs, and it made me feel comfortable most anywhere I ate or drank. With the faded images of Belmonte, Manolete and Joselito El Gallo peering down on me from the walls, it was as though I was among old friends.

The bullfight season in Sevilla begins with the two weeks of corridas held in conjunction with the *Feria de Abril* in early spring. There is always a fight held on Easter Sunday, and then, beginning a week or so later depending on the calendar, fourteen or fifteen days of consecutive corridas. The number has grown through the years.

On just about every weekend from the end of February to the beginning of October, a *feria* is being celebrated somewhere in Spain, and usually one of the principal features of it is the bullfighting. Valencia adds a music festival, Pamplona has the *encierro,* the running of the bulls through the streets of the city on the morning of each bullfight, and most of the Andalusian ferias include show horses, plenty of *fino* sherry and all-night dancing and commotion in private tents called *casetas.* In taurine terms, Sevilla's is the third major feria on the calendar each year, and either the most important one or second in importance to Madrid's month-long bullfight marathon, San Ysidro, depending on your geographic orientation.

Plenty of foreign aficionados, Americans and Brits and Frenchmen and Swedes, come to town for the feria, but when I arrived this year, on a rainy winter afternoon with a terrible chill in the air, there were few foreigners and the local taurine community had bunkered down for the off-season. The city's two football teams, the mediocre Sevilla club and the popular but hapless Betis, were in the midst of typical seasons. Regional elections, approaching in early summer, were a topic of conversation, and Expo '92, awarded to Sevilla several years before but still three years away, already occupied a daily four-page special section in one of the newspapers, even though almost no work had been done on the site itself.

But it didn't take long before I found people willing to talk about bullfighting. On the first sunny day I went to see La Maestranza, the *plaza de toros* of Sevilla: the grandest and most famous bullring in the world, a shrine with the hulking grace of a cathedral, painted white and trimmed with gold, set fronting the Guadalquivir River in the center of the city. At a bar nearby, a chunky, ruddy-faced man named Pepe Sánchez showed me highlights from his collection of taurine materials: genuine carteles from the beginning of the century including many of the important fights, such as the *alternativa* ceremony of Joselito El Gallo, black-and-white photos of Domingo Ortega in action, and the great Belmonte, nearly ten thousand items in all, he claimed. His dream is to publish a coffee-table book in the United States with several hundred of his bullfight posters.

Pepe Sánchez had a small but successful exhibition at the Sheraton in New York once. "People went crazy," he said. "I found I could get more for a bullfight cartel than for a famous painting. You want to know the reason? A painter, even Goya, only has his own point of view, his own interpretation. He's a great painter, but you have to accept his interpretation. But these carteles are authentic, the originals. You can see exactly how it was."

Pepe Sánchez wanted me to abandon my project and throw my lot in with him. He said he'd let me write captions for his book, which was sure to outsell anything I could come up with. "Matadors today are boring, not like the old days," he said. "Besides, Americans like pictures. Stick with me because I have the originals. While you're telling them about Manzanares and Espartaco [two active matadors], I'm going to be showing them Juan Belmonte and Joselito. Tell me the truth, whose book do you think is going to sell better?"

Pepe Sánchez didn't convince me to collaborate. But he did drive home the point that most of the people in Sevilla I had heard of were already dead.

So I went to visit them.

2

THE CEMETERY

AT A SINGLE gravesite in a cemetery on the northern fringe of Sevilla lie the mortal remains of three of the most successful bullfighters of this century. Another monument is being constructed to a fourth. And the tomb of Juan Belmonte is a short distance away.

The cemetery is in the Macarena district, about a fifteen-minute drive from downtown. It's easy to spot the entrance once you get near because the row of waiting taxis stretches through the iron gateway and into the street. They're for visitors who came by foot or by bus but are too tired or stricken or distracted to return that way.

Atop the gravesite of the three bullfighters is a statue of a procession bearing an open casket. This is Joselito El Gallo, who died of trauma eight days after his twenty-fifth birthday, gored by a Viuda de Ortega bull in Talavera de la Reina, which is on the road from Badajoz to Madrid. The date, set in a metal plaque, was May 16, 1920.

Joselito was the last great bullfighter to use a simple style without ornamentation and his seven years of concurrent majesty with Juan Belmonte were a true golden age. There are many Spaniards who consider Joselito the greatest bullfighter who ever lived. A young matador named José Arroyo has recently emerged using the same nickname and to some it is tantamount to blasphemy. Just about every Spanish man, woman, and child knows about the original Joselito, and the majority could tell you details of his life. Of course, true bullfight aficionados know everything about him and especially about the tragedy: the name of the bull that killed him, the time of day, the intricate series of passes he performed just prior to his death.

His genius manifested itself in technical proficiency. Killing bulls came easy to Joselito, or at least appeared to. Rarely was his effort evident. His death was a terrible surprise to all of Spain, which had considered him invulnerable and had feared instead for the life of Belmonte.

I have collected some numbers to reinforce my appreciation of Joselito. For instance: in seven full years as a matador, Joselito fought and killed all six bulls in a corrida twenty-two times, rather than alternating with two other matadors as is nearly always the case. On 257 occasions he appeared with Belmonte. He fought 81 times in Madrid, 64 in Barcelona, 58 in Sevilla and 49 in Valencia, and those statistics are notable because succeeding in the big cities is the truest test of a bullfighter. He understood bulls and the geometry of bullfighting and was able to do whatever he wanted with almost any bull—and yet he was killed in the ring. That lesson is learned early by every bullfighter.

To Joselito's right is the gravestone of Ignacio Sánchez Mejías. He was born June 4, 1891, and he died August 23, 1934. Sánchez Mejías had little natural grace, and limited ability as a bullfighter, but he brought such pluck and valor to the corrida that he became the favorite matador of Andalusia, of which Sevilla is the capital.

He started his career as Belmonte's *banderillero,* what is called a peon or subaltern, but against all advice went out on his own as a matador. He retired with health and fortune intact but was persuaded to make a comeback—a fatal mistake. He was a great friend of the poet Federico García Lorca, and after Sánchez Mejías died of a goring Lorca wrote *Llanto por Ignacio Sánchez Mejías* which is arguably the most famous poem composed in Spanish in this century. Its haunting refrain, ". . . at five in the afternoon," *a las cinco de la tarde,* denotes the hour of Sánchez Mejías's death.

Entombed to the left of Joselito is his brother, Rafael Gómez, also called El Gallo, which means the rooster. Born on July 16, 1882, Rafael El Gallo was for many years as elegant and graceful a bullfighter as anyone has seen. He was unusually prudent and would often decline to fight bulls he felt might be out to harm him. His caution served him well: he lived until 1960 and died a hallowed figure.

■■■

A few steps down the path I see a vast hole in the earth with concrete girders protruding and cream-colored bricks piled to either side. A small sign has been hand-lettered in pencil and leans against the brick. Don't ask, it says. This is for Paquirri.

His is a sad story, and stunningly modern. It's easy to think of the death of Joselito happening in some sepia-toned time of poor sanitary conditions and general confusion, but there is no sloughing off Paquirri's death. It happened in the middle of the Reagan era, days after the Los Angeles Olympics: a recent event.

Francisco Rivera, called Paquirri, as handsome as a movie star and married to a popular singer, was tossed and wounded in Pozoblanco on September 26, 1984. Medical help was delayed because the local hospital was under construction and the nearest city, Córdoba, was eighty kilometers away on rough road. Paquirri survived the ambulance ride but died on arrival. He was thirty-six.

Early in his career he had married Carmen Ordóñez, the daughter of the matador Antonio Ordóñez. He discarded Carmen in a scandalous divorce because he had fallen in love with a willowy black-haired entertainer named Isabel Pantoja. The strength of his bullfighting was always in his daring and the force of his will but after he married La Pantoja there were whispers that he was no longer willing to take the same risks because now life was going too well for him. It is said two things can make cowards out of brave bullfighters: a serious goring and a contented marriage.

There had been talk of retirement all that season and the corrida in Pozoblanco would likely have been his last. He had been married to La Pantoja a year when he died, and she has never recovered from the loss. She's still a tremendously popular entertainer, probably more popular than before because of the profundity of the tragedy, and you can see her now performing as far away as Miami, singing songs about Paquirri and crying onstage.

It's not only La Pantoja who still mourns. Paquirri's death remains very much in the national consciousness. This year I was reading a magazine on a bus in Sevilla when a middle-aged woman sat down beside me. When she saw the magazine was about bullfighting she shook her head. "What a shame about Paquirri," she said.

It's a short walk from Paquirri's monument to the grave of Belmonte.

The tomb is a modernesque sculpture of many-faceted black marble resting on a thick white stone base. It looks like no other gravesite I've seen and says simply 1892–1962 Juan Belmonte. Three bunches of carnations, one red, one pink, and one white, have been placed on its shiny black surface.

Juan Belmonte was the transcendant figure in the history of bullfighting. He changed everything. His style was absolutely the opposite of Joselito's and in opposition to all the rules of classical *toreo*. In his 1953 book *What Is Torear?* bullfight critic Gregorio Corrochano wrote: "The toreo of Joselito astonished with its mastery, its extension, its dominion . . . its facility solving whatever problems were presented by the bull in the plaza. The toreo of Belmonte surprised us with just the opposite, by the unexplainable: he bothered us with the impossible; it hurt to see him *torear*."

In the end it was Joselito, the invulnerable one, who was caught and killed by a bull. Belmonte lived on in an apartment overlooking the Guadalquivir River in the center of Sevilla, five blocks from La Maestranza and in a massive country home outside the city with its own bullring and bulls he used to cape at night.

And then, when he was seventy years old and the most renowned citizen in Sevilla and, save Franco, perhaps all of Spain, Belmonte put a gun to his head and killed himself, just as his friend Ernest Hemingway had done the year before.

■ ■ ■

When I first came to Sevilla three years ago, in 1986, to learn about bullfighting, I searched for and found the American matador John Fulton, whose relentless love for the bullfight is as consuming as any Spaniard's. Fulton has essentially wagered his life on success in this most intransigent of arenas, and he has endured. After three decades, even his detractors admire his tenacity.

This hardly satisfies him, for he had set his sights on what you might call immortality, an acknowledged greatness, a place beside Joselito, Belmonte, Rafael El Gallo and the rest, refusing to admit that for him such a thing was impossible. He ran up against a fundamental truth: that he who would be considered a great bullfighter had best be Spanish born.

It's true that the Mexican Carlos Arruza was considered the equal of Manolete for several years before Manolete's untimely death on the horns of a Miura bull in 1947, but today Arruza's name is not often mentioned. Currently there is a Portuguese matador of quality competing in Spanish rings and one Venezuelan and at least two Frenchmen, but none could be considered great.

And one who arrives in the world in Philadelphia, U.S.A., out of Hungarian and Italian parentage, and decides at age nineteen to become a bullfighter because he is infatuated with an old Tyrone Power movie that represents the life as glamorous and exotic and rewarding, and comes to Spain with no money and no connections to seek knowledge and respect and fame and maybe fortune, that man is attempting to buck such long odds and overcome such obtrusive and variegated difficulties that the nicest thing anyone could call him is foolish.

John Fulton came anyway and essentially beat the odds—but in the end he didn't. Because even though he was the first American to graduate from *novillero* to full matador in Spain, a ceremonial advancement known as the alternativa, and although he had several indisputable triumphs such as cutting an ear with a Miura in Sevilla, the wall of prejudice eventually proved unassailable and his noble character is today speckled with bitterness.

His is fifty-seven years old and tall—some say too tall for a matador—with a handsome, wide-open face and a receding hairline and protuberant ears, and he lives in a spacious house in the southern part of Sevilla not far from the rich section. He supports himself as a painter and sculptor. Some of the painting is done in bull's blood.

Fulton has not officially retired as a matador and still hopes to fight again but he hasn't appeared in a full corrida in Spain in a decade and now a comeback is all but impossible. He continues to train often with a mechanical bull, however. It is instructive to note that he has been working on his autobiography for some time and plans to publish it with the title *John Quixote*. The comparison is apt, except that the windmills he tilted at tilted back.

The studio where his work is displayed is on the Plaza de la Alianza in the oldest and most beautiful quarter of town, the Barrio de Santa Cruz. His adopted Gypsy son, Federico, works there and prospective matadors looking for a break are often around. Through both his kindness and his karma, Fulton seems to attract the luckless.

Those who have read *Iberia*, James Michener's magnificent nonfiction volume on Spain, have already found John Fulton. There he is on page 69 of the Fawcett paperback edition dancing in an attic during the feria, and later Michener praises him for his generosity and describes his struggles during his early days as a bullfighter, "stone broke and trying to make his way in one of the toughest professions in the world. . . .

"How Fulton supported himself during those bleak and wonderful years I do not know," Michener writes. "Most of us who trespassed on his hospitality managed in some way or other to leave behind donations: one brought the wine, another anchovies, another the cheese. Hemingway made his contributions by check; a delightful woman from Cleveland made hers by throwing memorable flamenco parties at which she gave John a fee for his professional help; I made mine by commissioning Fulton to paint me a picture, for I judged that he had more chance to succeed as an artist than as a matador. I was right."

Those words were published in 1968 and on Christmas Day of that year, an unorthodox date for a corrida, Fulton triumphed with the Miura in Sevilla. He was thirty-six years old.

"I took my alternativa in Sevilla and did well and fought around here and did well," he says now. "I went to Mexico and I fought with all the stars and I came back and confirmed my alternativa in Madrid and I still couldn't get another fight in Sevilla. And then one day they organized a benefit fight and one of the guys on the card dropped out when he learned that the bull he had to fight was a Miura. So they asked me and I cut the only ear of the afternoon," an ear being a trophy awarded for a fine performance.

"Now, if I had been some Spaniard, any Spaniard, that would have assured me of a fight in the April feria. But I have never been able to get any kind of fight in Sevilla since then."

He tells me that a friend has sent him a clipping of an interview with a Spanish painter, a fool of the most parochial stamp, who believes that in order to paint bulls one must be Spanish.

"Then you go out and prove that not only can you paint them, you can fight them," Fulton says. "And they say, God, what are we going to do now? I mean, let's face it, the Miuras are the killer bulls, man. Some snot-nosed kid from Philadelphia goes out there and swings his ass off with them and that means either one of two things. Either John Fulton really is a good bullfighter or the Miura bulls are a piece of shit."

I tell him neither of those things could be true, the way the Spaniards think.

"Right," he says. "So they ignore it. And that's the frustrating part."

The Christmas corrida was twenty-one years ago but the frustration has festered. John Fulton, respected by his peers as a man and as an artist, has become the spiritual leader of a cadre of English-speaking aficionados, professional men, men of some wealth and substance, who revere him because he has done what they haven't dared dream of. He is also an accomplished painter and a loving father and grandfather, with a winsome California blonde for a companion and a multitude of friends and well-wishers.

All of this is important to him, but not of the ultimate importance. "Only when I am bullfighting," Fulton says, "do I feel truly full."

3

WHAT THE PAPERS SAY

JOHN Fulton's studio is a good place to visit before lunch. His son Federico can usually be persuaded to lock the door and accompany me around the corner for a beer and a tapa. He has to be back by two o'clock to close the studio for the afternoon meal and siesta. It reopens again at five unless business hasn't been good in the morning or Federico has something else to do, or there is a bullfight in La Maestranza he has tickets to.

Federico has a broad, handsome face and dark, curly hair. He had stunning looks as a child that were captured in some photographs by Robert Vavra, but lately he has put on weight. He speaks English and Spanish fluently and is caring and friendly to almost everyone, but he has a raging temper I have only heard about. "A Gypsy trait," he says, and shrugs. He has swiftly become a good friend but if he were my son I might not give him charge of my business because financial concerns aren't his priority. He has a young Gypsy wife and a baby daughter and they seem to eat well enough . . . so let him lock the door and get a noontime beer. It is the way of Sevilla.

But we don't go for a beer when I arrive the morning after my trip to the cemetery. Matt Carney has died in Ireland and there are letters to be written and arrangements to be made. Carney is a Californian who came to Paris to write a book and stayed. He became a model, and over the years he earned a reputation as the most skilled foreigner at running with the bulls during the feria of Sanfermines at Pamplona every year. Some say he was better than the Spaniards, too. He had a celebrated barroom incident with Hemingway involving a wineskin and some drunken, profane comments, and many more celebrated barroom incidents with just about everyone he knew. "He was one of those few people you meet who truly was larger than life," his friend and fellow bull-runner Joe Distler once told me.

Carney never did finish the book, but he became a legend in Pamplona among all the people who care about bulls. "He would sit for hours surrounded by American college students, having a conversation nobody else could have possibly cared about," Distler said. "Everyone he met instantly became his friend."

Now he is dead of throat cancer. He was sixty-something, a legend, gone before I knew him.

"He never said he was afraid of the bulls and he never said it was dangerous," Federico says now. "He only used to say that it was great fun."

The door jangles and John Fulton arrives, walking toward us in the back room with his splay-footed walk. He's with a novice bullfighter, a novillero, whom we call Manolito: a tiny Mexican, maybe five foot three, whose flat Indian features and size give him an Oriental look. His full name is Manolo Cortés but there is another matador by that name and so this one is stuck with the diminutive, aside from its obvious appropriateness. Truth be told, the two of them—big John, all expansive gestures, and Manolito, small and secretive—look rather silly together.

Federico is John's true adopted son, but John has all but adopted Manolito, too. He lives at John's house, eats John's food, drives John's car. John is enamored of Manolito's style of bullfighting and spends time and money helping him. We all believe Manolito will have a short memory if he ever does become successful, and John will be out of luck as usual. It's a moot point so far; Manolito hasn't even been able to get a fight.

John and Manolito, the two bullfighters, call each other "maestro" and talk bullfighting—in Spanish, since Manolito speaks no English. Today the topic is the feria schedule. This year's carteles—a word meaning the matadors scheduled to fight on a given day, as well as the poster announcing the same—have recently been published in the newspapers. This is something we're all interested in and hot conversation around town: who's coming this year and who isn't, what combinations of matadors make up the important fights, and with which brands of bulls. Everyone has strong feelings about this because everyone has his favorite bullfighters and varying prejudices about the rest. Sometimes I get the feeling that the true national fiesta of Spain isn't bullfighting, but talking about it.

There is only one true *máxima figura* currently active in bullfighting today, a man named Juan Antonio Ruiz. He's from the town of Espartinas in the province of Sevilla and he calls himself Espartaco, which means Spartacus. By any measure, nobody is more successful. Just twenty-seven years old, he commands the most money and most consistently performs well. Yet there is argument about the depth of his work; you will hear it said that he does not have the soul of an artist. Neither Manolo nor John is an aficionado of his style, although both readily admit his stature and importance.

I usually defend Espartaco; I'm an *espartaquista,* a fan of his, although I understand how his toreo is lacking. He is more of an athlete than an artist, but watching him does something to me, and that's the true test. If you feel something, an emotional tug, when watching a bullfighter of any reputation, never let anyone tell you that feeling isn't valid. It would be like someone trying to disparage your favorite song; bullfighting is that personal.

As expected, Espartaco will be fighting four times in the feria and so will Curro Romero, who is Fulton's age and a Sevilla legend but almost never shows his skill anymore. Miguel Baez, called Litri, the twenty-year-old son of a matador and one of the up-and-coming generation of what Fulton calls "rock 'n' roll bullfighters," has three dates, and that's something of a surprise. He hasn't really earned them, but he's handsome and charismatic.

But the biggest news is the absence of three of Spain's better matadors: José Mari Manzanares, Roberto Domínguez and Juan Mora. "Manzanares probably asked for a certain type of bull," Federico says. "He often does that and usually they accommodate him, but sometimes they don't."

"He's a faggot," says Manolito, who tends to become cantankerous when discussing bullfighters more successful than he is, which is just about all of them. "A *maricón.*"

"Domínguez may not have wanted to appear on a cartel with some other matadors," Federico says. "He might be afraid of looking bad, or he might just be superstitious. Maybe the last time there was a certain combination of matadors something bad happened. Also, I heard a few of them were asking too much money and the impresario decided to shut them out to teach them a lesson."

"It's always money," says Manolito.

There are probably several hundred conversations just like this one going on all over Sevilla right now. Today's edition of the Andalusian newspaper *El Correo* says that true aficionados are already disappointed with the feria, which is still nearly two months away. I'm disappointed that Manzanares won't be here. An artistic torero, he's renowned for doing well in Sevilla, where artistry is valued (and when I check the statistics later I see that the reputation is correct: he's cut fifteen ears here during the feria over eleven years).

Manzanares always appears in Madrid at the San Ysidro feria in May or June but he's often a bust, and the local aficionados there have developed a marked belligerence toward his brand of toreo, which only makes him perform worse. I'll have to catch him elsewhere, maybe in his hometown of Alicante on the Mediterranean coast, to see him at his best. Mora, whom I've never seen, has been here three years without success but is developing a terrific reputation throughout the country. Domínguez, from Valladolid in the north of Spain, has only been here once during the feria, in 1978, but last September at La Maestranza he put together what John calls as complete a performance with a bull as he's seen in a decade. John describes this now and his eyes glisten. It is as if the passes are rolling on a projector in his mind. He finishes and everyone is quiet.

"It seems to be they'd want him back after a performance like that," I say.

"That's logical," John snaps. I have unknowingly plugged into his bitterness. "You can't go by logic when you're dealing with bullfighting. Bullfighting has its own logic—and its own politics. And the politics get worse every year."

■ ■ ■

Because bullfighting is a spectacle, not a sport, it doesn't appear in the sports pages of the newspapers. This surprises some people when they first come to Spain. Instead, bullfighting is in a section all its own, usually near, but not included in, the section for the arts.

There are a half-dozen daily newspapers for sale in Sevilla, and I buy three of them regularly at a kiosk surrounded by blossoming orange trees alongside the Plaza de Museo, a block and a half from my small apartment. *El Correo* circulates only in Andalusia and has a four-page bullfighting supplement every Tuesday. *Diario 16* is from Madrid but publishes an Andalusian edition and also has a Tuesday supplement. It's the most liberal of the important daily papers, and you'd be surprised how often political orientation extends to taurine matters too. *ABC* is the conservative paper, also out of Madrid, but it too has an Andalusian edition. It has no supplements but its Sunday magazine *Blanco y Negro* favors the bullfights and often includes long stories on matadors, with color photos. And its bullfight critic, Vicente Zabala, is the most imaginative and entertaining I've read. He's relatively unbiased and happens to share most of my taurine sensibilities. (*ABC* is the Spanish newspaper I have seen most often in the United States. Hotaling's, off Times Square in New York, usually has two or three different issues available for $1.75 each, a small price for a fix of bullfight news.)

I don't read *El País* because it has no separate regional edition and is heavily oriented toward Madrid, in bullfight matters as in everything else. It also runs bullfight news only occasionally, while each of the others prints a story on the corrida five or six days a week and every day during the major ferias. Joaquín Vidal, the bullfight critic for *El País,* is a controversial figure. He likes to compare today's matadors to the giants of the last century, Lagartijo and Pepe-Hillo and Frascuelo. He nearly always concludes that anything today's heroes accomplish the old-timers could have done better, and with bigger and more dangerous bulls. There have been ferias at which every bullfight critic but Vidal hailed a conquering torero as a true artist, while Vidal panned him as not worthy to wear the same suit of lights as the old-timers.

Ever since the carteles for the feria were announced, all of these newspapers have been running opinion pieces and editorials denouncing them. Most run on the editorial page, underneath support for Salman Rushdie or criticism of the Basque rebels. I hardly need add there are differences of opinion. *Diario 16* is irate at the exclusion of Manzanares and a fourth matador, Ortega Cano, while Zabala of *ABC* writes that of all of them Roberto Domínguez deserves to be here most. *El Correo,* in a full-page story by Antonio Lorca, introduces a new criticism: the matadors, contracted as always by the impresario of the bullring, have been badly grouped. Nearly all of the second week's corridas promise to be subpar. Lorca also believes Domínguez and Manzanares should have been contracted here not just for one corrida, but for three afternoons each.

The same page carries Manzanares's reaction to his exclusion. "I can't explain it, I can't accept it," he says. "I didn't have any idea that this year I wouldn't be fighting in Sevilla, in a bullring in which I have done almost everything."

The next day, the bullfight weekly *Toros '92* comes out with a fantasy feria, carteles suggested by readers, voted on, and tabulated. It's a meaningless exercise—I'm sure the executives of La Maestranza don't even read it—but it fuels conversation in the bullfight bars and with John and Federico in the gallery. In something of a compromise move, the editors have put Manzanares and Domínguez in two corridas each. Juan Mora is there once, as is Pepe Luis Vázquez, the son of a popular Sevillano matador of the fifties and sixties. And in a decision guaranteed to please their readers, Espartaco and Curro Romero, the current hero and the legend, each have four appearances, just as they do in real life.

■ ■ ■

The official feria carteles have been pasted on walls around the city. Postering is how most of the advertising is done in Sevilla. There are radio and television commercials and ads in newspapers and magazines, but most people don't quite believe in the existence of an event unless they see a poster announcing it on a wall.

There are designated places to put the posters and mostly the rules are followed. The art of placing posters is strategic. You want your posters up in advance, of course, but if you put them up too far in advance they will have been postered over long before the event arrives. Posters are usually put up in the dead of night. It is rare to see anyone actually slathering the back of a poster with the lumpy, viscous glue and slapping it on the wall—or, more likely, atop another poster. As with graffiti, you walk outside in the morning and the new additions hit you head-on with their ugliness or artistry.

This morning, heading up Calle Reyes Católicos for tea at the bullfight bar Los Tres Reyes, I see the feria carteles for the first time. Last year, in one of the rare strokes of good luck that has befallen him, John Fulton was chosen to paint the official cartel and responded with what I consider to be his best work. The original is on the wall in his studio. But this year he was out of the country when the decision was made, and anyway,

Escacena, who had churned out a series of amateurish feria posters in previous years, was said to have loudly protested the impropriety of awarding such a task to a foreigner. Escacena was duly contracted for this year's work.

Seeing the official cartel now, three of them sandwiched between a gaudy green poster advertising the Sevilla marathon and a somber-looking announcement of a classical music series sponsored by a bank, I agree with Fulton's biased assessment: it is a monstrosity. John's work captured the essence of Sevilla—La Maestranza, backed by the cathedral tower La Giralda, set against the blue sky. Escacena's muddle could be anywhere. It's a mass of watery dots that is probably a crowd, a bull curving around a matador like a Volkswagen bug taking a corner at high speed, done with a lack of detail and an utter absence of personality.

John was amused rather than enraged by Escacena's poster; he's after a bigger prize. La Maestranza is sponsoring an art competition with a broad bullfight theme. First place means twenty-five thousand dollars and plenty of publicity. John has finished sketching his entry and is beginning to paint. It features a girl in traditional Gypsy dress (Federico's wife, Angelita, is the model) standing in an archway of La Maestranza with the cathedral, as usual, in the background. In front of her are crests and portraits that symbolize stages in the history of the bullring. There is a matador's cap and a sword in the foreground.

One of the important people at the bullring has made it clear that he's eager to see John's entry, so all of us believe he has a good chance of winning, but John is wary.

"You don't know how these things work," he says, and laughs. "With my luck, the brother of some director over at La Maestranza will enter. And that will be that."

■■■

Fulton's fatalism, though good-humored, is deflating. But it comes from experience. He arrived in Spain in 1959 with all the idealism of youth. His perseverance has made him something of a public figure around town and certainly in the bullfight world. At Borbujos's speech he was recognized and acknowledged by nearly everyone there. He knows the journalists well and did a short television interview that night, answering questions about the feria. But even some of those who treat him with the most respect, who call him maestro and ask for his opinion on taurine matters of the day, would likely disparage his work as a matador in private. There's a difference between knowing about the bulls, as even the staunchest Spaniard admits Hemingway did, and being able to fight a bull with true *arte*.

The contrast between his own situation and that of Curro Duran has made Fulton wistful. "If I were Spanish, maybe I would have had a fan club," he says. "My own peña. And maybe some impresario would have said, hmmmmm, if I put John Fulton on the cartel he'll pull in at least five hundred fans. Instead, my hometown was thousands of miles away.

"I left my home, my family, my country, my girlfriend and my job opportunities to come over in a hostile atmosphere to do something nobody wanted me to do except me," he says. "When I had a bad afternoon I didn't have a place to go home to, a place where somebody could put their arm around me and wipe away my tears and tell me not to worry because it happens to the greatest. I had to go it alone.

"And my biggest frustration is not having been given enough opportunities—and I don't mean given as in a gift. I was never afforded or could never worm out of them enough opportunities in one season or two seasons to know whether I could have been a great matador. If you fight once in March and once in October, there's no carryover, or very little. They would always say, If you do well and cut ears you'll get another fight and more money. But it seemed every time I did well I never got another fight."

Fulton wasn't the first American to fight bulls in Spain, just the first to take his alternativa here. The most famous American matador is Sidney Franklin. He had several successful seasons in the early 1930s, successful at first as a novelty but later because he was a fine killer and proficient with the cape. And his association with Hemingway didn't hurt his success.

"His timing was perfect," John says. He has made a study of all the Americans to fight bulls in Spain, and knows about nearly all of the many who have tried it in Mexico, too. Comparing their stories to his is a hobby. "Sidney Franklin made his debut on a Sunday dedicated to the United States during the Hispanic-Iberian Fair of 1929," he says. "It was a pretty good showcase. Nobody had ever heard of him but he had been fighting eight years as a novillero in Mexico. And in those days they liked Americans.

"By the time I got here, the base program had started and there were all kinds of military personnel here. The American military is never a very attractive cross section of society, as you know. And the Spaniards disliked the whole idea of having an American military base in Spain. They said, The Americans are trying to take over our country and now with this guy they're trying to take over bullfighting.

"I had a situation in Madrid that was just a disaster. Some airmen got drunk on a Friday night in a bar downtown and started a scene and I made my debut on that Sunday. I mean, I was just stuck. They didn't want to know anything."

From time to time someone meets Fulton and decides to champion his cause, and occasionally it's a person of wealth or prestige. Writer Cornelius Ryan was in Spain once doing a story on Belmonte for *Reader's Digest* and was astonished to learn that John lacked the necessary six thousand dollars to continue his bullfighting career. This was apparently a small sum to Ryan, who remarked that he had recently squandered a similar amount investing in a Hungarian restaurant in Hong Kong.

Fulton distinctly remembers Ryan's promising to send money but the money never came and Ryan never called. "You have an obligation to your family to stop chasing fame and fortune behind a cloud in a bullring," Ryan said when John found him.

When Fulton's confidence was at its lowest he managed to get invited to Juan Belmonte's ranch. It was through the American ambassador, who was being honored at a party. There was a bullfighting exhibition with aspiring matadors and Fulton walked in with all the others looking to get discovered. After the rest had fought, the ambassador asked if an American in attendance could be given a chance.

"I was planning to ask Belmonte if he thought I had the ability to make it even as a bad matador," John says. "And if Belmonte said no I was going to be on the next boat home."

Fulton handled his bull well. Later, Belmonte approached him, threw his arm around a shoulder and addressed the nearby guests. "If I didn't know this kid's last name, you would think he came from Andalusia, not Philadelphia," Belmonte said.

"I have thought about that moment again and again through the years, whenever I doubted my ability," Fulton says now, "and there are many times when it has sustained me."

I ask him if he believes his experience has at least softened the Spanish resistance against the next talented American who comes along wanting to be a bullfighter.

He takes no time to consider.

"No," he says. "No way."

4

THE TICKET LINE

A VISITOR to Spain who wants to see a bullfight will rarely have a problem getting tickets. If money is no object, he'll never have a problem. There are always tickets available for those who will pay enough. The average bullfight ticket costs more than you might expect, however. A mid-range seat for a bullfight in Sevilla during the feria costs about thirty dollars, while the most expensive costs a hundred.

Those are the list prices, but nearly all the tickets sold on the day of a bullfight are sold at the resale booths, or *reventas*. These are booths set up along the major streets in town and around the bullring that sell tickets at a 20 percent premium. During the feria, when all the corridas are technically sold out, the *reventa* is the only recourse.

When the *reventa* is out of tickets, one must patronize a scalper, and scalpers are the same all over the world, unfortunately—whether hawking opera tickets outside La Scala in Milan, hockey tickets in the crisp frost of a Montreal evening or bullfight tickets, sun and shade. It is a case of supply and demand, and prices unbound by limits.

I plan to see all nineteen of the corridas during the feria and whatever else the Maestranza schedules while I'm here. So it's worth my while to buy an *abono,* the equivalent of a season ticket. Eighteen of the nineteen corridas during the feria are included in the *abono,* as well as three or four others during the summer. I'll get the same seat every time, the option to purchase that seat for any other bullfights at the Maestranza, and a discount from list price.

There's a set time and place for the purchase of an *abono*. Those who had them last year are allowed to come to the ticket window at the bullring and renew. A week later, new *abonos* are put on sale.

I had stopped in the Maestranza offices a month ago to talk to Señor Hugenio, who handles public relations. He brushed aside my request for a media credential but volunteered to personally expedite my order if I returned at ten o'clock this morning. I do, and find a line extending down the block. Hugenio helps me out all right. He writes a note on a scrap of paper that says, in essence, Take this man's money and let him buy an *abono*.

"Just get at the end of the line and when you get to the window, hand the man this," he says.

"But I can do that just as well without the slip of paper," I say. "What do I need this for? I can speak Spanish."

Hugenio shrugs.

The line, it turns out, had started forming before sunrise. Instead of helping me Hugenio has misled me and now I'll have to wait all morning. And there's another quirk in the system. The windows close at two o'clock and don't reopen until six. If I don't get in by two, I could easily be here until nightfall.

The line extends from the ticket window out along the tree-lined street on La Maestranza's backside. It's not orderly; at places there are five men standing abreast. Worse, there is almost no movement. I calculate that it is taking ten minutes to complete each transaction, which must by necessity be simple: each person is limited to one *abono*. But as I inch closer, it becomes clear why the wait is so long. Each person can buy just one seat, and everyone is intimately familiar with the bullring, so decisions aren't made lightly. Complete information is needed; this is too important to be left to chance or approximation.

"What about *tendido nueve, fila dos?*" someone asks, quoting a specific section and row number.

"I'll check," says the man behind the window—and he does, for a full five minutes.

"Nothing free," he says on returning, and the process starts again.

Nowhere is waiting in line more an active pastime than in Spain. At any moment, as many people in the line are moving as are standing still.

It's not that they seek undue advantage, for cutting a place or two closer over the course of five hours is hardly worth the effort. But the natural Spanish gregariousness forces interaction, for time endured might as well be time enjoyed. This leads to wandering.

I have brought several newspapers and a book, and I tuck my notebook and the papers under my arm and try to read. But a sense of uneasiness makes me glance up after a page and I find I'm now three bodies farther from the ticket window, even though the same man is still hunched beneath the iron grill negotiating for his seats and no actual line movement has taken place.

By noon the line has become a virtual huddle, less orderly than a rugby scrum. Nobody knows the actual sequence but everyone has memorized the appearance of the patron he's directly behind. Some people are holding spaces for a half-dozen others, which makes the wait more agonizing as the absent ones tend to arrive at the exact moment they are due at the window.

As a foreigner, the only one in evidence, it's easy for me to start conversations. Soon everyone wants to talk to me, and many do, some from nearby and others from far-flung places near the end of the line. Most are men, and the conversations concern bullfighting, of course. There are only a few women in line and very few young people of either sex, but the man directly behind me has brought his teenage daughter.

"She's the biggest aficionado in the family and the one who knows where all the good seats are," he says, introducing a smiling girl with pigtails. "I figured it was worth her missing a day of school to get us good tickets."

"Who's your favorite matador?" I ask her.

"Espartaco," she says immediately. "And Litri, too." Everyone smiles benevolently, although if she had been a man, or even a boy, her choices would have been the source of instant debate.

By two o'clock I have progressed inside the iron gate into a covered foyer leading to the Maestranza offices, but I'm still ten places from the window itself. But now I benefit from an oddity in the regulations: although ticket sales are supposed to close for siesta at two, anyone who has made it past the gate is allowed to stay and make his purchase.

In the end, with help from the teenage girl, I buy a five hundred dollar seat on the sun side about two-thirds of the way up the grandstand in *tendido* 11. I'm assured by all that it is the best I could have done for the money I have paid, which is about one-quarter of the price of the best in the house, the first-row *barrera* seats in the shade. Those cost more than two thousand dollars.

With my *abono* tucked safely inside my wallet, signed and notarized, my signature matching a duplicate in the lined and bound register kept behind the window (another reason why each transaction took so long), I shake hands all around. I'm not the outsider I was several hours before, but almost a Sevillano: a season-ticket holder at the local bullring, which happens to be the best known in all of Spain.

■■■

Later that afternoon I visit the gallery. Federico inspects the *abono* carefully; the design differs each year, and this is probably the first of this year's he's seen. It's a piece of cardboard folded in half, with a stunning aerial shot of the Maestranza and the surrounding streets, the area of downtown called El Arenal. Federico confirms that I have done well for my money, although he cautions that no seats on the sun side of the bullring can ever be considered good.

I know this, and it's not for reasons of comfort. Ninety percent of the action usually takes place across the ring, under the president's box in the shade. That's where the important people sit, the bull ranchers and taurine journalists and sometimes even royalty, and 90 percent of all bulls are fought there. Chasing a cloth in the heat of the Spanish sun can quickly tire even the most robust animal, and most bulls need to be coddled as long as possible so they retain enough energy to finish the fight. Bulls also tend to become entrenched in certain spots, called *querencias,* from which they charge sporadically and defensively. It is dangerous to fight a bull in its *querencia* because what the bull is doing, in effect, is staking out ground for its last stand. A matador must take care to draw a bull away from its *querencias,* and many times a bull's strongest *querencia* will be located at the mouth of the *toril,* the dark chute that leads from the pens to the inside of the bullring and is almost always located in the middle of the sun seats. This is probably because the bull remembers the cool, dark pen as the last place it felt truly secure before it was sent out into the ring to be tricked and stuck and prodded while fighting for its life.

Although he's the adopted son of a full matador, Federico isn't accustomed to the expensive seats in a bullring. For the first eight years of his life he lived in a Gypsy encampment and couldn't read or write a word in any language. He spoke a dialect of Hungarian and just a few sentences of Spanish.

Federico is a full-blooded Gypsy, which doesn't just mean that he moves around a lot. The Gypsies are a race of people across Europe with a common language—Romany—and a common culture. Nowhere is their tradition stronger than in Spain, perhaps because of bullfighting and flamenco, the twin halves of Gypsy art. Many of the best matadors of the past and several of today have Gypsy blood, and an even higher percentage of the most artistic flamenco dancers do. Yet nowhere are Gypsies more prejudiced against than here. Citizens otherwise liberal and open-minded rail against the Gypsies, calling them dirty and dishonest. It's true that Gypsies are mostly poor and often beg but owning a car and a house and living in a rich section of Madrid or Sevilla doesn't make one any less a Gypsy.

I came to Spain knowing little about Gypsies, except that Joselito El Gallo was one and Cagancho and Gitanillo de Triana, whose nickname means "little Gypsy." I didn't know that Gypsies have different blood, that they are "as different from whites as Miuras from Guardiolas," as Federico puts it. "A Gypsy is a different breed of person, better at some things, worse at others," he says. And he's convinced Gypsies make the best bullfighters.

Federico begins to tell me the story of his transformation from an illiterate, barefoot Gypsy child to the son of an unmarried American matador. It is a particularly slow day and Federico has time to talk. Actually, the day is more than slow, it's inert. The gallery hasn't made a sale of any kind in a week. There are no customers and the air inside is cool. Federico talks about meeting John Fulton and Robert Vavra for the first time.

Fulton and Vavra were searching the Gypsy camps for a young boy to pose for photographs for a coffee-table book on Gypsies. The picture they had in their heads was Mowgli, from Kipling's *Jungle Book*.

"At that age I kind of looked like him," Federico says. "I was wild and my hair was kind of like his, although his hair was probably very beautiful and clean and mine was dirty and full of dust and oil, because sometimes when we didn't have water to comb out our hair my mother would use olive oil or the grease that we used for the wheels of the wagon."

Fulton and Vavra took Federico to the Cota Doñana, a wildlife reserve

south of here where the photographs were to be taken. They paid
Federico's parents for the privilege of using their son as a model. His
life there bore no similarity to the Gypsy camp. They lived in a huge
house and ate what were for Federico astoundingly rich meals. And the
accouterments of the modern world, ballpoint pens and toasters and the
rest, were like mystical instruments.

Fulton taught Federico to write his name, and soon had him painting.
Some of his early efforts remain on the walls of the gallery, sketches of
birds and animals, natural and without artifice in a style wholly his own.
They are good enough to make me wonder why Federico doesn't paint
now. He tells me he just doesn't have the urge. That's a Gypsy trait, he
says. There's seldom a compelling enough reason to do anything if you
don't feel like it.

Eventually Federico returned to his parents, who had settled on the
outskirts of Madrid. His father, an alcoholic with a tendency toward
violence, warned him to stop wasting his time on books and help the
other brothers beg for rags. Instead Federico chose escape. Fulton directed him to a friend in Madrid and that began a year-long intrigue
like something you read in a spy novel. From Madrid Federico was
taken to Málaga and from there to Ronda, where, he says, he was
recognized in a bar from a newspaper clipping. He changed his appearance with a haircut and fake eyeglasses. Six months of hiding in
Sevilla followed while adoption papers could be processed.

Before legally adopting Federico, Fulton had to convince the author-
ities that a foreign single male living alone, with no steady income, could
support a Gypsy child. That John was trying to make it as a bullfighter
only led to more questions about his sanity. He was asked to bring three
witnesses to speak on his behalf. He brought Félix Moreno de la Cova,
a bull breeder who was the mayor of Sevilla, and Fermin, the famous
bullfight tailor from Madrid, and a marquis who was trying to present
himself as the head of the government. "It was all very impressive," says
Federico.

"Now I'm legally adopted by him and I have his last name," he says.
"I'm married to a beautiful Gypsy girl and I have a beautiful daughter.
And I'm waiting to have a boy, for a special reason. Not just to have a
boy, but a bullfighter named after my dad.

"It's kind of a little revenge against the Spanish people, the way they
treated him. They always said a man with the name John Fulton could
never be a bullfighter, and that a foreigner could never be a bullfighter.

Well, this kid is going to carry John Fulton's name, and even though that's a foreign name he'll have full Gypsy blood. It'll say John Fulton on the bullfighting carteles, but they'll have to admit he's good.

"I want to have a boy soon so my dad can say, Look, kid, this is the way you fight a bull. I want my dad young enough so he can still go out in the country and show him everything he has learned. Everything, in all those years of practice."

5

TESTING BULLS

THE ESSENCE of bullfighting is the bull. A bad bull is worthless for even the most talented matador, while an artless, even timorous, matador can succeed with a noble bull that charges consistently and predictably, "as if on rails," as the expression goes.

A good fighting bull is large, aggressive even when wounded and brave in that it will charge repeatedly without hesitating. Such bulls aren't produced randomly. Breeding is as much a part of bullfighting as of thoroughbred horse racing, and bull ranches occupy vast tracts of prime land around Spain: in the lowlands of southern Andalusia, in the hills of Extremadura, on the plateau surrounding Madrid, in Navarra to the far north and in Salamanca bordering on Aragon. Millions of potentially productive areas, all in private hands, are used for bull-grazing instead of producing food for the vast underclass of the country. Those who defend the bullfight respond that without the sprawling ranches, called *ganaderías,* which are set aside for the breeding and development of fighting bulls, the *toro bravo* would have ceased to exist long ago.

Of the necessary qualities in a fighting bull, the most important is bravery. A small bull or a bull with badly formed horns can still give a good performance in a *novillada* or in a full corrida in a small town, and the sense of danger will be there if the bull is brave enough. But if the bull refuses to charge, trotting aimlessly around the ring, or if it charges irregularly, hesitating or pausing mid-thrust to lift its head and consider its options, or, worst of all, if it retreats into a defensive position with its back to the barrera in a spot in which it feels comfortable, its *querencia,* and awaits the matador there, the spectacle won't be enjoyable. If the matador is pigheaded or desperate or ignorant enough, it will be bloody.

Accordingly, bulls are bred for bravery. But there are other, less noble, characteristics that can be bred into a bull. Since the time of Joselito and Belmonte, bulls have been bred smaller and smaller, their horns closer together and their natures more docile, so that many of today's wild bulls would have seemed tame or otherwise unsuitable a half-century ago.

The bulls have changed because bullfighting has changed. Today's public wants to be entertained, and the matadors oblige. Passes that formerly would have been considered flamboyant, even baroque, certainly unnecessary, have become staples. The bullfighting sensibility of today's aficionados was created by watching such adornment and the aficionados are willing to let matadors fight less threatening bulls, even bulls with shaved horns, in order to get it. Twirling capes, spinning toreros . . . it would be easy for a casual spectator to conclude that such spectacle *is* the bullfight.

This change in attitude can be traced to Belmonte, who first showed the world the breathtaking gymnastics that a man can perform with a bull. It happened by accident: bowlegged, not the least bit athletic, Belmonte was forced to work closer to the bull than anyone before him, to bring the bull to him instead of merely passing it. After that, simply dominating a wild animal didn't thrill the masses enough. That was fine as long as you were watching Belmonte, for he had the skill and bravery to work his magic with the huge, fierce, unpredictable bulls while avoiding a goring. But matadors since haven't had such genius. To obtain the desired effect the characteristics of the bulls have therefore been watered down, with much of their size and ferocity bred out.

Belmonte well understood the revolution he caused. "The fighting bull of today is a product of civilization, a standard, industrialized article," he wrote in his 1937 autobiography. "Its development has been one-sided, toward making the fight more pleasing to the eye." One can only imagine what he would say now.

There are bulls remaining of a more traditional caste, but almost nobody will fight them. The bulls of Don Eduardo Miura are reputed to be the best fighters in Spain; and of the hundred-odd active matadors in Spain, perhaps half a dozen regularly agree to perform with them. Espartaco, for example, proved himself last year at a charity corrida fighting six Miuras by himself, and although he didn't cut an ear, he performed admirably. But it may be a long time before we see Espartaco in a ring with a Miura again. Manili, Ruiz Miguel, Tomás Campuzano and Victor Mendes often agree to face Miuras these days, out of some combination of pride and necessity, and if you see the Miuras fighting at a major feria it's a good bet you'll have one of those four and probably two of them among the three matadors on your cartel. There is a long list of matadors you assuredly won't see.

Several other strains of bulls have qualities similar to those of the Miuras, most notably the Victorino Martins and the María Luisa Domínguez branch of the Guardiolas. But again, most matadors who have a choice—that is to say, the most popular and sought-after matadors— will demand bulls that are not so dangerous. In that way expectations will be lower, for critics are especially harsh on matadors who waste noble bulls with lackluster or hesitant performances.

A few matadors have the artistry to actually raise the quality of an unsuitable bull, taking an animal that starts the corrida reluctant to charge (the bullfighting term is *manso,* meaning tame or mild), slowly and carefully giving it confidence and eventually constructing a serviceable *faena.* It's inspiring to see such a performance, and bullfight critics and knowledgeable spectators appreciate the art, but it is success in a minor key. It doesn't compare to seeing a matador triumph with a Miura.

Bulls are intelligent animals and learn quickly, and one of the immutable laws of the corrida is that a bull in a bullring must be encountering a dismounted man with a cape for the first time in its life. A quarter-hour of passes is enough to convince the bull that the man, not the cloth, is the enemy; that's why the longer a faena continues, the more difficult and dangerous it becomes. But at the same time that the bull is uncovering the ruse of the cape and the muleta, its physical powers are diminishing. At about the moment the bull comes to understand enough to kill a man, it should be weakened to the extent that the matador can kill it first. That algebra provides much of the inherent beauty of the spectacle. The increasing danger of the passes validates the emotion.

Stories are told about aspiring matadors sneaking onto ranches and caping young bulls by moonlight to perfect their technique. This isn't a common practice—for one thing, it is exceptionally difficult to separate a single bull from a herd, which is necessary to make it charge—but from time to time youngsters are discovered lurking with cloth and stick in the pastures of a *ganadería,* and when caught they are severely punished. It goes beyond trespassing and the fear of a damaged horn or hoof: bulls that have been fought, however primitively, appear just the same as pristine fighting bulls—until they arrive in the ring. Then, encountering a man for a second time, they become a mortal danger to the matador and a disgrace to the breeder.

Because of this limitation there is one great difference between breeding wild bulls and breeding champion horses. In thoroughbred racing, the finest and most successful males retire from racing and have prolific, immensely profitable careers as stud horses. But there is no second act in the life of the *toro bravo.* A bull that appears in a corrida finishes the day dead, no matter how inspiring his performance. (There are a very few exceptions: once every decade or so, a bull appears of such nobility and *casta* that the matador asks for and receives permission to spare its life. It happens so seldom as to be statistically insignificant.) There is no way to know how a bull will react when it charges into a plaza de toros, and once you realize how good it is, it is too late to use it for breeding because it has about fifteen minutes left to live and is otherwise occupied. As a result, the male bloodlines of the fighting bull involve mostly guesswork and purely physical characteristics. Bravery must be bred in on the female side.

Female bovines are checked for bravery during a ceremony called a *tienta,* or *tentadero,* meaning testing. These are held irregularly during the spring and summer at ranches throughout Spain. A picador is hired and matadors, novilleros and well-connected aspirants are invited to come to the *ganadería* and work the cows. Sometimes urchins eager for a chance to perform arrive uninvited, and often the breeder will let them cape a cow at the end of the day. Some successful matadors have been discovered this way, but not many.

During a *tienta* each cow is temporarily wounded by the picadors, who drive a metal shaft under its hide from the safety of a horse's back. Then a torero works it with the red cloth muleta to see how eager it is to continue fighting. Those who react aggressively enough are included in the mating pool. Those who don't will soon provide an evening's meal for the ranch.

The afternoon's work gives matadors and those who want to become matadors good practice with live animals, and sometimes they'll manage to impress influential people. Usually it is enough for a bullfighter to work up a sweat, get the kick of making some passes with the muleta and drink beers or sherry as the sun sets, knowing that another day of life has been lived—precariously, but well.

■■■

When John Fulton invites me to a *tienta* I accept instantly. Years ago, a breeder named Alonso Moreno de la Cova helped John take his first tentative steps toward credibility. The two have remained friends, although the old man can be contrary and eccentric. Don Alonso has some cows that are ready to be tested and he has asked John to come—and to bring Manolito, the tiny Mexican. Manolito's manager will also be there. He's a retired banderillero and gregarious, off-center character named Vicente Navarro whom we call Navarrito. That was his professional name and it has become his nickname, too.

Navarrito has known John for more than a quarter-century. When John took his alternativa in Sevilla in 1963, Navarrito was a banderillero for him. He knows a bit of English and delights in startling me by shouting it out at random times. "Close the window!" he yells, once we are on the highway, and "Son of a bitch!" when a white SEAT cuts in front of us on the open road. He has an oversized pear-shaped head with tufts of black hair and a belly like a coal stove. He looks like a cartoon character.

Navarrito used to drink to excess and now he doesn't drink alcohol at all. It's a good thing; from the stories I've heard he was a terrible drunk. He was a Communist when that was illegal in Spain and was in a bar once loudly expounding his opinion when two uniformed officers of the Guardia Civil arrived toting clubs and guns. The Guardia Civil is Spain's rural armed militia and it represents the final word in matters of law and order. Officers are respected, and even feared, but not by a drunken Navarrito. His greeting for them was a shout: "When I have my first son, I'm going to name him Lenin! Lenin Navarro!"

After the ensuing commotion the Guardia Civil decided to remove Navarrito from the bar—for his own good, as well as everyone else's. Utterly drunk, he slugged one of them in the face. This is close to a capital offense in Spain: people have been locked up for a long time, or worse, for punching a member of the Guardia. Navarrito was fortunate.

They released him twelve hours later, not long before he was scheduled to place banderillas for John. On the other hand, they had worked him over so well that he could barely move his arms or walk. Advised to enter a hospital, he summoned up the strength to work the corrida successfully, even artfully. The adventure sounds unlikely but John insists he was there to see it. "Stories like that are what bullfighting is all about," he says.

In his forties now, Navarrito has become quite respectable. He has been retired since 1987, and agreed to serve as Manolito's manager because John's connections weren't helping. Navarrito can be found every day just before noon sitting at a sidewalk table outside the Tres Reyes bar, drinking strong coffee and talking bullfighting.

It's past four o'clock when we reach Moreno's ranch, near Lora del Río out the Córdoba highway. We turn down a dirt road that bisects two jade-green hills and make our way to a whitewashed brick structure, a small bullring. We climb a three-story stone platform and look down. The walls of the *plaza de tienta* have been painted deep red, and the sand is brown, smooth and uniform. There are vivid colors in every direction. Behind are verdant hills stretching to the horizon. Off to the right are hills of brown-black naked earth that has been sown with seeds. All the land we can see in every direction belongs to Don Alonso.

The surroundings are quiet and the air smells fresh, a welcome change from the congestion of the city. It's warm in the sun but cool in the shade on the middle level of the viewing platform, where chairs have been set out for us. The sky is huge here. Straight ahead over the bullring, several miles distant, a lone house is set against the horizon.

Alonso Moreno's is one of nearly three hundred bull ranches in Spain. Each will send bulls to an average of seven or eight corridas a year, although the number can vary enormously. Don Alonso's bulls make the feria carteles in Sevilla from time to time, and he usually has a corrida in Madrid.

Soon about half a dozen cars are parked by the ring. An aspiring novillero called Chiquilín has come from Córdoba with his manager and some friends. He's the great-grandson of Lagartijo, one of bullfighting's legendary Four Caliphs of Córdoba. Chiquilín is scheduled to debut as a professional bullfighter this spring, and he, like Manolito, is wearing *traje corto,* a form of modified evening dress that toreros wear in festivals, less formal than the full suit of lights. Chiquilín looks young, scared, lanky and almost distinguished in the dark vest and white shirt. Manolito looks small.

The picador arrives on his horse, trotting up the dirt lane. Another novillero comes, shaking hands all around, dressed in a polo shirt and loafers like a prep school student. Don Alonso rolls up in a four-wheel-drive Jeep. He's wearing a cowboy hat and looks Texan.

The first cow, branded number 697 across its flank, comes charging out of the makeshift toril braying and snorting. Even though it is a cow and not fully mature, the sense of danger is palpable. It's not like seeing a full-sized bull in the ring, but the horns are frightening and it builds up plenty of speed when it charges. Stories are plentiful about matadors getting badly gored at *tentaderos* (and at least one killed: the distinguished Antonio Bienvenida), and it is easy to see how.

Chiquilín works the cow with the cape, moving the cow toward the center of the ring and then closer to the picador, who is sitting atop his horse gesturing and grunting. From where I sit I can hear the cow and even smell it; we're that close.

"If she were an excellent cow she would charge from that distance," John tells me as the animal stares at the picador. "She's not an excellent cow."

Nor is Chiquilín an excellent torero, even though his bloodlines are probably better than the cow's. The cow finally takes the pic twice and Don Alonso tells Chiquilín to work it as best he can with the muleta. Don Alonso is interested in seeing how readily it charges, but we're all watching Chiquilín. We know he's scheduled to appear in a novillada in Umbrete in the middle of the month and in Carmona a week later.

The cow is lackluster and Chiquilín seems to have little idea what to do with it. Don Alonso has lost interest and starts identifying for his visitors some of the crops he's growing—onions, sugar beets, sunflower seeds. If Don Alonso is like most *ganaderos,* the money he makes comes from his crops, not his bulls. Raising bulls is a hobby, expensive and high profile, and it usually doesn't turn a profit. "I'm going to harvest four million kilos of onions this year," he tells me.

John calls my attention back to the ring. The cow has developed a definite *querencia.* This is easy to recognize. When charging left to right it sprints on past Chiquilín for several yards and only then turns around for the return. But when going right to left it almost immediately comes back the other way. Clearly, it feels most comfortable over there.

A matador has to be able to recognize where a bull has made its *querencia* and then to draw it out. The latter can be accomplished with a series of passes or by dragging the cape along the ground with one hand. Chiquilín permits this cow to ensconce itself exactly where it wants to be, and then he makes an even worse mistake. When he lines up the cow for a mock killing, which is done with the palm of the hand in place of a sword, he manages to get himself directly between the cow and its *querencia*. "You think he's in the right place?" John asks me. Before I reply, the cow charges directly at its *querencia*—and at Chiquilín. The teenager is soon dancing on the end of a horn, pushing the bucking cow away with his hands. Manolito and some of the others run out flashing capes to distract the cow and Chiquilín scampers to safety, dejected but unbloodied.

Manolito handles the second cow. After it has charged the picador three times, Don Alonso calls for Manolito to take the muleta. Manolito executes some graceful passes but there are thirty or forty seconds between charges as he struggles to pique the cow's interest and it is clear the cow won't serve. "Kill it, hombre!" Don Alonso calls, asking for the mock *estocada* that ends the cow's time in the ring, but Manolito works another pass. "Now!" exhorts Alonso. He's seen enough to know that the cow isn't usable for breeding and he doesn't want to waste any more time. Manolito profiles and executes a simulated kill, deftly running his hand to the end of the cow's tail.

The *tienta* continues in this manner for another hour as several more cows are tested. Some pass, some don't. The day is languid and everyone seems to be sleepy in the heat of the afternoon. Alonso has been talking about his crops with some of his guests. Suddenly he turns back toward the bullring and yells for John to work one of the cows.

John hadn't been expecting this, I know, and he politely declines. I'm disappointed. Hemingway saw John Fulton fight a bull and Michener did and Juan Belmonte. This is only a *tienta,* but if I don't see John with the muleta here I don't know when I will. Don Alonso asks again, and this time John feels obligated. He walks down the steps and into the ring and Manolito hands him the muleta. He takes the stance of a matador and his stomach hangs over his belt, but with his first pass it's evident he is more accomplished and more graceful than anyone we've seen today. He has a tricky moment when the cow catches him in the leg and when he fights it off blood from the side of her body spatters on his white shirt. But he recovers nicely, works three brisk *naturales* with the left hand and passes the muleta on.

"That's my dope, my fix," John tells me later. "Alonso is such a weirdo. I told him no, I'm old, I'm out of shape, but he insisted. You know, he has invited me out here plenty of times and then not let me fight. Today, when I had no intention of doing anything, he insists."

Navarrito is rambunctious on the long ride home and Manolito is morose. John is pensive. Thinking back on the afternoon, I wish I'd had a camera to record John's passes on film. John Fulton isn't one of history's great bullfighters, of course. He's more a curiosity than anything else. But I'm an American aficionado, and he's the best bullfighter we have. He's fifty-seven years old and who knows how many bulls he has left?

Later, Federico asks if I caped any cows and I tell him no. Although I want to know the sensation of time stopping and death being cheated as the animal thunders by, it doesn't seem worth risking serious injury— or even serious embarrassment. I have enough respect for toreo not to try it myself as some foolish stunt. I'm sure Don Alonso would have let me try with some harmless younger animals if I had asked, and that would have been fine, an apt simulation of the experience. But caping bulls isn't my dream and I'm hesitant to use up anyone else's opportunity, or their good fortune. They need it more than I do.

6

FIRST OF THE
SEASON

SINCE arriving in Spain I have
stayed mostly in Sevilla, or close to it. Except for the *tienta* I haven't
had a reason to stray more than an hour in any direction, nor easy means
to do so. Now I find myself rolling down a shoulderless road on a Sunday
morning, skirting potholes, headed toward the Portuguese border in the
black SEAT Ibiza. There's a bullfight at the end of this journey, three
more hours away.

The car belongs to Rosa, a mathematics teacher at a local high school.
She's trying to get the tape player to function while I drive, but her
inquisitive little brother has dismantled it and rebuilt it and now it
doesn't fit. She accepts defeat and looks out the window at the small
towns flashing by.

Four hours is a long way to drive for a bullfight, but this is early in
the season and there isn't anything closer. Besides, we both have an
interest in Litri, the fourth-generation bullfighter who has a chance to
attain prominence this year. He's just twenty but has been given three
dates in Sevilla so the opportunity is there for a breakthrough. Until
now he has mostly earned a reputation for being young and handsome.
Teenage girls from all over Spain have taped his picture to their walls.

Such popularity doesn't mean he can't also be a serious bullfighter,
although some of the more cynical aficionados think it does. It doesn't

help that Litri uses a controversial style of bullfighting called *tremendismo,* as his father did. When done expertly it is as valid as any toreo but it tends to emphasize crowd-pleasing at the expense of technical proficiency. As performed by the vast majority of toreros, it looks tawdry.

We're headed for Olivenza, a town in Extremadura not far from Portugal. The road was level and well-marked for the first forty-five minutes out of Sevilla but at Aracena we turned left and it worsened. Now the scenery is spectacular. There are occasional towns, whitewashed, starkly set against the bright blue sky. This is mountainous country and the road veers and dips. The potholes get bigger and the driving gets harder.

There are olive trees on both sides of the road as we approach our destination, and a meadow of yellow and white flowers. My Michelin guide tells me Olivenza is laid out in the Portuguese fashion but I don't know what this means. Rosa, a typically parochial Sevillana, doesn't know, either. We hunt down the bullring and buy the cheapest tickets we can find: general admission in the sun. They're 2,200 pesetas each, nearly twenty dollars. After a meal at one of the two restaurants in town, we return at five o'clock. Passing through a portal with our tickets, we immediately climb a ramp of matted grass and enter at the highest point of the bullring. There is a view of the town at the top of the ramp and, inside, rows of stone seats all the way around.

■ ■ ■

Like most Sevillanos, Rosa has a rudimentary knowledge of bullfighting. She has seen only a few bullfights in person and none in recent years, because it's just too expensive to scalp a ticket at La Maestranza and her family doesn't buy an *abono,* but bullfighting's basics are second nature to her. She has known since she was old enough to walk that the corrida is constructed like a three-act play (six three-act plays, actually, since six bulls are disposed of in an afternoon) and that each act is called a *tercio.* The killing of each bull takes place in formal, ritualized fashion, starting with the picadors on horseback, who stab the bull with a pointed lance to weaken it so it lowers its head; continuing with the banderilleros, who place sticks wrapped in colorful paper just under the hide, mostly for ornamentation but also to reinvigorate the animal after the numbing pain of the pics; and ending with the matador alone with the bull in the sand. Dressed in the most ornate costume, paid the most money and given the most esteem, the matador leads the bull around his body with the muleta, a piece of red cloth draped over a stick—the phase of bullfighting foreigners think of when they hear the word.

Rosa has seen her brothers imitate those movements countless times, one pretending to be a bullfighter, another a bull. She has seen artful kills on television and terrifying gorings. She has read the gossip about Espartaco and El Cordobés and the rest in the glossy magazines and had her schoolgirl crush on Paquirri. This does not make her an expert— just a typical citizen of Spain and especially of Sevilla. She does not understand the nuance of the corrida, nor does she pretend to. And so, as we sit on the hard stone seats waiting for the clock to strike five and the proceedings to begin, it is she asking me about Litri and his chances for fame and fortune and a distinguished career.

Litri, just twenty years old, is the son of a renowned *tremendista* bullfighter of the sixties and the latest in a long line of bullfighters dating back to the last century. His given name is Miguel Baez, and in the newspaper profiles his mother calls him by the diminutive Miki. *Tremendismo* was evolved almost to the point of absurdity by Manuel Benítez, nicknamed El Cordobés, in the 1960s and 1970s, and the best way to understand the style is to know his story.

El Cordobés was a starving urchin from Palma del Río who desired fame and fortune so badly, he didn't mind getting gored to achieve it. He was sent to the hospital more than thirty times in his career, but now lives in a huge mansion outside of Córdoba. They say he is one of the richest men in Spain. This doesn't mean he was an artistically successful bullfighter, though. Actually, most knowledgeable aficionados despised him for his tricks and their popularity among the casual spectators, who assumed that the most dangerous-seeming maneuvers were indeed the most dangerous.

El Cordobés would turn his back to the bull after mesmerizing it with the muleta, which is something any matador can do and means nothing, but he did it with such flair that the crowd would respond. He liked to place his own banderillas, as some matadors do, but he would sometimes snap them in half and in half again until they were little more than pencil-sized points. That's dangerous, all right—and foolish. But he also had an innate understanding of a bull and its capabilities; a peculiarly accurate sense of exactly how daring he could afford to be with each particular animal.

At times his yearning for public adulation would prod him into attempting stunts that had never been seen in a bullring before. It was during those moments, intoxicated by the hysteria of the crowd, that he would either succeed marvelously or be gored and carried to the infirmary.

There is talk from time to time about a comeback by El Cordobés, but it will never happen. He fought bulls to get rich, and now he doesn't need the money. And he would have trouble regularly getting bulls with shaved horns as he did in his prime.

Litri is no Cordobés, for sure. Cordobés's main motivation was financial, but Litri has grown up in a privileged position. It's part of the paradox of bullfighting that sons of successful matadors often become matadors because they have the opportunity to spend time on bull ranches and learn the passes from the best; and yet, the best bullfighters are the hungriest. But Litri has incentive to perform well, a different sort of hunger in his belly. In his second season as a full matador, he's out to prove that he's an honest bullfighter in his own right, not just his father's son. There happen to be several others in his position just now: Rafi Camino, the son of the great Paco Camino, who took his alternativa in a double ceremony with Litri and has been nurtured by his father to the point where he must now succeed or fail on his own; Julio Aparicio, son of the *figura* of the same name, who is still a novice but has great potential; and Pepe Luis Vázquez, who is still trying to make his own name after nearly a decade of bullfighting but remains overshadowed by the name of *his* famous father.

■ ■ ■

During a bullfight the matadors or novilleros on the *cartel* perform in the order of their seniority. The one who has been a matador the longest kills the first and fourth bulls, the next longest the second and fifth, and the one with the least seniority the third and sixth. (The only time this changes is for the alternativa ceremony, when the most senior matador hands the muleta to the graduating novillero and asks him to kill the first bull.) Even though much of the crowd has come to see Litri, we have to sit through Luis Reina and Rafael de la Viña first.

Reina is from nearby Badajoz, and three different peñas have posted signs in the bullring in his honor. The bulls are from some local *ganadería,* and nobody expects much from them. The first one trots out, large and slow. Since this is a third-class ring, no weights are posted, but I estimate it weighs about 520 kilos. The biggest bulls in Pamplona and Madrid can weigh as much as 700 kilos, or 1,500-odd pounds, and there are minimum standards for how much a fighting bull has to weigh in order to perform for a first-, second-, or third-class ring. Any animal less than 420 kilos is a *novillo* regardless of its age and is fought by novilleros or in a festival, a bullfighting exhibition for charity.

Reina does some valid work with the cape and then sets out to attack the bull from his knees. This is one of the many maneuvers used to thrill the largely ignorant bullfight populace in a small country town such as Olivenza, which will have only one or two corridas a year. On his feet now, he passes the bull in a straight line, like a traffic cop waving vehicles past. Reina achieved a small measure of fame a year ago when he arrived at this very bullring having sold advertising space on his suit of lights, a transgression bordering on the blasphemous. Evidently he figured the notoriety would help his career. Seeing him fight now, it is easy to understand why he resorted to such a gimmick. His *estocada,* or sword thrust, is low and off to the right side. He needs to execute several *descabellos,* pokes to the spinal cord with a short sword that is specifically used to put a suffering animal out of its misery, before the bull finally expires. But this being a small town and Reina a local, he is awarded an undeserved ear by the president.

An ear is supposed to be awarded only when at least half the crowd demonstrates its approval of the matador's work by waving white handkerchiefs; any additional prizes are given at the discretion of the president, who sits majestically in a special box usually in the middle of the shade section. He is treated as royalty even though in most towns he is nothing more than a police chief.

Two ears and a tail is the best a matador can do with a bull, and you'll see that awarded maybe once a generation at a first-class ring such as that of Madrid or Sevilla. But here, in a pueblo, ears and even tails come cheap. Awarding them benefits everybody. The promoter will be able to boast that six ears and two tails, say, were cut at his bullring last Sunday, while the bullfighters will be photographed holding the ears aloft or leaving the ring on someone's shoulders and the picture will run as an advertisement in one of the bullfight weeklies and anyone who wasn't there will see it and perhaps be impressed.

Rosa knows this, and she doesn't take it seriously when Reina parades around the ring with his ear after a performance that was anything but a triumph. Even reporting the prizes awarded at a corrida such as this one is foolish. But if you see a matador cut an ear at the feria in Sevilla, for example, you will have witnessed something, because in the eighteen fights held at La Maestranza in 1988 there were a total of fourteen ears awarded and no tails, and in twelve novilladas there were eight ears awarded and no tails. The numbers in Madrid are similar: thirty-nine corridas during all of 1988, twenty ears and no tails; seventeen novilladas, eight ears, no tails. One matador, Espartaco, earned four of the fourteen ears awarded in Sevilla. Another, Manili, earned five of the twenty in Madrid.

Today's second matador, Rafael de la Viña, has drawn a reprehensible bull: weak, with little visible muscle. It falls six times during de la Viña's faena, but then the matador gets careless and gets caught during the kill. The bull rips de la Viña's pants cleanly from the cuff nearly to the waist, and the excitement earns the matador two undeserved ears.

It is Litri's turn. He fought in Castellón at the feria there yesterday (matadors are renowned for crisscrossing the country overnight in order to earn more money) and cut an ear, but was overshadowed by José Arroyo, the new Joselito, who has four years as a full matador behind him although he's just Litri's age. Joselito cut four ears in Castellón and earned a five-column headline on the bullfight page of *El Correo*.

Capework, the hallmark of a mature matador, isn't Litri's strength, and he gets the first *tercio* over quickly. Litri can't do much with the muleta and ends up passing the bull from a distance, putting together an uninspired faena and killing gracefully but a bit low. He earns polite applause.

Reina's second bull then refuses to leave the *toril,* the passageway which leads outward from the pens, and when it does emerge, we wish it hadn't. De la Viña's second bull is even worse. The matador has borrowed olive-green pants from somebody, and, perhaps to avoid losing them, too, he works the bull from such a distance that when it does decide to charge he has to strain to pass it. Why take a chance, he figures? With the two ears he was awarded earlier he has already upstaged Litri, unless Litri can do something spectacular with his second bull—and most of the locals can't tell the difference, anyway.

This last bull is slightly better. It buckles under a pic but rallies and spills the horse into the sand, showing at least some strength and tenacity. Litri handles the muleta smoothly. He shows a series of passes with his feet together, working with the right hand, and then drops to his knees and faces the bull with the muleta up around his neck. This is *tremendismo,* and the crowd responds. His passes are much closer than Reina's, the most valid we've seen all afternoon. Litri profiles and kills but lands the sword much too low, in the left lung. The bull loses a good quantity of blood from its mouth, a sure sign that a lung has been punctured. Litri gets an ear, and all three matadors leave on shoulders. We file out, shaking our heads.

■■■

On the ride home Rosa asks for my opinion. Like the vast majority of bullfights, this one was mostly terrible, with just a handful of moments to make the trip worthwhile. That's the way most of them are. Aficionados continue to attend them on the chance that they'll see something better—a few transcendent passes, maybe one superb kill. Rarely will any single matador in a given afternoon excel with both cape and muleta, then top it off by killing well. But every now and again you see a bit of the perfect performance.

I tell Rosa there was little good capework today, a couple of sets of banderillas well placed, and a few, very few, passes of real merit, in which the bull was made to bend around the body in pursuit of the muleta, guided in a sweeping arc with grace and control. Not once all afternoon did I feel the shortness of breath that comes during a truly artful faena, the matador pushing to its aesthetic limit his control of the untamed beast. Not once did we see a bull killed the way it is supposed to be killed: the sudden and dramatic fusion of man and animal into a single entity, leaving a moment later a vast emptiness where the emotion was and the animal staggering and then dead, its blood clotting and staining the sand.

But this was a bullfight in a third-class ring in the early part of March. What did I expect?

Still, the journey was worth the effort. We did see Litri work the bull close from his knees, and Rosa enjoyed the pageantry and the excitement. It's always fun to see a new bullring and a new town, and we even manage to get the tape player working for the ride back. There is little more to say about the bullfight, so instead we have Paul McCartney and the Andalusian band Patanegra booming into the chilly March night.

7

MEETING
ESPARTACO

THE FOLLOWING SUNDAY
we try again. Curro Duran is fighting a festival in a suburb called Alcalá de Guadaira, for the benefit of Sevilla's itinerant Gypsy population. I take the hourly bus there with four Americans I know, students here for the semester, and meet Rosa outside the bullring.

A festival is different from a full corrida in that the horns of the bulls are usually blunted and the bulls are likely to be flawed, or the smaller novillos. Usually, six or seven toreros will fight one bull each. It's difficult enough to convince a bullfighter to risk his life for charity, and killing one animal, with a certain amount of the danger removed, is about all most will agree to. Matadors and novilleros are often mixed on this type of cartel, and among those here is a promising teenager named Domingo Valderrama, one of the few bullfighters smaller than Manolito. He's a wizard with the muleta but has trouble killing, and that has held him back. The only time I've seen him previously, in a novillada in a village, he ruined a valid faena with a low sword thrust into his animal's flank.

There is always greater value in trying to kill the bull in the proper place, the triangle of exposed hide just below the neck, and to fail, however ignominiously, than to slink past and stab the bull in the side, risking nothing. A severe *bajonazo* will often puncture the bull's lung, causing its life to slip away agonizingly as it spits up blood, and such messy killings contribute to the impression that the corrida is brutal and inhumane, for a bull dying that death is clearly suffering. However, killing in the correct fashion requires exposing your own flesh to the bull's horn, and if you go up and over with perfect form, the horn will likely be positioned just inches from your heart at the moment the sword makes contact with the bull's hide. For that reason, killing properly and well is the bravest and most difficult thing a bullfighter can do. Some matadors, even highly regarded ones, never quite do it correctly.

Our group settles into seats in the sun. The small plaza de toros is situated beside a highway in the midst of a residential area and has lights strung across it like spokes of a wheel, for use during night corridas and other exhibitions. Above the top of the arena literally dozens of television aerials are visible.

Duran is the third matador on the cartel, and he's better than I expected he'd be from his reputation and the small-town atmosphere at his peña. With the cape he's self-assured and in control, letting the bull do the work, and he snaps off a classic *media verónica,* gracefully turning the cape inward so it slaps against his thigh. The faena that follows is simple but smooth. Duran, too, was left off the feria carteles even though he's from the area. He's good enough to fight in the Feria de Abril, but not so talented that his absence is a major omission, except home in Utrera, and he knows this. Still, his pride is wounded. This cozy bullring in a modern suburb is as close as he's likely to get to La Maestranza this year and he wants to prove his worth to the aficionados and journalists of Sevilla.

Duran's best passes are the backhanded *pases de pecho,* which are done only with the left hand. These usually end a series of *naturales,* in which the muleta is held low and the matador turns with the bull's charge and, if we're lucky, guides the animal around his body. The *natural,* also done only with the left hand, is the basic pass in bullfighting. If you can do it well, you can earn a living in a suit of lights even if you can do little else.

When the bull starts to veer toward the muleta, Duran works one more series and then kills on his second *estocada,* up and over the blunted horns, earning two ears and a *vuelta* around the arena. Along the way he gets caps tossed to him, several wineskins and a bunch of flowers. Over near our side of the stands, the cheap seats, a fan throws a crutch. Duran laughs and hands it back.

This crowd, suburbanites, is better dressed, better behaved and more sophisticated than those in Olivenza—and more difficult to please. There is usually a correlation between the size and location of a town and the sophistication of its aficionados, and the crowd in a first-class bullfight during a major feria is the most demanding of all, with the exception of Pamplona during the feria of San Fermín, because by late afternoon there everyone is too drunk to know the difference between good toreo and bad. Raucous bands play in the stands, distracting attention, and usually by the time of the *encierro* the next morning almost nobody can remember what happened the afternoon before—and the intervening evening is lost forever.

Domingo Valderrama is the last of the six toreros to work and the only novillero (even in a festival, the order is determined by seniority). He's a tiny kid, nineteen years old but looking years younger, and his cape and hat appear preposterously large on him. He removes his hat for his faena and we see his big, wide eyes clearly. I fear for him, he looks so young—but that is clearly part of his appeal. "They're going to let that boy fight?" Rosa asks. "Does his mother know?"

His faena is decent but he needs six sword thrusts to kill the bull. "I don't think he's tall enough to reach it," Rosa says. My American friends, unaccustomed to the spectacle, are hooting at Valderrama until we tell them to stop. The teenager is trying to kill correctly; he just hasn't mastered that aspect of his craft. By the time the bull dies the emotion of the afternoon is gone, and we leave the bullring talking quietly.

Crossing the street through the traffic, Rosa spots a casually dressed young man walking some ten paces ahead of us. *"Mira!"* she yells. "Look!"

It is Juan Antonio Ruiz—Espartaco, the most famous active matador in Spain. But he doesn't look famous—just familiar. The first time I saw him, on an oven-hot Sunday in July 1987, at the plaza de toros of Jérez de la Frontera, just a few streets away from where sherry was invented and where all the major sherry companies in Spain still have their warehouses, Espartaco with sheer determination cut an ear with a Santiago Martín Sánchez bull that could only be described as schizophrenic. In doing so he overshadowed two legends, the aging, temperamental Gypsy Rafael de Paula and the innovative and controversial genius Paco Ojeda, who has since retired.

Ever since that afternoon, when I've thought of the allure of bullfighting, Espartaco's face has flashed through my mind. I see his eyes narrowed in concentration while citing a bull, the lines at the corners belying the youth of a man not yet thirty; or his contagious grin as he steps around the ring waving to fans after a superior performance. The face is framed by an absurdly bad haircut, bangs chopped straight across the forehead, that manages to make him both handsome and homely at the same time. Of course, it is impossible to forget the face; it is in every issue of every bullfight magazine and plastered on walls around the country whenever he is fighting nearby. With Paquirri dead and Franco gone and the drab socialists in power and the national football team unfulfilling, he is the closest thing Spain has to a hero these days. Here he is, walking his familiar stiff-legged walk just ahead of us, his lips set in a line: a serious look for a serious man who has already sacrificed his youth—and may one day sacrifice his life—for success and his art.

He stops when an older man, thin and wrinkled, taps him on the shoulder. We're close enough to hear him address Espartaco in the familiar form, the second person singular, without the unseemly awe most Americans have in the presence of television stars and athletes. After a brief conversation, the man pumps his hand firmly and walks off and I step up. I explain that I am an American aficionado writing a book.

"I have seen you fight several times," I say, "and I'm looking forward to your four appearances in Sevilla." He seems extraordinarily polite, and thanks me with sincerity. I add that I've recently seen his brother, a novillero called Espartaco Chico, in a festival. That day, several months ago in a temporary bullring in a quiet village called Umbrete, Espartaco Chico had performed so dreadfully with his animal that shame compelled him to purchase the spare novillo with his own money and try again. He fought the second one at the end of the day, butchering it almost equally. I do not tell Espartaco this, only that I saw his brother kill two bulls.

"The first and the last," Espartaco says, raising a finger. *El primero y el último.* "I was there, too. A day of bad luck."

Another group passes and greetings are exchanged and the informality of it all is striking. Standing on a sidewalk, chatting with anyone who wanders by, is this man who earns several million dollars annually by risking his life, an entertainer and public figure and a role model. From nowhere a young girl in a pink dress emerges and hands him a flower, a single rose, and he grins and thanks her and she rushes off, embarrassed. The American students, surely the only people in sight who don't recognize Espartaco, start showing their impatience, and Rosa, shy and tongue-tied, is peeking meekly around my back. There is nothing more to say except "Good luck." I shake hands and move on.

"Who was that?" one of the Americans asks Rosa in his halting Spanish.

"The king," she answers, and we laugh. "*Sí, hombre*. That was the king of Spain."

■ ■ ■

Since bullfighting became a public entertainment several centuries back there have been bullfighting bars. Spanish society demands it. The corrida lends itself to subjective discussion, and what better way to discuss anything than over a tapa and some *fino* in a local tavern?

In Madrid, Hemingway used to drink and talk bullfighting at the Hotel Victoria, and most aficionados maintain it is still the best bullfight bar in the city. But Madrid is a huge place and bullfighting is one of many, many pursuits. You could be there on the day of a major bullfight, walking down the tree-lined Paseo del Prado toward the great museum or sitting beside the rowboats sipping a beer in the middle of Parque Retiro or shopping in the luxurious stores that line Calle Serrano, and have no idea that a bullfight was taking place.

Sevilla is different. Drinking and talking bullfighting are the two great local passions, and they're almost inevitably intertwined. In a sense, nearly every bar in Sevilla is a bullfight bar. I once tried to catalogue the carteles and photos on the walls of the bars I went to but ultimately abandoned the project. There are too many places to drink and most are overflowing with memorabilia. One entry reads: "Casa Ramón, Plaza de los Venerables—many framed photos including three of Pepe Luis Vargas in action, five showing Curro Romero with the muleta (two of those autographed), one of Lucio Sandin; and two carteles of the feria, one from 1932 with little pictures down the sides of Chicuelo, Nicanor Villalta, Marcial Lalanda, Cagancho and Domingo Ortega, among others, and the other without pictures, from 1944." And another: "Bar Nido de Robín, Calle Harinas—framed photos of El Yiyo and Espartaco, two of Curro Romero (both autographed) and one with an illegible signature of a banderillero; a framed feria cartel from 1985, a cartel from a 1958 festival that included Manolo Vázquez, Antonete, Juan Bienvenida and Paco Camino; a 1953 cartel; and a 1944 cartel from Sevilla that includes

Luis Miguel Dominguín." The notes went on like that for twenty pages until I decided I'd rather spend my time in bars drinking and talking than scribbling in a notebook.

Here in Sevilla much of the real bullfight crowd congregates at Los Tres Reyes on Calle Reyes Católicos, across from the Hotel Becquer, which is where most of the matadors used to stay before a new policy kicked them out. After a great success the ruckus in the lobby was unpardonable and the other patrons complained. Also, there was usually damage done. John Fulton tells me he has seen signs outside hotels in Mexico that say "No Pets or Bullfighters."

There is a restaurant upstairs at Los Tres Reyes, a balcony overlooking the street and glassed in because of the air-conditioning, but I have never eaten there nor known anyone who has. The action is downstairs. The barroom itself is a single misshapen room. Everything is marble: white, black, and gray—with the exception of a column in the middle covered with brown panels. Serrano hams, a delicacy of the region, hang along one wall. On another is the massive stuffed head of a seven-year-old bull that was killed in La Maestranza in 1895, with a plaque that provides the pertinent details. There are five photos of Paquirri together in a frame, and in the back, a pencil drawing of Manolete, looking somber as usual.

Most important, there are always at least two or three current bullfight posters on the walls, carteles for the coming weeks from all over Spain and the south of France. If you arrive in Sevilla and want to know where to find a corrida on the coming weekend, this is where you find out. Even the bullfight weeklies aren't entirely up-to-date in announcing corridas. New ones are scheduled somewhere in Spain practically every day in the summer, though usually not near enough to Sevilla to justify pasting posters all over town. But the people who run Los Tres Reyes get hold of them and put them up. It's necessary to come by the bar at least every couple of days to see the new carteles, if for no other reason than to plan your weekend trips out of town.

Late mornings, bullfight aficionados, managers and agents gather for coffee and the nominal Sevilla breakfast of bread and butter and jam and perhaps a slice of Serrano ham. Contracts are negotiated and deals are struck. Midday, much of the same crowd stops by for a tapa and a beer. You can get *cola de toro,* bull's tail, which looks and tastes like short ribs. A big plate of beets costs seventy cents and beef in tomato sauce is a dollar.

I often come to the Tres Reyes at night, too, although it isn't as crowded. Tonight I walk in and see a huge cartel that has been posted for a corrida in Écija, with Curro Romero, Manzanares and Manili. It isn't long before I have a dispute going between a jagged-toothed Sevillano and a volatile aficionado from Bilbao, a man in his forties, with a big belly and huge forearms. The latter is down for a few days on business and he knew where to stop for his gin and Coke and a bull-fighting discussion. It begins when I inquire about the cartel in Écija, which seems enticing now that Manzanares isn't coming to Sevilla.

"Manzanares, that asshole," says the man from Bilbao. "What do you care about him? Curro Romero is the only true man on that cartel."

That is absurd. Manili triumphed with the Miuras in Madrid last year and Manzanares is acknowledged as a classy, if erratic, performer, practically a *figura*. But Spaniards love to begin arguments by disparaging other people's manhood and sexual preferences. Words are used injudiciously and illogically, without regard for applicability.

"Actually," offers the Andalusian now, "I agree with the *Norteamericano*. Curro Romero is a fat old man."

The discussion degenerates into an exchange of sexually explicit insults, always directed toward the other's admired torero and never the man himself. Nobody wins the argument because such an argument is unwinnable. Somebody will come by and ask if anyone there happened to see Litri in Olivenza last week, and if nobody did, the performance, however mediocre it might have been, suddenly becomes an all-time classic, every pass a marvel, unless the man is no *litrista* but a detractor, in which case the little *maricón* has no validity whatsoever as a torero and his passes were ten feet from his body and the bull was probably drugged anyway and just wait until the little snot gets to Sevilla. It goes on like that all night.

The Andalusian leaves, and the man from Bilbao and I talk on, fast friends now despite our taurine disagreement. He tells me about running with the bulls in Pamplona during *sanfermines*. "I do it every year," he says. "You have to try. It's unlike anything in the world."

I finish my beer and wish him well. I tell him I'll run with him in Pamplona soon, maybe next year.

"But that won't be possible," he says. "I have a fatal malady."

"What?" I wonder if my Spanish has failed me.

"I'm going to die in September," he says, and not a bit morosely. "The doctors told me."

"I don't believe it," I say. What else is there to say?

"It's true. Cirrhosis of the liver. If I don't drop dead by September I'm definitely gone by March. Six months to a year, they said."

"But that's terrible! Maybe they're wrong."

"No, they're not wrong. But it's not so terrible either. We all have to die sometime, right?"

The next day, Federico Fulton tells me he attended a funeral for an in-law who had died suddenly on stage playing flamenco guitar, felled by cirrhosis of the liver at age fifty-seven.

"It happens all the time in Spain," Federico says. "That's because everyone drinks so much."

That day I limit myself to a small glass of Rioja.

■■■

The Sunday after seeing Espartaco on the street in Alcalá de Guadaira I set out to see him on purpose in Jaén—and to see Litri, too. It will be the first direct competition of these supposed rivals this season, and the cartel is sweetened by the presence of Manzanares. There are those who believe that Manzanares is capable of the best toreo in Spain. He has what Espartaco lacks—the soul of an artist—but no consistency: he fights well, it is said, only when he cares to. He also rarely fights bulls from the prestigious ganaderías, one reason the Madrid taurine community, which is oriented more toward the bull than toward the matador, disdains him.

The bulls in Jaén will be from Alonso Moreno's ranch. John Fulton called him last night and told him I'd be arriving on the noontime bus from Sevilla. He passed along instructions to meet at his hotel.

It's a four-hour bus ride from Sevilla to Jaén. I borrow an alarm clock and rise at seven, then walk the twenty minutes from my apartment to the bus station. It's cold and the streets are practically empty. I walk through the Plaza del Museo and out Calle Alfonso XIII, turning right at Sierpes, the well-known pedestrian path. There are no pedestrians here now, and the kiosk at which I often buy my bullfight magazines is shut tight. It seems earlier than it is because the sun is low in the sky. Despite the warmth of the afternoons here it is still just March, and Sevilla is about as far west in its time zone as any major city in the world. Logically, we should be in the next time zone west, Portugal's, and it should only be about quarter after six right now. But all of Spain, save the Canary Islands, runs on the same time for the sake of conven-

ience, so it gets light later here and stays light past ten o'clock in May,
June and July. For that reason, bullfights here begin at 6:30 or even 7:00
P.M. in the summer months. It is not until then that the sun has sunk
low enough for even minimal comfort.

I hasten down Sierpes, past a slot-machine parlor that stands where
Juan Belmonte's favorite bar used to be, and past one of my favorite
Sevilla peculiarities: the Enrique Sanchis El Cronometro. It has to be
one of the best places in the world to set a watch. Mounted high above
the street like a vast headboard, in dark wood, golden piping, and neon,
is a sign for a local clock shop. Embedded in it are five clocks of identical
facing, a large one on top and four smaller ones across the bottom, all
ticking in synchronicity, exact to the second.

You may have seen in fancy international hotels or television news-
rooms a row of clocks along a wall, each displaying the time in a different
part of the world. This is similar, except that at the Enrique Sanchis El
Cronometro there is no interest in what the time is in other cities. People
here don't concern themselves much with the outside world. They don't
read foreign papers and they don't eat much ethnic food. V. S. Pritchett
wrote in *The Spanish Temper* that the true passion of the Spaniard is
provinciality, that "he turns his back. His lack of curiosity amounts to
a religion." The Sevillanos are the most uninterested of all. Their in-
troversion is almost a source of pride.

As a result, nobody considers it the slightest bit strange that all five
clocks are set to Sevilla time.

■ ■ ■

An hour out of Jaén, the skies are overcast, and there is wind whistling
against the side of the bus. Bullfighting is nakedly vulnerable to the
elements. A football game in freezing, snowy weather, a World Series
game on a cold October night—these may suffer artistically, but they
will still provide a result, and separating winners from losers is, after
all, the prime purpose of a sporting event. But if an afternoon is windy
or chilly, or if drizzle has made footing uncertain, a torero has a valid
excuse to be lethargic, unimaginative, even cowardly.

Jaén is a terraced city that has been built on hills, so that if you occupy
the penthouse apartment of one of the many new buildings on the
outskirts of downtown you can look out your living room at an unin-
terrupted vista of fields and trees below you, but chances are you'll get
headlights through your bedroom window at night from the street above.

Walking toward the bullring, a sound truck passes me, advertising the fight, which is some five hours away. *Manzanares ... Espartaco .. Litri ... cinco y media en la tarde.* Around the corner is the plaza de toros made of dusty red brick and white concrete, built in 1962 in a modernistic style which today looks nostalgically antiquated, like many apartment buildings of the same era. As I approach the ticket window there is a commotion inside. I hear yelling and the slamming of a door, and the ticket seller disappears around the back. Moments later, he strides around the corner.

"The bullfight has been canceled," he says, eyes flashing. He gives me no time to ask questions. "Why canceled? Canceled because the bulls are bad!" There is no further explanation, and he slams the ticket window shut. "Maybe next week," he sneers, bolting the window closed, "we'll have better luck."

At the hotel they tell me that Don Alonso left for home early that morning. My bus ride home takes six hours and the olive groves and pungent cigarette smoke combine to nauseate me. No more trips for a while, I resolve—but then, none will be necessary. Curro Romero, Espartaco and Joselito will begin the bullfight season in Sevilla in a week, on the afternoon of Easter Sunday.

Leaving the bus station in Sevilla I see the streets crowded for the first night of Holy Week, people massed in anticipation of the ornate floats, and I'm certain I'm not the only person there thinking that the flickering of candles and the smell of the incense and the passionate singing in the streets, ancient and stunning and impressive, are also harbingers of the approaching spring—and of bullfighting in La Maestranza just seven days away.

PART TWO

THE FERIA

1

CREATING A
RIVALRY

EASTER Sunday dawns cool and overcast in Sevilla. As bullfight time nears, the wind is gusting, sailing advertising handbills into legs and hubcaps in the crowded streets. With an hour to go I find myself outside a bar at a table across from La Maestranza with John Fusco, a painter friend who lives half the year in Madrid and the other half in Maine. He has taken the train to Sevilla for three weeks of bullfights. We raise toasts of Magno cognac, mine to a memorable afternoon from our three matadors—while Fusco, whose orientation is taurine, proposes a drink to a corrida of massive bulls of steady *casta* and large horns. Nearby, a man rendered momentarily motionless by the crush of patrons overhears and lifts his own glass. "Let's drink to good weather," he says, his voice raised over the clamor. "Without that, nothing else matters."

For weeks the feeling of expectation for the first bullfight of the season has been palpable in Sevilla, and it has grown daily in intensity. The image of Jose Arroyo, "Joselito," just twenty years old and bearing that famous nickname, has been postered all over town. You can't turn a corner without seeing a Joselito poster on a wall or a photo of him in the window of a bar.

Joselito is from Madrid, where he was raised in poverty, and Fusco is an aficionado of his work. But the barrage of publicity angers Fusco, who thinks the kid can't possibly live up to all this billing. Fusco is nervous about Joselito, nervous about the wind and the overcast sky, nervous about everything. He sees some fifty bullfights a year but says he still sometimes vomits beforehand, which is a reason for the Magno: to calm his nerves. He's short, with straight black hair and a ratty blue windbreaker and a few generic-looking short-sleeve shirts. Thirty years old this week, he's the son of a New York doctor; he moved to Paris after graduating college. I don't know how he became interested in bullfighting; like most American aficionados he just stumbled upon it, then confirmed his alternativa of *afición* with frenzied readings of *The Sun Also Rises* and *Death in the Afternoon*. Fusco is the most opinionated person I know and he enjoys expressing his opinions. Every discussion becomes a philosophical ballet. Bullfighting is his passion, and in taurine terms he's a devout reactionary. He reads Joaquín Vidal in *El País* and nods with each radical polemic. I tell him he's nostalgic for a past he never knew.

Surprisingly, Fusco is indecisive on perhaps the fundamental bullfight issue of the era, at least in Andalusia. Curro Romero, the aging matador we will be seeing in La Maestranza this afternoon, has been polarizing opinions here for several decades. Now in his fifties, Curro will be terrible ten, fifteen, twenty bullfights in a row, wasting good bulls, ignoring bad bulls, making cursory stabs at the animals, killing shamelessly, running away—and then he'll get a bull he feels comfortable with and for maybe a couple of passes with the cape or a series with the muleta, *time stops*. That's how people describe it.

Nobody who has ever seen him perform at his best disagrees that when Curro is good, he's magical, maybe as good as anyone ever was. It's the difference between the Andalusian temperament and that of the rest of the world that Sevillanos are willing to wait months and spend hundreds of dollars for the chance of seeing Curro good for a few moments. Everyone else would have lost patience long ago.

Even as a young man Curro rarely performed at his best. Michener writes about seeing him numerous times before first seeing him good, and that was in the mid-1960s. In fact, the argument about Curro's worth has been raging ever since he took the alternativa on March 18, 1959, thirty years ago last week—long before either Espartaco or Joselito was born. But these days, even his so-called triumphs never consist of more than a few passes: Curro hasn't cut an ear in a major plaza in five years.

An aficionado I know, a tax collector from Sevilla, once told me:

"Curro Romero may be bad, very bad. But he may have one or two passes in an afternoon that are worth everyone else's faena." That seemed like saying a writer can have one or two sentences in an otherwise worthless book that are worth the book, but the tax collector became frustrated with me when I told him that. He said I was an American and I didn't understand, and that you can't compare writing, which is an unemotional art, to bullfighting. I went to Federico Fulton for an explanation. Federico is an unabashed *currista,* which is what fans of Curro are called, and he explained it this way: "He can be very bad with the cape, but at times he uses the cape, or sometimes the muleta, so slowly that the bull slows up, too, until finally Curro has it walking in the middle of a charge. You'll know it when you see it—it's incredible."

I find it difficult to conceive of a single pass so brilliant and artful that it makes an entire two-hour, fifty-dollar corrida worthwhile, but then I've never seen Curro good. "I used to think the same way as you do, and sometimes I still do," Fusco tells me now, downing his Magno in a gulp. "I'm no *currista*. But last year I saw him make seven passes that were simply fantastic. Unbelievable. Everyone was standing with tears in their eyes, their hair on end. It was electrifying, and since then I've had to reexamine my opinion. There are times when I feel he is simply worthless, the most shameless of them all, and then I remember those seven passes."

■■■

Forty minutes before the corrida, the streets and sidewalks outside La Maestranza are nearly impossible to navigate. There are people milling in the street, some shouting, waving, laughing, some in a rush to get inside the plaza, others lingering, conversing; mostly males, many dressed up in suits and ties. Hawkers are selling nuts and candy off plastic white card tables. Every bar in the area is overloaded with people and there are people staggering out into the street, not drunk but pushed from the doorways by the shifting overflow. On the street itself, wide and tree-lined, auto traffic is nearly impossible because of the commotion. Fusco and I take a difficult lap around the bullring, pushing our way through the crowd, and then we give up on atmosphere and go inside to wait on the hard stone seats.

Fusco has purchased individual tickets from the *reventa* for nearly every fight of the feria; today's put him up in the *grada* seats, the covered section above the *tendidos*. His sightline will be reasonably good because the bullring is small and there really aren't any bad seats; people are surprised to hear that the famous Maestranza, arguably the best-known bullring in the world, is one of the smaller big-city plazas in Spain. Even the *gradas* aren't very far away from the sand. This isn't true in Madrid, for example, or in several Mexican bullrings that cater to tourists and hold some twenty thousand people. At those places, you can find yourself so distant that it is impossible to know if a matador's passes are valid or not—but there the good seats are cheaper.

When you first start seeing bullfights it's advisable to sit far enough away to take in the whole panorama of the spectacle, and also not to be shocked by the vitality of the animal and its ensuing death. Then, as your *afición* gets more accomplished, you should do what you can to sit as close as possible, close enough so that when the bull emerges from the toril and into the light you can sense its size and ferocity and the danger, and when the matador passes the bull you can hear him grunt and the animal bellow and see the blood shining on its flank, and you can gauge the distance between the man and the horn. Later, when you are an expert, you can sit higher and catch every detail of the toreo, such as how far away from the barrera the matador is positioning himself or the geometry involved in preparing the bull for the placing of the banderillas.

I have my *abono* and the same seat for every fight. It is a *tendido abono,* better than the *gradas* but not as good as the barreras, just in front of a railing, one section to the left of the toril—a sun seat, to be sure, but not a bad one. Every seat is filled and La Maestranza looks her best. It is not an arena designed for spectator comfort, however. We each have very little room. The rows of stone have been divided into seats with painted lines, and the divisions are not wide, having been drawn both for maximum profit and the smaller dimensions of the bullfight patrons of several centuries ago. The man next to me, Leonardo, will be my neighbor for the duration of the feria. He's a businessman, in his late forties, and dressed fashionably. Behind me, Enrique and Antonio, older men, are talking up Curro. Antonio has his knees resting against the small of my back. I'm doing the same to the man in front. Leonardo takes a deep breath—he's nervous, too. "La Maestranza is old, older than the United States," he says to me.

The sky is clearing, but the wind has picked up: bad news. Wind is more detrimental to a bullfight than rain. Rain is unpleasant for spectators and matadors alike, but wind can kill. A gust can lift a cape or a muleta and make it sail without the torero's intention and a bull may charge at the waving cloth. If the torero happens to be standing behind it, he gets gored.

The Torrealta bulls we will see today have a reputation for being finely tuned. If they're on, they can be great. But often an entire batch of them, all six, prove worthless, despite their fine presentation. Curro Romero's first bull, the first bull of the season in Sevilla, is named Mandarin. It trots out of the toril and stands in front of us, considering. It weighs 544 kilos—approximately 1,200 pounds—and has large horns. Curro, resplendent in his purple-and-black suit of lights, waves the cape at the bull while stepping backward and then the picadors come riding in. Mandarin spills the horse on the first pic, but the second is long and damaging.

Curro's work with the muleta is worthless. He passes the bull as he trots backward, and by the end of the pass the bull is in Cádiz and Curro is in Alicante. *"Sinvergüenza,* Curro," someone yells: Shameless. Aside from the occasional insult, the crowd is completely silent, intent on the spectacle. This happens only in Sevilla. Anyone who tries to talk during a faena gets hushed until he stops. There is total concentration on what is happening in the ring, as if it were an opera. It is an affectation one quickly comes to appreciate.

Curro, having waved at the bull for maybe three minutes, takes the sword, profiles, and sinks a *bajonazo,* a low kill, in the animal's flank. There is whistling as it is dragged off.

Espartaco removes the bad flavor. Working with a 514-kilo bull called Arabesco, he performs a long series of maneuvers with the cape, then athletically steers the bull toward the picadors. "Athletic" is the perfect adjective for him: he's the optimal bullfighter for an American to like because he is so athletic. He has the grace of a center fielder, the presence of a quarterback. Standing in the ring, leaning against the barrera, he doesn't even look like a bullfighter, and his personality is more that of the athlete than the artist. Many matadors have, and cultivate, a reputation for temperamental behavior on the sand, but Espartaco is determined to give a good performance every time, with every bull, to the point where it hurts his growth as a bullfighter.

Because he is so consistent, he is contracted by dozens of pueblos every year to appear on the cartel in their one and only corrida. If the townspeople are going to pay their hard-earned money to see one bullfight in a year they're going to want to see something good, and Espartaco just about guarantees two faenas' worth of entertainment. But the bull-fight crowds in pueblos aren't discerning, and instead of being satisfied with solid, traditional toreo Espartaco will sometimes resort to a bit of *tremendismo* to give the people what he perceives is their money's worth. With his talent, he doesn't need to. His toreo has everything now but profundity, and he must concentrate on attaining that if he is to become a serious artist of the first rank. Through the years Espartaco has become less of a *tremendista* and more serious, and every season he wins converts who realize he is a matador to be taken seriously. But if you catch him in a small town with a difficult bull, he's still likely to ham it up.

Here in Sevilla there are no such concerns. This is where Espartaco is at his most serious and best. Several times he has been named *gran triunfador* of the feria, and several times he has been carried out of the *puerta grande,* which only happens here when you cut three ears in a day. (In Madrid, for whatever reason, the tradition has evolved differently. There, you need to cut just two ears in an afternoon to go out the front door on shoulders.) La Maestranza is Espartaco's home bullring, the closest major ring to his home in Espartinas, and even though his style is not the classic style of Sevilla, he is among supporters here.

Espartaco's faena is superb. With complete silence in the plaza, he works an accomplished series with the right hand, then switches to the left. La Maestranza's brass band, seated in the *gradas* up over my right shoulder, begins to play a pasodoble, an official sign of acknowledgment that the matador is performing well. The most renowned matadors have their own pasodobles, bits of music composed especially for them, and then there are a dozen or so pasodobles from the past that everyone knows. They sell this music on cassette tapes outside the bullring and in the tourist shops near the cathedral and on Calle Sierpes. Buy a tape and listen to it while driving down some American highway or in your American living room, and it brings back the sensation of the bullfight better than any book or photograph ever could.

As the pasodoble plays Espartaco is passing the bull cleanly with the left hand, guiding it past his body. (What he doesn't often do—what few matadors often do with regularity—is pull the bull around his body in the classic style. Still, he is able to link his passes because his *mandar,* his ability to provoke a charge, is exceptional.) Passes performed with the muleta in the left hand are more difficult and valid than those performed with the muleta in the right because of a simple geometric fact: the sword is always kept in the right hand, so when the muleta is also held in the right hand it is draped not just over the balancing stick but over the sword as well, extending the face of the cloth. But when the muleta is in the left hand, the matador has a face of cloth the length of the stick to work with, and nothing more—so he is positioned that much closer to the animal. Many matadors are hesitant about attempting anything too difficult with the left hand, but the left-handed *pase de pecho* and *natural* are the cleanest, starkest and prettiest passes in bull-fighting when done well.

Espartaco works extremely well with the left hand: even his detractors don't doubt his courage. His best pass of this faena is a slow backhanded pass from the left side, with the bull almost coming to a stop before trotting through. It is a wonderful pass and the crowd appreciates it. He then *naturales* all the way around his body and walks away to great applause.

The work is brutishly done but done well and with no emotional tricks. He has slowed the bull now and he profiles and kills it, thrusting the sword all the way in. The bull is tough and lingers, and a *descabello* is needed, but it is administered gracefully, the bull's spinal cord severed with a single stroke to end its misery, and the white handkerchiefs are waving in the wind all around the arena so the president of the bullring flips down his own handkerchief from his *palco:* an ear. Espartaco, grinning hugely, takes a victory lap and receives the requisite flowers, hats and other items thrown from the stands with more or less precision.

Joselito's first bull, called Escopetero, is black with a white underbelly, and it leaves the toril charging fiercely, with plenty of gas. Joselito, though still so young, is adept with the cape. He capes the bull slowly and smoothly, wrapping it around himself as the bull whizzes by, earning a series of *Olés* from the crowd. The crowd yelling Olé! at a bullfighter is a popular sign of recognition, just as the music playing is a more official sign. After the banderillas are placed, Joselito takes the muleta. There is pressure on him to live up to the publicity. He dedicates the bull to the crowd from the middle of the ring—usually done when a matador has seen something he likes in the bull and is reasonably con-fident of success—but then he can't get his animal to charge regularly.

Once a faena starts, the matador has maybe two series of passes to establish dominance, and if he doesn't, the bull will. During the course of a faena, either man or animal will grow stronger and the other weaker, and how that is determined is partly through the mood a matador conveys. Joselito can't get this hesitant bull to charge consistently, and soon it is evident that the bull is in control of the faena. It stops halfway through the passes now and looks ominously at Joselito, then hooks its horns upward. The bull is confident and dangerous now and must be killed and Joselito quickly kills it.

Every bull is different and must be approached with a different style and intention. Espartaco understands this and it is one of the strengths of his toreo, but Joselito doesn't, not yet. With a good bull Joselito can be astounding: he cut two ears off each of two bulls at the Feria de Castellón. But with a difficult bull, he hasn't yet found the secret. Leonardo leans over. "When the bull won't let you torear," he says, *"hay que lidiarlo."* When it won't let you control it with the passes, you have to truly fight it, dominate it with your personality.

■■■

Now the rotation begins again. Curro Romero gets his second bull, and when he shows us six quick verónicas with the cape, nothing extraordinary but at least an effort, there is expectation in the crowd. The aficionados of La Maestranza aren't looking for much from Curro. I don't believe they expect a faena such as he was capable of years ago, just a pass or two to jog the memory—a momentary flashback. They want to confirm what they felt seeing Curro at his best years ago and to quiet the growing legion of doubters. These days, there is a moment of realization with each bull Curro fights when it becomes clear he is abdicating his responsibility yet again, that he is refusing to torear with validity and honesty. When that moment comes later rather than sooner—say, two minutes into the proceedings rather than fifteen seconds—hope is sparked throughout the arena. You can almost hear the thought going through everyone's head: maybe this bull will be the one he feels secure with, the one he decides to fight the way he used to.

After the bull shows its mettle by dumping the picador off his horse it suffers under a vicious pic and soon Curro is taking his mincing steps in the other direction. He waves the cape as if to begin one of his slow verónicas but his feet obey some different, more primal, command, some neural override, and they take him farther and farther from the animal. The whistling starts again. With the muleta, Curro works a series of *pases de castigo,* and soon the bull seems listless and refuses to charge. Curro looks into the crowd, seeking validation that the bull is indeed unfightable, but nobody buys the act. They saw the bull a moment ago, how it charged and how it moved, and they have seen Curro in action too often before to be tricked. They're forgiving, and will be ready to again believe in the impossible by the time they see Curro's next fight next week, but they aren't fools.

What has actually happened, as a series of newspaper photos will plainly show the next day, is that Curro has used the *pase de castigo* to ruin the bull. In this pass the bull is made to double back on himself, and as he does Curro sticks the point of the sword through the folds of the muleta and into the ribs of the bull. The *pase de castigo,* done correctly—that is to say, without the stabbing—is a valid tactic used to further weaken a still-raging animal. Performed by Curro today, it is butchery, worthy of the meat counter.

Finally the bull folds its legs under itself and falls to the ground of its own accord, refusing to participate further. With the bull lying on the sand, Curro waves the muleta across its face a few times, then gets it standing again and tries to kill it with a disgraceful running stab. The slaughter mercifully ends with a *descabello,* and the catcalls come long and loud from the crowd. Shameless!

■ ■ ■

It falls to Espartaco again to remove the stench of Curro's faena, but this time he doesn't get the same cooperation from the breeder. His second bull is small, brown in front and darker in the back, and it charges erratically. While Espartaco attempts to solve its personality with a series of verónicas, it catches him on the leg briefly. He retreats, unbloodied, waving off his peons who have sprinted out with capes flapping to distract the animal. The bull takes two pics and manages to injure one of its horns. It hooks upward with the other one and looks like a little ram, fencing at the muleta. Espartaco works quite close to the bull and manages to send it past his body with a nice *derechazo,* the right-side equivalent of a *natural,* but the animal starts to wander off soon after and there isn't anything to be done. It is an inferior animal, unfightable in any artistic fashion, and nothing remains but to kill it.

By this time the bull has decided not to charge at all and Espartaco is forced to attempt a kill while it remains inert. There are several ways a matador can attempt to kill a bull. Because this bull isn't charging well, Espartaco will be killing *volapié,* or flying, running toward the bull with the sword extended in front of his body and then going in, up and over the horns. When the bull meets the man along the way, it is killing *al encuentro.* Killing *recibiendo* is almost a lost art today. To kill *recibiendo,* receiving, the matador remains stationary, incites the bull with his cape, receives its charge and only then goes in over the horns with the sword and kills. It is difficult and quite dramatic, and presupposes that the bull has been fought in such a manner that it still has a swift and true charge left in it at that final stage of the faena. Masters of the *estocada* start preparing for a *recibiendo* kill as soon as they sense the bull is apt and worthy, sometimes as early as their first series of verónicas.

Espartaco's first two tries hit bone and bounce out, but the bull meets the matador halfway on the third try and the *estocada* is perfect. The bull is dragged out by horses and whistled at, an insult to the Torrealta *ganadería,* but Espartaco, who gave his athletic and creative best, gets applause—stronger applause than he would receive in a pueblo, where his effort at valid toreo would not have been appreciated by so many. He has already moved behind the *burladero* to prepare for the arrival of Joselito's second bull, the sixth and last of the afternoon, but the applause continues and he returns to the sand to acknowledge it by blowing a kiss. He seems almost ashamed.

One bull to go: Aguador, 526 kilos. Joselito's capework is smooth and dramatic and bodes well for the faena. But the bull is weakened by the pic-ing and Joselito can't find a way to provoke it. He reluctantly trades the mock, lightweight sword used during the faena for the real sword used to kill, and hits bone twice before puncturing a lung. The bull dies spurting blood from its mouth.

■■■

As the senior matador, Curro Romero is the first to walk across the sand and to the exit, and after the way he has performed, it is a long walk. Upon entering La Maestranza spectators are able to rent plastic-covered foam cushions used to ease the discomfort of the stone seats, and now two of the cushions fly from the seats and rain down on the sand, narrowly missing Curro. There is a lull and then two more come, and soon a barrage, this well-dressed and largely sober crowd expressing its frustration after seeing the limitless possibilities of emotion and art aborted by Curro's fear. Somehow, none of the cushions hit Curro—it must be the same Providence that has enabled him to continue his bullfighting career into late middle age, long after every objective stan- dard says he should have retired—and he continues through the barrera and out the side door, head held high. One of the peons in his cuadrilla tips his hat to the crowd in sarcastic gesture as he disappears under the archway.

"Curro showed more courage walking out than at any other time during the day," Fusco would say later, at our corrida postmortem over Cruzcampo beer at Los Tres Reyes. "Espartaco was fantastic, Joselito did some good work with the cape and Curro was Curro. It's more value than you get in most of the bullfights you see."

Espartaco follows Curro to good applause, and Joselito, despite his failings, receives the same. Sevilla's crowd is demanding, but it isn't cruel. Midway across the arena, Espartaco stops walking and turns, then motions for Joselito to join him so the two can walk out of the bullring together.

Joselito has been primed for a rivalry by the huge public relations campaign, so he declines the offer. He wants no part of a show of friendship, even though it is Espartaco's reputation that has been enhanced today, not his own.

2

A WEEK OF
DISCUSSION

THE ORANGE TREES are heavy with fruit along the Plaza del Museo these days. The man inside the kiosk there knows me by now. He has my selection of newspapers ready when I arrive on Monday morning: *ABC, Diario 16* and *El Correo.*

"Espartaco, and not much else, eh?" he says, handing me my papers and my change.

"What did Zabala say?" I ask him.

"Zabala?" He laughs. "He called Curro a fraud."

I take the papers home and sit on my terrace and sift through the coverage of the previous day's corrida. Opinion, for once, is more or less unanimous: Espartaco had given his usual quality performance, Joselito was unmemorable, the bulls were subpar, the picadors overeager and Curro a disgrace. "Once again, the publicists and promoters have made fools of themselves," says Emilio Parejo of *Diario 16,* while Carlos Crivell of *El Correo* praises Espartaco and bemoans the bulls. I save Zabala for last because I know he'll be the most interesting. He spends the first third of his piece villifying the bulls and the picadors, and then he turns his bile on Curro:

"But that doesn't justify the complete lack of desire of Curro, who should not be able to walk out into a plaza de toros, despite the innate art he may have, with this predisposition toward indolence. Your writer knows quite well what Curro represents to Sevilla and, indeed, to bull-fighting, but that still can't counterbalance such a shameless exhibition in the plaza. Curro's second bull had nobility and style, to which Romero placed a few artfully destructive verónicas, especially a pair on the left side, and wasted the animal completely. It appears natural that when a bull has bad tendencies, a bullfighter of Curro's stamp would tremble a little—it has been that way his whole life. But what escapes logic is that inveterate terror which manifests itself in Curro's coming to the plaza ready to kill the bulls in any way possible. It smells badly of fraud. I'm not saying such a giant should have the desires of a kid who's just starting, or that he should be able to keep up with a bull as lively as the fourth yesterday, but Sevilla deserves better treatment, at least some reciprocation for the care it has given him."

I can't help but smile thinking of the arguments this paragraph will provoke. It could only have been written by a critic whose newspaper circulates nationwide, for one based in Andalusia would be too scared of reprisal. I fold up my papers and head to the Bar Cairo for lunch: *punta de solomillo,* some cheap red wine, and the latest installment of the unending debate.

■■■

Because Easter falls so early this year, the daily bullfights don't begin for another week and a half. There is a corrida this Sunday, the second of the season, but that leaves a whole week for nothing but talk about Curro, Espartaco and Joselito and what did and didn't happen. This city is made for talking, has perfected the art, so the topic doesn't become stale. As usual, there is revisionist history at work. Whereas on Monday Curro is a shameless son of a whore, by Thursday the *curristas* are looking to his next corrida eight days away because he'll be fighting bulls he has been successful with before, the Domecqs. It takes a day or two for the crustier aficionados to forget Espartaco's success, but by midweek he's being criticized for a lack of *arte* in Sunday's performance. "A real *figura* would have had two ears with that first bull," a bartender at Tres Reyes tells me over a glass of Cruzcampo beer on Wednesday. "Oh, to have seen Ordóñez with that bull!"

As for Joselito, the opinion on the street is that he's a product of Madrileño hype, more bullshit from the capital. But he does have another try at La Maestranza in two weeks.

Tuesday morning, having given the corrida a day to settle, I head to

John Fulton's gallery. Federico is gone for the day, off driving somebody somewhere, and he hadn't attended the bullfight anyway because tickets were scarce and expensive. But John was there. He was generally disgusted with the afternoon but has some praise for Espartaco, who isn't usually one of his favorites. He believes the picadors ruined the bulls, that Curro is more of a disgrace than ever, and that Joselito has no business thinking he can be a rival of Espartaco's. There is an Australian expatriate rummaging in the shop, and an Englishwoman who works part-time for John, and we share our disbelief at Sevilla's love affair with Curro. It is inconceivable that he should still be so popular. John, who first told Michener how good Curro was in the early 1960s, reminds us that there was a time when he was quite talented. "But that was many years ago," he says. "Most of the *curristas* today never even saw him fight back then, so I don't know what they're waiting to see."

Tuesday is the day the newspapers have the weekly bullfight supplements, and they each provide four more pages of nuance and interpretation. Opinion among the bullfight critics seems to be that Joselito blew his chance. "Opportunity Lost" is the headline in *Diario 16.* John Fulton sees it and takes great umbrage. He believes Joselito is the finest of the young generation of bullfighters and thinks Sevilla's failure to embrace him says more about the city than about the matador.

As the week between bullfights passes by, too slowly, Fusco is becoming disenchanted with Sevilla. The weather is cold and damp, and Sevilla, unlike some cities, doesn't wear bad weather well. A rainy day is an opportunity for romance or sweet melancholy in Paris or San Francisco or London, but not here. The dreariness makes it seem frumpy and unoriginal. Sevilla is at its best dressed in the harsh primary colors of the hot sun, the white buildings glinting light along the river. Without sunlight, this can be a joyless place.

Fusco is accustomed to the tumult of Madrid, so the pace of life here seems dull. There isn't much theater and few movies other than the Spanish potboilers and American imports badly dubbed, and the renowned art museum just a few yards from my apartment is closed indefinitely for repairs. In general, Sevilla is not a city that offers up its charms easily, although it is a striking city. Tourists who come for a day or two are enchanted; most residents would live nowhere else. But those who come just to see the bullfights or stay for a week or two doing research or seeing friends have trouble solving the place unless they return often enough to truly know it, and their discomfort in the meantime colors their perception. If Fusco feels this, he's in good company. "One is never accepted in Sevilla," Michener wrote in *Iberia*. "I have spent much time in that city, during feria and otherwise, and I have rarely received either hospitality or courtesy." And Hemingway, in his 1960 book, *The Dangerous Summer,* about the Antonio Ordóñez–Luis Miguel Dominguín rivalry, wrote this: "Neither of us cared truly for Sevilla. This is heresy in Andalusia and in bullfighting. People who care about bullfighting are supposed to have a mystic feeling about Sevilla. But I had come to believe over many years that there are more bad bullfights there in proportion to those given than in any other city." Fusco is not a fan of *The Dangerous Summer,* but he takes to quoting me that passage as the week goes by.

■■■

My small apartment on Calle García Ramos has no television, but Fusco has one in Madrid so he's up on all the bullfight programs. He watches "Tendido Cero," the weekly highlight show, each Wednesday at 10:00 p.m., and has been following the wildly successful weekly situation comedy about a Sevillano bullfighter called "Juncal." He also watches the televised corridas when they're shown, which isn't as often as it used to be. The new director of RTVE, Radiotelevision Española, is a Catalán who is vocally antiviolence, and in his mind the evils of the medium include bullfighting. He has sharply curtailed the number of corridas nationally televised, as well as boxing matches and graphic crime shows. But every now and then you can still catch a bullfight on RTVE, and the new commercial channel in Andalusia, Canal Sur, has announced plans to show some, too.

There is no television where Fusco is staying here, a *hostal* tucked away on a side street just outside the Barrio de Santa Cruz, so we meet Wednesday night to have some supper and watch "Tendido Cero" at an odd bar I sometimes frequent on Calle Albuera. It has terrible food but cheap beer and wine and a color television. The film clips are from the previous Sunday. We see Tomás Campuzano fail miserably in Madrid, Litri earn a vuelta with a Domecq bull in Málaga, and about thirty seconds of Curro running away from the bulls in La Maestranza.

A few days later we reconvene at Bar Albuera to see the televised *mano a mano* from Murcia between Manzanares and Ortega Cano, two of the best matadors in Spain—and two we won't be seeing in Sevilla. Alejandro, the bartender, is in a contentious mood and begins a discussion comparing Manzanares and Espartaco. Although other customers are clamoring for service, Alejandro ignores them; he's busy making us a diagram of Manzanares's *pases de pecho* with folded paper napkins.

Watching at the Bar Albuera is a poor simulation of attending a bullfight. Perhaps because of RTVE's sensitivity to violence, most of the camera shots are long range, so the viewer at home gets the equivalent of the worst seat in the house. And, although the television is turned up loud (this is practically a state law in Spain: if you are watching television, it must be at full volume), the other bartender insists on playing the radio. There is lively music with lots of percussion, and then from behind the bar a blender starts to grind ice. When the blender stops, the hundred-peseta slot machine behind us kicks into action, blaring its own electronic melodies. On the screen, the first bull splits a hoof after the banderillas have been placed and can't charge and Manzanares has to kill it almost at once, and the second bull is fat and has a broken horn. Hammering has begun outside the front door. Fusco, more depressed than ever, is ready to leave but Ortega Cano is working his first bull well. His passes are linked and his *temple* is perfect: the bull's horns appear to be guided by the muleta, which precedes them by just a couple of inches.

Ortega Cano was a *tremendista* who was nearly killed several years ago in Zaragoza when a bull stuck a horn into his chest two inches from his heart. At that point, he decided that if he was going to risk his life killing bulls he might as well do it seriously and from then on he became one of the most interesting and capable toreros around. With a good bull, he's as likely to be brilliant as anyone fighting today. This bull is good. Ortega Cano kills it flawlessly on the first try and earns two ears, then takes one of the slowest vueltas around a bullring I have ever seen. I stand and stretch and use the bathroom and order a beer and pay my sixty pesetas, and when I sit back down Ortega Cano is still making his way around the ring, catching bouquets of flowers and waving.

Manzanares's second bull looks equally impressive, but before he gets a chance to work with it an *espontáneo* enters the ring. *Espontáneos* are spectators who sneak a muleta into the bullring and jump in, illegally, to show their bravery and their talents. Many are aspiring matadors looking to impress. They can do real damage to a matador's faena by wasting the bull with inept passes. Most important, they are exposing themselves to real danger. El Cordobés made a comeback several years after he first retired and he was fighting a bull when an *espontáneo* emerged. The crowd, remembering that Cordobés had started his career in similar fashion, exhorted the matador to let the novice show his stuff, and Cordobés acceded. The *espontáneo* was killed by the bull and Cordobés was blamed in the newspapers for the death because he had encouraged the boy. He re-retired immediately and hasn't fought since.

Today's *espontáneo* waves his muleta around and gets carried off after a few passes. The camera zooms in. He is wan and pale, like Lee Harvey Oswald. Moments later, the bull cracks its horn against the barrera. The crowd petitions for a substitute but doesn't get one, and Manzanares kills this animal with dispatch.

What follows are some of the most enjoyable minutes of bullfighting Fusco and I have seen, even though the emotion is badly transmitted by television and the radio has gotten louder and Alejandro insists on making comparisons between Manzanares and everyone else who has ever fought a bull. Ortega Cano works a reluctant bull with his right hand and then his left, building the animal's confidence until he is able to link his passes, working closer and closer, finishing each series with a flourish and killing flawlessly. He receives two ears and there is petition for a tail. Manzanares finally gets to fight a healthy bull and does well, earning an ear. And then Ortega Cano works another faena that is close to perfect. He kills *recibiendo,* letting the bull come to him, and receives two ears and a tail, the first time I have seen this in a reputable bullring. For the day he has been awarded six ears and a tail. He takes the slowest vuelta maybe in the history of bullfighting, a vuelta that makes his earlier one look like a mad dash, and as we leave Fusco and I agree that Ortega Cano is as good as anyone currently fighting bulls in Spain and that Canorea, the impresario of the Sevilla bullring, looks rather stupid tonight.

■ ■ ■

There is something of a tradition here that the second bullfight of the season should feature lesser-known, if not downright mediocre, bullfighters. It is not a tradition that is popular with the aficionados, but on the other hand they usually get to see an intensely fought corrida, since the three matadors who have been signed for the afternoon likely as not have most of their season unbooked and need to impress in order to secure future fights. It is quite popular with the impresario, because these nonentities usually come cheap.

In keeping with that tradition, José Luis Parada, Franco Cadena and Álvaro Amores come to La Maestranza on a gloomy Sunday afternoon.

Parada is nearly forty years old, took his alternativa more than twenty years ago, hasn't fought in Sevilla since 1983 and hasn't fought anywhere in several years. Before his hiatus he was known for an efficient, classical style marred by an inability to kill well. Cadena, twenty-nine, from across the river in Triana, is a former protegé of John Fulton's who, Fulton tells me, hasn't learned anything about bullfighting since he was a novillero. Amores, twenty-six, is debuting in Sevilla and fought just three times last year. In one of the three, in Barcelona, he performed to rave notices. Nevertheless, it is disheartening that these matadors are performing in the Maestranza during the Feria de Abril, while Ortega Cano, Manzanares, Roberto Domínguez and Juan Mora aren't.

I spend the afternoon at the Bodegón de Torre de Oro, which is the unofficial meetingplace for the foreign aficionados during the feria. It's a cavernous room with long wooden tables and a bar along one wall and bartenders who have been catering to the bullfight crowd for years. The bar is several blocks from the bullring and just down the street from the Torre de Oro itself, which the government of the city formerly used to collect tolls and taxes along the Guadalquivir. Nights during the feria the Americans and Brits and Swedes all reconvene here to talk about the corrida they've seen and argue and order *raciones* of shrimp in garlic or mushrooms in garlic or *cola de toro* and Cruzcampos in short glasses. Few of the foreigners are in town yet, but John Fulton is there and Fusco and Federico and several others, including an Israeli woman who is writing a travel guide to Sevilla in German.

The big news is that Manolito, the tiny novillero, has apparently lined up some fights in Madrid through the connections of the irrepressible Navarrito. The plan, according to John, is to have Manolito take the alternativa and become a full matador by the fall. This seems preposterous because Manolito has yet to fight his first novillada in Spain. I can't believe he'll be ready.

John Fulton disagrees. He tells me toreros today take the alternativa as if they were taking an aspirin. "There used to be an apprenticeship, but it's not like that anymore," he says. "You can't make any money as a novillero and it's so goddamn difficult to get fights. If I was managing a Litri or one of these guys I'd rush him on through to the alternativa, too. The bulls aren't all that much bigger than you face as a novillero, and their quality is usually a lot higher."

Fusco and I have our glasses of Magno and then at six o'clock we all walk along the river to the bullring. The day had been brilliant earlier but now it is dark and dismal. The wind is fierce and there is rain in the forecast. The weather and the wind and the pressure on the matadors to perform well make the afternoon rather foreboding. Everybody is thinking it but no one wants to say it: it is afternoons like this when *cornadas* happen—a matador getting caught on the horns of a bull and ending up in the hospital, or worse. And these are Conde de la Maza bulls, of unsteady *casta,* known to be unpredictable.

It turns out that our fears are groundless, and we do see one *faena* of quality. Parada nearly cuts an ear with the fourth bull. First, Pepín Fernández, his peon, places a perfect pair of banderillas, striped green and white for Andalusia, and earns the strongest applause of the day. Then Parada constructs an emotional faena, all the more emotional for its imperfections. He passes the bull slowly and closely with his right hand, guiding it past the body by squaring his shoulders to the bull and stepping forward, then pulling it around with the muleta. *Cargando la suerte,* this is called—taking charge of the pass. It is precisely what Espartaco doesn't do, and why some aficionados claim the real emotion is missing from his toreo. Soon the music is playing and Parada puts together a series of *naturales,* not smooth but effective. Absolute control seems just beyond his grasp but he dominates the bull during all the necessary moments and he is a crowd favorite, classical in style and an underdog. A good kill would have earned him an ear but the scouting report was right: he hits bone, never letting go of the sword, and then hits a *media estocada* in a spot a bit lower than the optimum. Still, there is plenty of petition for an ear, and in a lesser plaza he would have received it, but the president of the bullring says no, and rightfully so.

Parada has to be content with a vuelta. He gets flowers and applause, and three-quarters of the way around the ring, not far from where I am sitting, someone hands him a pair of live white doves. He cradles them in his hands, holding them aloft as if they were the ears of the bull. Then he walks to the center of the ring and releases them and they fly off, brilliantly white against the darkened sky.

That was the highlight of the day. Amores was caught by his first bull under the right arm but not hurt, then disposed of his animal quickly, and his second faena, with the final bull of the day, was so atrocious that the crowd actually started yelling "No!" as he stumbled through his passes. Most spectators left the arena before the kill. Cadena was, if possible, worse. His first bull hooked to the left and the matador had no idea how to compensate. He continually appeared on the verge of

getting caught, which is the opposite of how good bullfighting is supposed
to look. "The bull pardoned his life all day," John Fulton would say
later. With his second bull Cadena nearly managed to get gored in the
chin. "This guy has no idea," said Leonardo, to my left. The crowd
whistled as it became clear Cadena had lost control of the fight. It is a
frightening sight to see, the bull doing the toreo and the man being
manipulated, reacting to the whims of the animal. The bull flicked the
muleta away and stomped on it; Cadena retreated.

The kill, too, was a travesty. "I was sitting five rows away," Federico
told me later, "and I saw his face go grayish-green when it came time
for the kill. And after he missed the first time, he just didn't care
anymore." In the end, Cadena needed six thrusts with the sword.

■■■

We meet at the Bodegón afterward, then head to the Bar Robles, near
the big cathedral. Fusco asks John Fulton a question comparing Litri to
his *tremendista* father and soon Fulton is giving a demonstration for us
of the proper geometric technique needed to link one pass to another.
It involves giving the bull room to charge, guiding it around your body,
and then leaving the muleta where it ends up and repositioning your
feet. Most matadors do it backward: they leave their feet in place and
pull the muleta back so that it's farther from the bull than they are.
That's why they have such trouble making the bull charge a second
time.

He then explains the principle behind inciting the charge in the first
place. John has made a study of all this; he didn't grow up with it, so,
to become a matador, he had to puzzle it out. He knows the principles
behind bullfighting probably better than all the famous matadors of this
century, because they learned by instinct and imitation at a young age,
while he, foreigner and autodidact, had to know the theory. A bull sees
best toward the ground, John says, "because that's where the grass is it
has to see to eat." Because the bull's eyes are spaced apart, its vision is
mostly peripheral. The idea is to stand in front of the bull and keep the
muleta in sight of its far eye, tilting it downward with a shake. If you
stand behind the bull and hold the muleta in front of its nose, it will
see you, and the space between you and the muleta, better than it will
see the muleta itself. John draws a diagram, simple geometry, to explain
the principle, and it is suddenly clear why Franco Cadena looked so out

of control all afternoon. "Franco Cadena doesn't even know there *is* a principle," John says.

During the demonstration a well-dressed blond woman in black pumps pushes through the knot of people that has collected toward the door, just as John completes a sweep with his imaginary muleta. "Watch it," he says, without looking her way. "You'll get gored." She sweeps on past and we follow with our eyes.

John's descriptions have been so vivid and intense that the bar has become a plaza de toros and we peons on the edge of the sand, watching enraptured as a taurine master shows his secrets. It is easy to imagine some half-ton Torrestrella, head lowered for the charge, emerging behind the woman's clicking heels and into the moonlit street.

3

THE
AFICIONADO'S
DILEMMA

IF ONLY the typical *toro bravo*
charged with the alacrity of that imaginary Torrestrella! If only the
average performance by a matador of repute had the verve and vitality
of John Fulton's impromptu demonstration!

Instead, you'll find a perplexing flaw in contemporary bullfighting:
work of quality is scarce. You might think that here in Sevilla, where
the bravest, most artful matadors in the world fight the best-bred
bulls before discerning, ardent spectators, it would be possible to see
good bullfighting much of the time. It isn't. Madrid, Bilbao, and everywhere else are no different; even at a first-class plaza, most bullfights
are bad.

That's not to say they aren't interesting, because each time you watch
a bullfight you notice something you haven't seen before, something as
eventful as a bull vaulting the barrera into the *callejón,* as insignificant
as a detail of capework, or as ancillary and irrelevant as José Luis Parada
releasing white doves into the darkened sky. There is always something
to capture and preserve in the mind's scrapbook. But, sad to say, there
usually isn't much good toreo.

This makes following the bulls more difficult than it ought to be.
Every aspiring aficionado, even the hardiest and least demanding, must

learn to rationalize away certain amounts of disgust. If he doesn't, he will soon move on to some simpler, more generous obsession.

In general, the longer you have been attending bullfights the lower your expectations. You arrive at a bullring for the hundredth time so skeptical as to be almost amused. You will leave it entertained, as a motion picture or a ball game might have entertained you, but you probably won't have been moved, metaphysically aroused, in the way that an emotional religious service can arouse you. *Yet that arousal is precisely what you are seeking.* Bullfighting at its best forces everyone who sees it to become keenly aware of his own mortality, which arguably should ennoble his being and enhance his life. It's serious stuff. Watching valid toreo is not supposed to be fun.

The scarcity of truly good bullfighting is essentially our fault, in the sense that any critical public eventually gets what it deserves. In financial terms, bullfighting is booming as never before; in 1989, some 41 million spectators will attend bullfights in Spain and the Americas. But as proportionally fewer of them have the ability to recognize and demand valid toreo, and more of them, that burgeoning mass of casual aficionados, are satisfied with pageantry and the scent of blood, the quality of bulls and bullfighting declines to match the public taste. This started at least as far back as Belmonte, and probably before that. "The bullfight has been transformed," wrote Spanish essayist Antonio Diaz-Cañabate. "It has gone from something serious, hard, arduous, exciting to become a vulgar, superficial, banal spectacle where deep down there is still the possibility of a bloody episode."

No serious aficionado I know would disagree, and yet the *afición* of these people never lapses. They fill the Maestranza for the important fights, and when late May comes they go to Madrid and fill Las Ventas. With expectation reduced nearly to nothing, they go for the scene and the gossip and because they can't imagine not going, and every now and then they see something worthwhile.

Fusco raged long into the night yesterday about how that attitude is aiding the continuing devaluation of the bullfight. He believes the only noble choice is to stop attending corridas, and to convince others to do the same. While such self-denial might lead to better bullfighting a generation from now, assuming that the breeding of negative characteristics into the bulls can be reversed, I'm not frustrated enough—or altruistic enough—to make the sacrifice. Today's watered-down bullfighting is better than no bullfighting at all. And I notice Fusco too is there every day, one city after another, year after year.

■ ■ ■

These thoughts wander across my mind as the matador Manolo Cortés wanders across the bullring, and I rationalize my own disgust. Fusco and I are sitting in barrera seats talking to a man who says his friend beside him is a torero. "But he's a bad one," our neighbor says. "He's afraid of the bulls."

In front of us Cortés is giving a sleepy performance with a small Palha bull, Portuguese bred. Fusco and I are bored, but the man next to me is beside himself with boredom. He tells us his friend will jump in the ring and fight a bull if we agree to bail him out of jail. The friend nods in agreement. He's ready to go.

"How much will it cost?" I ask.

"Thirty thousand pesetas."

Fusco turns to me. "Maybe we should agree to do it, then not pay," he says, laughing. "It can't be worse than this."

The Maestranza is about two-thirds full on a gray and windy Thursday evening. It's the first official corrida of the feria and the third of the season, and three holes have been dutifully punched in my *abono*. There is a bullfight scheduled for each of the next eleven afternoons, and a morning novillada a week from Saturday. Fusco, buying his tickets daily and on a budget, had planned to skip this fight. Of the three matadors, Cortés, José Luis Galloso and Ruiz Miguel, only the last promised anything of interest. I had already moved down from my *tendido* to an open barrera seat when Fusco appeared.

"I wasn't going to come," he said. "And then I was just going to sit in the *gradas*. But somebody rushed up and offered me a great deal on a *tendido*. And now here I am in a barrera."

He's starting to regret it. The day is chilly and the action torpid. Cortés kills his bull without our even noticing, and the next one, named Varino, emerges from the toril. Then Ruiz Miguel steps onto the sand with his cape bunched between his arms, his eyes following the burly black animal to gauge its tendencies—and the chatter stops. Even our would-be *espontáneo* is watching.

Francisco Ruiz Miguel is forty years old, a serious and well-respected bullfighter, and this is his last season. His final appearance at the Feria de Abril, barring the inevitable comeback, will be a week from Sunday when he fights in the annual corrida here with the Miura bulls. Ruiz Miguel cut a tail off a Miura in a memorable corrida at La Maestranza in April of 1972, the last time a tail has been cut by anyone here, and neither he nor the aficionados have ever forgotten that. He has made much of his living and his reputation fighting Miuras ever since.

We don't have to wait for the Miuras to see him with a good bull. Little Varino weighs just 480 kilos but attacks the cape with a confident power, a locomotive barreling down familiar track. Ruiz Miguel's style is staccato, all stops and starts. It serves to keep a recalcitrant bull in motion, but this one needs no such encouragement. Varino responds eagerly to the capework, then charges the picador from nearly twice the normal distance. It continues to buck even under the weight of an unrelenting pic, and its untrammeled aggression earns it an ovation. The bull needs little prodding to return for a second pic and again drives at the horse even with the metal digging into its flesh. The music starts playing, one of the few times I have heard it during the pic-ing—and the only time we will hear it all day. The bull takes a third pic and the crowd roars in appreciation, and when it attacks its way through the placing of the banderillas the anticipation for the faena grows.

Ruiz Miguel has a knack for getting stubborn bulls to charge, and for willing his way with the big, bold, dangerous Miuras. But as his faena unfolds, it becomes clear he doesn't quite have the artistry to deal with a good and simple bull, noble and eager. Perhaps earlier in his career he did, but now he doesn't. And the wind, which has plagued us all week, is again gusting hard. Three times it forces Ruiz Miguel to stop in the middle of a series and adjust his muleta. His passes are linked, but not much emotion is being transmitted, and even though he kills well it is clear he hasn't accomplished enough with this bull to earn an ear. The aficionados of Sevilla are very demanding with good bulls ("They see them so infrequently here," says Fusco), and Ruiz Miguel has not performed at the level of the animal. Several weeks from now, Varino will be named the best bull of the feria.

One of the bulls that follows is also quite good, and two others are stubborn but interesting. These Palhas have more to them than the other bulls we've seen this year, but they're difficult to fight, and with these matadors, and this wind, they inspire no memorable work. On the way out I see Enrique, the gentleman in his sixties who sits behind me at my regular seat, and he shrugs and explains the afternoon away with a bullfighting truism: *Cuando hay toros, no hay toreros, y cuando hay toreros, no hay toros.* "When there are bulls, there are no bullfighters . . . and when there are bullfighters, there are no bulls."

We head into the street battling a lingering unpleasantness. There often comes after a bad bullfight a certain empty feeling, a hollowness in the psyche. Watch a crowd file from the portals of the plaza: its dissatisfaction will be evident. In part you're seeing the melancholy of what-might-have-been, of expectation soured and potential squandered (along with a substantial sum of money). But mingled with the disappointment is the uncomfortable sensation of having witnessed living creatures unjustifiably slaughtered in a public spectacle—slaughtered, it came to pass, purely for the sake of entertainment. It is unjustifiable because mere entertainment can never justify bullfighting. If all bullfighting offered anyone was two hours of diversion in the sun, it should be banned at once.

For moral men to sanction such destruction, the process must at least occasionally provide us with something substantial and important and spiritual in return, something unavailable within the bounds of daily life. It didn't today, but now and then it does. The presence of death in the plaza, summoned most appealingly by good toreo but with equal impact by a goring, infuses each of us with the awareness of our own eventual demise. And yet, in what seems to be a contradiction, we will also—if we're lucky—see death stopped, negated, delayed, seemingly overcome, as the matador successfully risks his life to control the beast with his art and his guile.

That explains both the jubilation and the discomfort you sense during an emotional faena; what most people discover is that the glimpse of immortality is quickly forgotten, while the troublesome feeling remains.

Ideally, then, you should leave a bullfight disquieted—with the melancholy that comes from an intimation of your own mortality, and with a memory of having been thrilled by what you have seen. If, leaving the bullring, you aren't at least vaguely aware of the tenuousness of man's existence, it wasn't a good bullfight. Unfortunately, that turns out to be most of the time.

Fusco and I head down Calle Dos de Mayo, nursing our hollowness and dissatisfaction, talking of tomorrow. Espartaco is fighting again and so is Curro, and the third matador is Litri. The salvation of following the bulls is that there is always another corrida on which to pin your hopes, and in Sevilla during feria there is always the Bodegón, to drink and to talk.

The discussion there lasts late into the night because the out-of-town aficionados, the *extranjeros,* have started to arrive. Espartaco's performance last Sunday becomes all the more emotional in the telling, and Curro wasn't simply bad, he was at his worst. It is all exaggeration and argument, and every bit as much a part of the *ambiente* of the corrida as anything that happened, or didn't happen, on the sand in the hot daylight hours long before.

■■■

Ernest Hemingway had both admiration and disdain for the matador Manuel Baez, called Litri, who fought with a foolish bravado and was caught and killed in Málaga in February of 1926 after just one season of alternativa. That Baez was a second-generation matador: his father, Miguel Baez, had an outstanding career around the turn of the century and was also called Litri. Hemingway described the younger, ill-fated Litri as "a prodigy of valor and wonderful reflexes, but insensate in his bravery and very ignorant in his fighting." Although he hadn't been properly trained as a novillero, Litri took the alternativa anyway and became a full matador. "For a year," Hemingway wrote, "he substituted bravery, luck and reflexes for knowledge.... We all spoke of him as *carne de toro,* or meat for the bulls, and it really did not make much difference when he took the alternativa since he fought with a nervous valor that could not last, and with his faulty technique he was certain to be destroyed."

Manuel Baez was fatally wounded at the beginning of his second season as a matador and he died before his wedding day. There was talk that his fiancée was carrying a child. A short time later she married her deceased boyfriend's father, Miguel Baez, the retired matador, himself a widower. The son she subsequently bore was named Miguel, and he too became a matador. While not the draw of El Cordobés, this Litri was a true *figura* in his time—popular, and one of the most talented and innovative of the *tremendistas.*

It is his son, also named Miguel and nicknamed Litri, whom we saw earlier this season and who will be fighting with Curro and Espartaco here tomorrow. The newest Litri took his alternativa in a unique ceremony in Nimes at the end of the 1987 season. He alternated with his father and another matador of great reputation from the previous generation, Paco Camino, and with Paco's son, Rafi, a highly regarded novillero who was also taking the alternativa. Both Litri *padre* and Paco

Camino came out of retirement for the day and each killed a single bull. The elder Litri served as *padrino* for his son and *testigo* for Rafi Camino, and Paco Camino did the opposite. Each of the famous fathers cut an ear with his only bull and the younger Litri cut an ear off each of his bulls, leaving only Rafi without a trophy from the memorable, if absurdly overhyped, occasion.

Whether Manuel Baez Litri is Miguel's grandfather or merely his great-uncle remains a mystery, but the two bullfighters have much in common. This Litri favors the *tremendista* of his forebearers but his style is still unkempt, and his tricks do not seem merely bold but truly dangerous. "There are times when I truly fear for that boy's life," says John Fulton. And, like Manuel Baez, Miguel has been criticized for taking the alternativa ceremony before he was ready to do so. Under the tutelage of his father, our Litri was nearly always given hand-picked novillos to fight during his apprenticeship, nothing too big or unorthodox, and there are many who believe this has not adequately prepared him for the much larger and more challenging animals he will see in first-class plazas throughout Spain.

There is another way in which Litri is nothing like Manuel, nor like his own father. Litri *padre,* now approaching middle age, has always been an unappealing-looking man and was especially so in his youth. Photos of him in *traje de luz* reveal sunken eyes, a large nose and prominent eyebrows. Manuel, too, was no matinee idol; Hemingway described him as a "bowlegged little boy" with "a face like a rabbit." But this youngest Litri, now twenty years old, is dark and stunningly handsome, and his looks have contributed significantly to his popularity and financial success as a matador. Teenage girls who know nothing of bullfighting adore him, and weep to the poster in their bedrooms each time they hear a disobedient bull has sent him to the hospital.

After Rosa and I saw Litri in Olivenza he surfaced in Valencia later in the month where he alternated with Espartaco and Ortega Cano and cut an ear. He then had two ears the following Saturday in a third-class ring in Hellin, in the provence of Alicante, and earned a vuelta with a Domecq bull in Málaga the following afternoon. The next Sunday, in Jaén, the rescheduled date of the postponed bullfight I had traveled to see, he cut an ear with each of his Alfonso Moreno bulls. As his first fight in the feria approaches he is being touted as the revelation of the season and the next true rival for Espartaco, Joselito being last week's vanquished rival and this week all but forgotten.

The hype is difficult to ignore, but what I see Thursday morning at the newspaper kiosk astonishes me: Litri's face, nearly actual size, filling the cover of the tabloid *ABC*. Granted, it's just a regional edition, but *ABC* is a conservative, even reactionary, publication—and young Miguel Baez a twenty-year-old bullfighter of uncertain ability. If he hadn't been nervous about the pressure of fighting during the feria, and of challenging Espartaco, he will be now.

I'm tempted to buy several copies of the newspaper. John Fulton has promised to introduce me to Litri later in the day, and I figure I'll arrive bearing gifts, because either the matador or his parents will surely want some extras for mementos. But as I fish in my pocket for more change, my plan suddenly strikes me as absurd. There are probably several hundred others, friends and family members and fan club officers, eagerly buying up every copy of *ABC* in sight.

If Litri succeeds in La Maestranza, he'll be swimming in cover pages by the end of the week. And I know enough about matadors and how seriously they take omens and superstitions to know this: If young Litri doesn't perform well this afternoon, if he exits the bullring not in triumph but to a disapproving or even hostile reaction from a crowd angered by yet another example of unwarranted hype, he won't ever want to see this edition of the newspaper again.

4

THE LATEST HERO

BULLFIGHTING thrives on rivalries between matadors. Managers and impresarios around the country foment and foster such competition, although occasionally rivalries emerge spontaneously through the aggressive ambition of one matador, or both, or from genuine dislike. In the end it doesn't matter as long as the toreo is honest and both matadors deserve the attention. The escalating duel between Antonio Ordóñez and his brother-in-law, Luis Miguel Dominguín, during the Dangerous Summer of 1959 was real enough, as was that between Dominguín and Manolete a generation before. Dominguín is even said to have sent Manolete to his death by inciting him to attempt toreo that was too difficult with dangerous bulls.

No bullfight rivalry ever received more attention than Belmonte against Joselito, but there were others before it of similar intensity, notably the competition between the elegant Lagartijo, an Andalusian with the looks and bearing of a Roman senator, and the crude and courageous Salvador Sánchez, called Frascuelo. This was during the second half of the last century and both matadors retired alive and ambulatory in middle age, Frascuelo in 1889 and Lagartijo four years later. That was followed by the tragic competition between Guerrita and a Sevillano called El Espartero as the century turned, an example of a rivalry created by public demand. It didn't last long. Espartero died young of a horn wound in Madrid.

It is rare throughout the history of bullfighting to find a transcendent talent who ruled his epoch alone. An important exception from hundreds of years ago is Pedro Romero, the first and most heroic of taurine legends, the grandson of the man who invented the muleta and the son of the first man to organize a cuadrilla of banderilleros and picadors under the matador's control. Hemingway appropriated Romero's name for use as his matador character in *The Sun Also Rises*. That Pedro Romero, "the best-looking boy I have ever seen," was a direct representation of Cayetano Ordóñez, called Niño de la Palma. Ordóñez was a handsome and masterful matador in the 1920s and was also the father of Antonio Ordóñez, of whom Hemingway wrote copiously and hagiographically in *The Dangerous Summer*—a tidy irony.

The real Pedro Romero emerged from Ronda in the eighteenth century, mastered modern bullfighting, killed nearly six thousand bulls in this thirty-year career without once suffering a horn wound, and died of natural causes at age eighty-four, all the while alone in stature and success. There are taurine historians who believe two younger matadors, Pepe-Hillo and Cosillares, could have evolved into Romero's equals, but each was killed before his prime.

When a rivalry is in earnest it is the best spur there can be to better bullfighting. It doesn't matter whether the matadors are friends or enemies outside the ring if each is determined to outdo the other and earn a reputation as the finest bullfighter in Spain. But when a rivalry is fabricated purely on personality, with a vast inequity in the caliber of toreo, it is both useless and dangerous. The young Litri, in just his second season of alternativa, has no business challenging Espartaco, and it is almost certain that nothing good will come from such a competition.

In fact, Litri has little to do with this rivalry. It was created by the bullring impresarios, the aficionados and the media, all of whom seek to manufacture some interest for the coming season. His father, who guides his career, well understands how detrimental it will be if comparisons are made now between Litri and Espartaco; the youth's reputation might need several seasons to recover. Even worse, if Litri truly comes to believe he can be the equal of Espartaco before he is physically or psychologically in the same category as a matador, it is a recipe for tragedy. This is more than supposition for Litri *padre,* it is family history, and he has been telling it to his son for weeks—but you can't stop aficionados from talking or the girls from swooning, and you can't prevent that winsome face from showing up on the cover of the newspaper.

Litri does seem aware of the danger. He was quoted in *El Correo* recently attempting to downplay the competition. "I'm going to fight for first place, but it's very difficult," he said. "Espartaco is number one, and it will be very hard to snatch that away. I lack years, and successes, to be considered a premier figure of toreo." Such wisdom is striking, but once inside the plaza, in front of ten thousand aficionados and the attention of the entire taurine world, he will be tempted to forget his own measured words.

■■■

Why can the bullfighting community find no better rivals for Espartaco than neophytes such as Joselito and Litri? The answer can be found in the Spanish political realities of the last two decades.

When Francisco Franco died in 1975 after thirty-six years of rule, Spain threw off the shackles of his dictatorship with a vengeance. While many Spaniards revered Franco while he lived and to this day believe his repressive regime was a necessary step in the transformation of the country, much of Spanish society rebelled against his legacy in the years after his death. The social radicalism most of the Western world experienced in the 1960s hadn't yet had an opportunity to manifest itself here, and Franco's demise belatedly provided one. His prohibitions— against the liberation of women, against freedom of expression in the arts, against affection in the streets—were aggressively overturned.

Bullfighting, which Franco had supported, was associated by the public with the ugliness of the dictatorship. It can even be said that the blood and carnage of the bullfight were reminiscent of the horrors of Spain's civil war, and the costumes and the rigid order of the spectacle, of Franco's domineering rule. At the same time, the stench of El Cordobés's avant-garde toreo was still in the air, its festering remains spoiling the perception of what bullfighting was supposed to be. As a result, the majority of the newly democratized citizens of the republic were disinclined to take an interest in what they perceived to be a dying spectacle. They preferred to look for new diversions, abandoning the past for the future.

Bullfighting's reprieve, oddly enough, may have been the death of

Paquirri in 1984. A single horn thrust by the bull Avispado offered a tragic reminder to the masses that genuine risk was involved inside the bullring—even if the bulls were getting smaller and less aggressive by the year, and even if the insidious practice of horn shaving was profligate throughout the country. Following Paquirri's death, bullfighting slowly started to become socially acceptable, and even fashionable. Some of the important members of the ruling Socialist party, thought to be philosophically opposed to the spectacle, were sighted at major bullfights. Most important, young boys throughout the nation, having invested their hero worship in football players and film stars for a decade, could again be seen running in the streets with bits of cloth, playing bull and bullfighter.

Espartaco, the son of a matador, was thirteen years old when Franco died—old enough to know that he wanted to fight bulls for a living. Bullfighting, he has said many times, was already set in his soul. Those who were younger than he at the time, twelve and ten and eight years old, largely looked elsewhere for a dream, and currently those tennis players and rock singers and prison inmates and whatever constitute a lost generation of bullfighters. Right now there are very few first-class bullfighters between the ages of twenty and twenty-eight. Litri was six when Franco died but fifteen when he heard the news that Paquirri had been killed in Pozoblanco. His generation is just now coming to maturity. Besides him, it includes Joselito, Fernando Cepeda, Rafi Camino, Niño de la Taurina and talented novilleros such as Julio Aparicio and Pepe Luis Martín. Nobody knows what level of toreo these youths will ultimately achieve, but there are knowledgeable aficionados who say this generation of bullfighters has the potential to be the best since the early 1960s, when Ordóñez and Litri *padre* and El Viti and Curro Romero and Paco Camino and Diego Puerta and others were together on the carteles.

That is the hope for the future. But these days there is nobody to truly challenge Espartaco. Of the older matadors, Manzanares, Ortega Cano and one or two others are each considered by some, especially those who don't like Espartaco's style, to be Spain's best, but time and again, in the eyes of the majority of aficionados, Espartaco has outperformed them with consistent success. Every year he manages to be *gran triunfador* of the majority of Spain's ferias, and that record cannot easily be argued with.

The major *figura* of that older group, and the one true rival Espartaco had, retired several years ago. Paco Ojeda, not yet forty years old, is as wealthy as he needs to be and lives leisurely on his horse farm. Insisting that the corrida requires him, absolutely cannot prosper without him, *Toros '92* clamors for his return almost weekly. The magazine may be right, but so far its arguments haven't convinced Ojeda to leave his easy chair.

■■■

For now we have to be content with Espartaco and these phantom rivals, Litri and Joselito and whoever else is dredged up in the weeks to come. After buying my newspapers I head down Calle Bailen toward the Tres Reyes, where John Fulton is supposed to meet me at noon. We're headed for the Hotel Alfonso XIII, the best hotel in town and one of the best in all of Spain, where Litri is staying tonight and where most of the top matadors stay.

I arrive at the Tres Reyes and see a crowd seated outside, drinking and eating. The men are nearly all wearing suits, looking important, and it's no wonder: most of the behind-the-scenes figures of big-time bullfighting are here, promoters and managers and retired toreros, sipping tea and chewing on bread. Blue-and-white bunting promoting La Ina sherry hangs from the ceiling, adding to the festive mood. Of course, the prices have increased for the feria. A ham sandwich and a glass of juice costs me 475 pesetas instead of the usual 300, and the bartender tells me it will only get worse, here and everywhere else in town. "You want good, cheap food?" he asks. "Go to Granada. Or try back here in May."

Some twenty minutes later than promised, which is punctual for Sevilla, John Fulton and Manolito drive up in the old station wagon, looking for Navarrito. Manolito has been signed to fight somewhere in Extremadura next month using the name Hernán Cortés, playing up the idea that he's descended from the conquistador—which, of course, he isn't. It's a smart move, because if Manolito does well with that name he'll be quite a hit when he returns to Mexico. The Mexicans have an inferiority complex about their bullfighters, and if a matador has taken the alternativa in Spain he immediately assumes great importance in Mexico. If he also happens to be Mexican born, he can be a hero.

Soon Navarrito is located and he and Manolito drive off, headed for a *tentadero*. John and I are going to see Litri, but we stop first at the Bar Nipal, a grimy place tucked away off a pedestrian passage between

Sierpes and Calle Tetuan. A group of white-haired well-dressed men are sitting around a table, drinking coffee and smoking cigars, and they look incongruous in the modest, almost seedy, surroundings.

I am introduced to two brothers of Alonso Moreno, Félix and Javier. Like Alonso they are both *ganaderos,* important figures in the taurine world, and John has come to show them a poster he has painted to advertise a corrida in La Algaba later this summer. The town is a short distance away from Sevilla, and the small plaza de toros there is constructed from wagon wheels. John has used this motif in his painting; he hands the work around and gets murmurs of praise. He has been working with some young novilleros out in the country and he intends to give the impresario of the La Algaba bullring the rights to the poster in exchange for placing both of the novilleros on the cartel. It is a noble and financially unwise gesture he can ill afford.

The Moreno brothers excuse themselves with hearty handshakes all around, and after they leave John introduces me to a famous old matador named Luis Fuentes Bejerano. Born in Madrid in 1903, Bejerano has been a fixture in Sevilla for more than half a century as both a bullfighter and a member of bullfighting society. Bejerano killed his first bull at the age of nine. About fifteen years ago, he killed a bull at Javier Moreno's ranch to commemorate his seventieth birthday, then killed a Saltillo novillo on his eightieth. Not long after, he suffered a stroke. "I don't know what kind of shape I'll be in when I'm ninety," he tells me.

Today his grip is firm and he bounces out of his chair to meet me, an aficionado and an American. "I was in New York during prohibition," he says. "It was the year 1927. You could get all the wine, whiskey, or sherry you wanted if you knew where to go." He had been on his way back from Mexico, he tells me, where he had been fighting bulls. "But after that I headed down to Havana for a while," he says. "Just to smoke some good cigars."

Bejerano is renowned around the city as Spain's oldest living matador, seven months older than Marcial Lalanda. In his prime he was renowned for his proficiency at killing bulls and is still referred to as an expert in that art. Despite his age he is lucid and opinionated. He no longer attends bullfights but still has opinions on all the current bullfighters and has no problem with Sevilla's love affair with Curro Romero. "The man has been carried out of the Puerta del Príncipe five times," he said. "What more does anyone need to know?"

Ten minutes later we are talking to Litri, a matador some half a dozen generations removed, sixty-five years Bejerano's junior. He is sitting at a table in the lobby of the Alfonso XIII, wearing a shiny silk shirt with a single gold chain and khaki pants. He's leafing through some black-and-white bullfighting photos. He jumps up to greet John and talks to him with deference. I try to imagine Litri in half a century or so, sitting in the Bar Nipal or somewhere similar, provided his daring and often foolish brand of toreo hasn't killed him first. "I was on the cover of the *ABC* before my twenty-first birthday," he might be saying.

Litri shakes my hand politely, too. He tells me he'd love to talk and I should come back and see him in the hotel at night after the corrida. We wish him luck and depart, back into the gloom of yet another gray day.

■■■

By five o'clock the wind has picked up and Fusco and I wander around La Maestranza chilly and miserable. We sit outside the bullring and watch the people walk by, bundled in coats and scarves. The crowd seems almost exclusively Spanish apart from our little group of *extranjeros.* A hawker approaches and tries to sell us something—the handbills that are distributed free at the door. "We're American, but we're not stupid," Fusco tells him. We take a short walk to see the weights of the bulls, which are taped to the outside wall of the arena. These Domecqs, *juan-pedros* to the bullfighting fraternity, will be the biggest animals we've seen this year; Litri's second bull is 563 kilos, while Curro's is just a kilo smaller. The odds of him even looking at a bull of that size are astronomical.

The trumpet sounds at 6:30 and the procession of cuadrillas makes its way across the bullring to pay its respects to the acting president, and by 6:35 we already know what Curro is planning to do with his first bull. He lets his banderillero take the first dozen or so swipes at it before he even emerges from behind the *burladero,* and then the bull charges and comes to a dead stop some three feet in front of Curro and gazes at him. It is as if the animal wants to say that it never could have guessed four years of grazing in the Domecq grasslands, readying itself for the climactic quarter-hour of his life, would have brought this parody of a matador standing before it now, his cape up near his shoulders protecting his body like a breastplate.

The bull stands there looking at Curro for a good long while, and Curro stands there holding his cape up, looking back. Bulls have plenty of native intelligence, and as this one trots off toward the far barrera it might even realize, as we all certainly do, that the chances are slight it will have the opportunity to die with any dignity.

With the muleta Curro doesn't really attempt passes, just leads the bull along while backpedaling. He exchanges swords after a cursory faena, profiles and cites, then runs past and stuffs in a *media estocada*. A *descabello* is needed, but it takes some time to get the bull to lie still and lower its head. It's small wonder; the bull has barely been fought and still has plenty of life in it. Curro walks off to jeers. Even Leonardo and Enrique, my *currista* seatmates, are disgusted.

Espartaco dedicates his first bull to the Madre del Rey, the mother of King Juan Carlos. She is sitting high above the ring in a velvet-draped box next to the president of the bullring. I hadn't noticed her there before and it strikes me as odd that Curro failed to dedicate his first bull to her, too, as is customary. Espartaco then works a faena of intensity. It is a masterpiece of *temple,* that skill of keeping the muleta just centimeters ahead of the bull's horns at all times. The result is an animal that appears perfectly tamed.

A drizzle starts to fall but Espartaco appears unaffected by it or by the steady wind. The music is playing and he switches swords and profiles immediately, but in his haste to earn an ear he rushes his *estocada* and hits bone; his second try does, too, and his third is a blatant *bajonazo*, so he settles for good applause and the waving white handkerchiefs from about a quarter of the spectators.

Now, Litri. His bull is small but fiery and it notches a makeshift X in the *burladero* with its left horn. Every bull favors its left side or its right side, just as people are left-handed or right-handed. It is one of the characteristics a smart matador watches for when the animal first emerges from the toril. He plots his course of action accordingly.

Litri shows some surprising artistry with the cape, finishing his first sequence by twirling it around his body as he passes it from hand to hand, a movement called a *revolera*. He does several of his trademark *litrazos,* a pass made famous by his father in which the matador cites the bull from a great distance by leaping in the air from behind his cape, then waves the cape to the side at the last moment, but these don't stir the spectators as much as the *revolera*. They're looking for profundity here, not novelty. He then leaves the bull a considerable distance from the picador, and it charges, and now the crowd applauds—for Litri's judgment, the bull's aggression, and a fine pic job.

Again, Litri leaves the bull some forty feet from the horse and again it charges and is well handled by the picador, the redoubtable Saavedra. The banderillas are placed well, as they usually are by Litri's peons. The members of the cuadrilla are paid out of the matador's take on a corrida by corrida basis, and since Litri is a popular and very active matador who will have fights at all the major ferias this year and all over Spain in the small towns and will earn plenty of money, he is able to get some of the best banderilleros and picadors to work for him by guaranteeing steady, well-paid employment. For us, it means a bonus when we see Litri fight. We know that even if he is bad, Montoliú and Leopoldo López will be placing sticks and Ambrosio Martín and Saavedra will be pic-ing and the *quites* and ancillary capework will be well performed.

The rain has stopped now and some sun is peeking through the heavy clouds and the stage seems set for a fine faena by Litri, who is walking the ring with confidence. He dedicates the bull to the Madre del Rey and begins his work. His bull is willing, but Litri, from ignorance or nerves, is unable to find its *distancia,* the optimum distance from the horns for the muleta. The result is a couple of fine passes inevitably followed by a jerky, unappealing one, and then a long wait while he tries to convince the bull to charge. It's clear he understands the problem and would like to gain control of the faena, but he can't. The rain, having held off as if to give the neophyte a chance, has seen enough and starts to fall again. It is a sad scene with the rain falling and the sky a deep gray and the matador, in shame now, trying to salvage something with the bull.

He works a series with his right hand and sets up the bull for a *pase de pecho* but he is too far away, and instead of charging the animal turns its back and wanders off, adding to the ignominy. Litri sees that it isn't going to get better, and switches swords, then kills about six inches low down the bull's left side. The crowd responds with a damning silence.

Curro's second bull is big and black and gorgeous—but why bother with the details? We do get four valid passes with the cape but then Curro swiftly reverts to form. The bull is so eager that it charges the picador a second and third time without interruption from Curro, who lets the peon make the initial *quite* and then stands aside and watches.

Curro then makes a dedication to the mother of the king—one bull too late. "I hoped the second bull would be better," he would say later, "but now that I've seen it I guess they were about equal." The faena seems to last no longer than the dedication. It's another fencing match, with the muleta serving more to parry the bull's thrusts than to incite a charge. Eventually the bull lowers itself to the ground and remains there, blinking, while Curro's peons pull its tail to get it standing again. I believe being a banderillero for Curro is the hardest job in bullfighting: you have to do all the difficult work, virtually fight the bulls yourself, and then dodge cushions on your way out of the ring.

Curro shoves in a *media estocada* on his third try, then administers the *descabello,* what is supposed to be the coup de grace. However, he can't find the right spot. He tries three times and then the crowd takes up the count, chanting with each thrust: *"Cuatro! Cinco! Seis! . . ."* Finally, after eight unsuccessful stabs at the defenseless animal, he pricks it a ninth time and, although missing the spinal cord, wounds it enough to kill it.

We see Espartaco build his reluctant second bull into a formidable opponent, land another subpar sword thrust and settle for a vuelta— and one of the better days a matador can have without cutting an ear. It is a surprising performance for him; even those who don't admire his toreo freely admit he is one of the most artful and precise killers in Spain. Then Litri, with everything to prove, gets the worst bull of the day and fights it with mounting despair. Eventually the animal stays on its feet long enough to be killed, and the afternoon is over.

Curro leaves the arena to the standard barrage of cushions, one hitting him flush in the face. Espartaco gets strong applause and the applause continues for Litri, kind applause, but tomorrow morning *Diario 16* will be less kind to the little *tremendista*. "Litri, nervous, bewildered and unsure of his style, suffered the great defeat of the afternoon in the first of his three appearances," it will say on the front page. The headline inside will read "A blotch on Litri's record." *El Correo* will be better, but not much: "Litri, valiant and yearning, performed like the color of his suit of lights—green."

That evening at the Hotel Alfonso XIII there is much commotion in the lobby as usual during feria—but no Litri. I start a conversation with one of his entourage, a relative of some sort, and am told the matador isn't seeing visitors. "Miki is feeling sick," the man says, and then twists his face into a grimace. "Physically sick or mentally sick, I couldn't tell you."

5

THE
EXTRANJEROS

CHARLES Patrick Scanlan is at his usual place in the Bodegón de Torre de Oro, a first-row table on the far side of a pillar, facing the long wooden bar. He's wearing his usual outfit, too: white panama hat with blue band, white trousers, sunglasses, blue double-breasted sportcoat, rep tie. A light-haired six-footer now in his fifties, Charles Patrick is usually the first *extranjero* at the Bodegón after each bullfight, and he probably was the last to leave it earlier in the day for the five-minute walk to La Maestranza. That's also a custom of his, and if you didn't catch sight of that white hat over in *tendido* 1, you might wonder if he had been to the bullfight at all.

Of all the characters that inhabit this odd and almost make-believe world of bull-following, all the Americans and Englishmen and others who spend much of every spring and summer in Spain traveling from one feria to another, from Sevilla to Madrid to Pamplona and on to Bilbao in September if it is an interesting season and maybe even shadowing a particular matador throughout the country in the summer and fall if someone is doing something special—of all of these people, acting out their present-day version of *The Sun Also Rises,* drinking and arguing and laughing their way through their summers, consumed by differing degrees of obsession with the bullfighting itself, Charles Patrick Scanlan might in many ways be considered the most representative. Without question he is the most recognizable, what with the hat and the sunglasses. Like many of the others, he is an expatriate. He has lived outside the U.S. since 1972 and currently lives in London. He also carries, maybe cultivates, an air of mystery, one that would fit in perfectly with the Jake Barnes crowd.

It is not clear precisely how Charles Patrick earns his living, or even whether he is fabulously well off or not well off at all. He purchases bullfight tickets for himself and many of the others months in advance and also books hotels, providing his friends with an invaluable service. He gets the best seat for himself—in the section where the bull breeders sit. He was raised in El Paso, Texas, and evidently fought as a novillero for a time across the Mexican border in Juárez, although he is taller than any bullfighter I have ever seen and must have looked silly alongside those undersized novillos. He has lived in Africa, South America and Spain, among other places, and I'm told he usually refers to himself as an accountant, though he was introduced to me simply as a businessman. He has known John Fulton since he was eighteen, and he understands plenty about bullfighting. Sit down with him and a pitcher of beer and a willing ear, and he'll be happy to tell you about it.

■ ■ ■

This time of year in Sevilla there are really two ferias, at least for a foreign aficionado. Bullfight lovers from all over the world have convened to drink and talk and see the corridas, and all of that takes place on this side of the river and has nothing to do with the grid of temporary streets named after famous dead bullfighters on the other side, and the all-night dancing and merrymaking that go on over there. The feria originated as a means for the citizens of the city to relax after the somber ceremony that accompanies Semana Santa here, to recover with debauchery and indolence from their liturgical hangovers, and even now, more than a century later, it remains far more insular than other, similarly raucous festivals.

But none of that concerns the foreigner who is drawn here for the bullfights. He never need visit the feria itself, and after his first few trips here he probably won't—unless he has good friends who are Sevillano. In that case, they will be insulted if he doesn't come and get drunk for at least a night or two—not that they'll be in a condition to notice him once he gets there.

During feria, all the bullfight business and most of the pleasure is transacted by visitors in two small areas of the city. One is the section of the Barrio de Santa Cruz that includes the Laurel restaurant, where the more well-to-do of the *extranjero* crowd eat their two o'clock meal most days, and also the Murillo hotel. The second neighborhood is the ten-block radius around La Maestranza that includes the Bodegón de Torre de Oro and Michener's old hangout, El Mesón, and the Romerito, for more drinking and the tempting but ultimately disgusting late-night meat-fat sandwiches called *pringás;* and, in the other direction, the Bar Cairo and the Tres Reyes. A little farther away is the Bar El Burladero at the Hotel Colón. It would be entirely possible to come here for feria, see the bulls every day and drink and talk all night long, and never go anywhere but those two areas, and many people have no qualms about doing that. "I have my *querencia,* just like a bull does," Charles Patrick told me once. "I get in the Barrio and I don't leave. I stay at the hotel and buy some wine and have friends up and eat my meals right down the street at the Laurel and never get anywhere else. I once lived at the Murillo for two years and the whole time I rarely left the Barrio at all."

Charles Patrick never has to wait long before the Bodegón fills with friends. By the time I arrive after trying to find Litri in the hotel lobby, just about everyone I know is already here. Pleas Campbell, a former TWA pilot from North Carolina who moved to Miami after a heart attack, is sitting across from Charles Patrick with a Tiparillo between his teeth and a young girl in his lap. He's the opposite of Charles Patrick in almost every way—the sloppiest dresser of the lot, the least urbane, the most accessible. He lived in Barcelona at one time and then in Marbella and he loves to shock the stuffier aficionados with purposefully heterodox opinions. He's a veteran of the bull-running in Pamplona and another old friend of Fulton's. Most of the English-speaking people who come here call themselves Fulton's friends, and that's all right, because Fulton is friendly with nearly everybody who hasn't tried to cheat him out of money, and sometimes with those people, too.

Tonight, Pleas is talking about the corrida with Joe Distler, who is best known around here as the most skillful bull-runner in Pamplona, the heir to Matt Carney's legacy. He's also an actor and an art collector and a former amateur boxer. Joe owns a restaurant in lower Manhattan with good food and art on the walls, and you can find him there most every Friday and Saturday night except during the summers, when he's in Europe—at his Pamplona apartment or his house by the water or traveling to a bullfight somewhere. He wears vests like some dapper old-time newspaperman, or like Mel Ferrer's Robert Cohn in the Pamplona scenes.

Years ago he used to find himself in plenty of loud arguments and fistfights just like Carney, his hero and mentor, but now he takes things easier. Distler can sit next to only certain people at a corrida or he'll spend the entire day trying to argue them over to his perspective to everyone's distraction, but at the Bodegón he's as likely to talk about professional boxing or books as about bullfighting. Right now he's talking to Pleas about women, and the brunette on Pleas's lap, some friend of a friend in town for a few days, is having a giggling fit.

Soon Michael Wigram arrives. He's an Englishman whose encyclopedic knowledge of the corrida is both astounding and oppressive. Tell him your opinion on a taurine matter and inevitably he'll draw on his private stock of bullfighting lore to disagree. "But Diego Puerta went eight ye–e–e–a–r–s without cutting an ear in Málaga, from sixty-seven to seventy-five," he'll say, or something similar. He always wears wool suits and often sweater vests beneath them, even in the warmest weather. I have never seen him without a tie. Michael speaks fluent Spanish but with an upper-class British accent. He can be intimidating but after a while he seems like some proper and stiff John Cleese character, all book learning and tweed. Wigram arrives with Noel Chandler, a Welshman, and Noel's girlfriend Nancy Fortier, who is from Atlanta and wonderfully idiosyncratic. She wears the most expensive clothing in the place, funky boutique stuff, has a voice like a little girl's and reads romantic fiction, and knows quite a bit about the bullfights, too.

From maybe a half-hour after every corrida until midnight or so, the Bodegón is filled with them, these people and maybe two dozen other regulars, and often the nights go much later than midnight, although groups are always breaking up to go to fancy dinners or to the Romerito for those unholy *pringás* or even to walk across the river to the feria. On average these people go to the feria maybe once a year, if that. Distler always makes it over for at least a night; I have a feeling Wigram never does. The theory is that it hasn't changed much in the twenty or thirty or more years each of them has been coming here, and they're right— it hasn't changed at all, which is sort of the point.

The talk here is often edifying, sometimes stultifying, usually argumentative. Tonight Charles Patrick is working on another installment of his life story. "I was down in Zaire computerizing a kitchen operation," he says to me. "I didn't rate high enough on the totem pole to get a four wheel drive vehicle, but I wanted one. I wanted to drive up into the mountains and see gorillas because I knew in my heart if I was close to them— say, from here to the door—they wouldn't bother me. Gorillas are a lot of bravado, beating their chests, and if you're foolish enough to try and fight one, you're in trouble. But if you mean them no harm, generally they mean you no harm."

Pleas has moved to the next table and is telling a tale about breaking into a ranch near Pamplona one year and caping some wild bulls by moonlight. The girl is off his lap now and talking with Steven, who lives in Singapore with an older English gentleman named Neville. Steven is quite rich, mostly from family money, wears print shirts from Bali and travels around Spain seeing some eighty bullfights a year. The first time he saw one he vomited during the *estocada,* and for the first few years of his *afición* he had to leave his seat for each *suerte de matar* because he couldn't stand to see the bull killed.

John Fulton walks in, all dressed up in a sportcoat and a tie but dripping wet from the rain. He and Wigram were at some function, a formal supper with a *ganadero.* Fulton has some interesting news: the veteran matador Rafael de Paula, who is sort of a Gypsy version of Curro Romero but somewhat younger and not quite so shameless, has made plans to kill six novillos in Pamplona at the end of May. Paula has asked Fulton to be his *sobresaliente,* his stand-in. Fulton will be the only other dressed matador on the premises and the man who must fight and kill the remainder of the bulls if Paula is gored or injured. Usually the *sobresaliente* is allowed at least a few passes with the cape and maybe even some work with the muleta. Fulton is thrilled to be making his return to a Spanish bullring, even at a festival, but he tries to downplay it—he's had too many disappointments before, and Paula is notoriously unreliable. Plenty can happen in the intervening weeks.

There had been some talk tonight about wandering down to the feria, but it is obvious from Fulton's drip-dry appearance that the rain is still falling. "You can count on it," says Federico. "Every year, no matter how good the weather was in March, the feria comes and the rain comes with it. *En Abril, aguas mil.*"

But even Federico has to admit this year is different. There hasn't been a good hot bullfighting day in several weeks, and you can usually rely on at least a half dozen of them. This year, it seems possible, even likely, the rain will never end.

■■■

There's a famous photo of a matador named Pepe Luis Vargas taken moments after he was gored in La Maestranza a few years ago. Mostly the photo is famous because Vargas put it on the cover of a book he wrote. In the photo you can see blood spurting upward several feet from the wound in his thigh while Vargas watches with dismay. The photo has given Vargas some notoriety among the more casual bullfighting public and he was scheduled to fight here in the feria on Sunday with Espartaco and Manili. It would have been a high-profile date for him, the most important corrida he's had since the goring.

Last Sunday, at a festival in a town called Villanueva de Marsan, Vargas broke his left wrist and was subsequently removed from this weekend's cartel. There was some sentiment for Pepe Luis Vázquez, left off the feria carteles for the first time in a decade, to replace him. Instead, José Luis Parada was chosen on the basis of his fine performance last Sunday.

We are all ready to see good bullfighting, memorable faenas and ears awarded, but the rain makes us wait. It comes in volume all day Saturday and washes out the corrida scheduled for that afternoon: Julio Robles, José Antonio Campuzano, and Fernando Cepeda with Ramón Sánchez bulls. That one is subsequently rescheduled for Sunday at 12:30, as a matinee, but when we get to La Maestranza the rain begins again and cancels it for good. It seems likely the regularly scheduled corrida will also be lost but by late afternoon the sky has brightened and the rain has subsided.

Fusco and I hear some disturbing news on the street as we walk to the bullring: the highly regarded Atanasio bulls have been rejected by the veterinarian. Two other *ganaderos,* Cobaleda and Moura, will contribute three bulls each. The two Atanasios that did pass inspection will serve as substitutes, if needed. We have our cognac at a bar across from the bullring and head to our seats, hoping the weather will hold, but with the damp sand bound to make footing difficult and the chill and the uncertain bulls, we're not expecting much—even with Parada, Manili and Espartaco, three interesting matadors, on the cartel.

The first bull has a bad right foot and must be replaced. The Atanasio substitute is called Alegaro and weighs 544 kilos. It trots to the center of the ring and takes up residence. Alegaro is unpredictable and wild and sends each banderillero vaulting over the barrera with unexpected charges. Once the third pair of banderilleros has been placed, it runs the full distance of the ring and finds a *querencia* a quarter-turn clockwise from the toril.

Parada starts his faena there. His success last weekend has become one of the stories of the young season and if he can repeat it here, his career, which has been static for a decade, will have been resurrected. He works the bull closely with the muleta, crossing in front of it with his feet and steering it around his body, but there is a dangerous feeling to the faena. Eventually Parada brings the bull out of the *querencia,* working more smoothly now, then changes swords and puts in a *media estocada,* but the bull shakes the sword free and stays on its feet. It returns to the *querencia,* and Parada, not wanting to risk a warning for taking too much time, decides to kill it there. He cites and profiles, in difficult territory, exposing himself to the defensive-minded bull, and though he escapes unscathed, again the sword won't stay. Three more *estocadas* go in and out before the *descabello* finally puts the animal to rest.

The second bull also ensconces itself in the middle of the ring and refuses to leave. It will be Manili's challenge to move it out. Manili, born Manuel Ruiz, is a matador devoid of finesse. For that reason he often fights the Miuras and the other large and more dangerous bulls. He has had major successes at Sevilla, Madrid, and Pamplona. No artist, he's just a tough, courageous, hardworking bullfighter. He has a big, flat face with eyes close together and he looks more like an Inca warrior than a Spaniard, but he comes from Andalusia. He is one of the few matadors who succeeds by intimidating a bull with his attitude. Some people diminish his achievements because he isn't aesthetic, but I love to see him fight. He grunts and sweats and works and finds a way to do the job.

Manili uses his cape to lead the bull toward the picador. The bull charges and spills the horse. It chops with its horns and for a moment it appears the bull is going to kill the horse, despite the heavy padding the horse is wearing to prevent that from happening. At the last moment, a banderillero leads the bull away with a deft *quite*. Manili comes to meet the bull in the center of the ring while the horse is being righted and he holds the animal's attention with capework. There is complete silence in the ring and the sun is glinting through the clouds.

When Manili takes up the muleta he dedicates the bull to the crowd and gets fine applause. You wouldn't think so because of his unrefined style, but Manili is something of a favorite here. He took his alternativa in Sevilla in 1976, cut ears off two Miuras here in 1982 and two years later was proclaimed *gran triunfador* of the feria. Five times he's been carried out the big door, having cut three ears in an afternoon.

It takes two series with the muleta to get the bull out of its *querencia*, and then Manili goes to work. He passes the bull again and again, almost brusquely but with profundity. *Temple* is not his strength—each pass seems dramatic, not smooth. With music playing, he ends the faena with a *remate* that dizzies the bull, then leans down and looks it in the eye. He kills with a *media estocada* and is awarded an ear—only the second we've seen in twenty-six bulls here this season.

The man who has earned the other one, Espartaco, is next, and I have that usual feeling of excitement I get whenever he steps onto the sand, a bit bowlegged, shaking out his cape. His bull, Bilbalero, is small but thick-necked, with a rich swell of muscle and a habit of bucking on its charge. It runs at the picador once and almost spills the horse, but clearly dislikes the sensation of the pic and refuses to charge again.

Espartaco's superb banderillero, El Ecijano, misreads the bull, finds himself in trouble, and has to shove in one stick while running past. On his next try, Ecijano places the green-and-white striped sticks gracefully and well, earning applause, but while darting away from the bull he slips and falls and in an instant the animal is directly above him. There is a gasp, ten thousand spectators sucking in breath, but as the bull lowers its horns to gore, Manili's cape appears from nowhere and the animal raises its head, startled. Manili flicks the cape again and the bull forgets Ecijano, who is still prone on the ground, and directs its rage toward the flapping cloth. Ecijano, on his feet now, runs toward the barrera as Manili, careful not to lose the bull's attention, works a slow, sober, almost gladiatorial pass with the cape. There is a standing ovation: Manili's *quite* has saved Ecijano from serious injury.

Espartaco takes the muleta. He works purposefully, solemnly, with focused intensity, and creates an emotional faena. This emotion is born not of artistry, as Parada's is, but of a man's raw dominance over a malevolent bull. He works right hand to left hand, patient and sure. "The reincarnation of Joselito El Gallo!" somebody shouts over the triumphant music. And then Espartaco profiles and kills about as perfectly as anyone can kill, straight up and in over the horns, the two forms becoming one and then parting, the sword remaining perpendicularly straight between the shoulder blades as the man emerges and triumphantly extends his arms to the crowd. He gets his second ear of the feria.

■■■

Parada's second faena is the best I have seen from him, yet there remains something I don't like about his work. Every fifth or sixth pass, maybe once a series, the bull catches the muleta, and almost catches him. It makes for exciting toreo, but good toreo is supposed to include control. Parada always seems to be fighting for control of the faena and sometimes fighting for his life. A *cogida* is an ever-present possibility. Even on his good passes—and some of them are brilliantly done—the muleta often gets caught on the bull's rump or brushes against its flank. By the end of his faena Parada has bull's blood all over his white suit of lights. He changes swords and misses with his first thrust, as usual, then hits cleanly with his second. There is strong petition for an ear, and he gets it, the third awarded today.

The fifth bull is huge, 582 kilos, dark brown with a light brown patch in the back. Every color combination has a different term to describe it in Spanish—this one happens to be *castaño*. A bull with a white patch around its neck forming a collar is *gargantilla,* while a bull with vertical lines from its back to its belly differing in color from the rest of the body, that's *chorreado.* There are literally hundreds of such words in the taurine dictionary, each describing a unique pattern. This bull is startlingly handsome, with big horns and a nice swell of muscle—the perfect fighting animal, except that it won't charge.

Manili struggles through a difficult faena. When he's not succeeding with a bull he can be an ugly bullfighter because his own movements aren't graceful. This bull is problematic and the rain is coming hard again, but Manili's kill is stupendous. He does it *al encuentro,* with the man and the bull moving simultaneously. They meet halfway and Manili goes up and over, dropping the sword in the perfect spot.

It is late now and getting dark and the lights go on. Espartaco's second bull, the last of the day, quickly loses its force. Moments into the faena it stumbles and rolls on its side, and it is clear there is no reason to continue with it. Espartaco hits bone on his first try and then goes in purposefully low to dispose of the bull, killing it in one swipe with a *bajonazo.* The bull has cushions thrown at it as it is dragged away, a sad end to a marvelous afternoon.

∎∎∎

At the Bodegón, long after midnight, the talk turns to bullfighting books. Charles Patrick, leaning close, tells me to study medicine before I start to write mine, because the study of medicine or some similar discipline is the only way to learn precision. He tells me he wrote ten thousand words in one sitting for a bullfight journal. "And they were damned good, too. Better bullfighting stuff than Michener ever wrote."

Michael Wigram perks up. This is one of his pet subjects; I have heard the Michener diatribe several times before. "Michener?" he says. "Why, Michener makes more errors about bullfighting than anyone. The preface to the American edition of Hemingway's *Dangerous Summer* must average more than an error a page. It's rare that you read a page of that and don't come across an error."

This ignites Noel Chandler. "In that preface, he says he's seen Ordóñez fight more than anyone," Chandler says in his thick Welsh accent. He turns to Wigram. It is as though the conversation is scripted. "Well, you and I saw Ordóñez at damn near every significant place he fought during those years, right? You know how easy it was to tell Michener was around—he was usually drunk, for one thing. I think if he had been there, we would have known about it. I don't remember seeing him at all during that time. I mean *not once*. Do you?"

"No," Wigram says, the corners of his mouth betraying a smile. "Actually, I don't."

6

THE GYPSY WAY

I HAVE WATCHED Rafael de Paula fight bulls before, but at the time I knew nothing about Gypsies. Two years ago, on a steamy afternoon in his hometown of Jérez de la Frontera, he cut an ear off a stately Andrés Garzon Duran bull. It is one of the few ears he has cut recently in a reputable bullring but it was richly deserved and no hometown gift.

That day Paula used a style of toreo I had never seen. It was elemental, as if from a textbook, and yet utterly natural; artistic, but without pretense or posturing. It was the Gypsy style of bullfighting at its best, I later discovered, but Paula can also be quite bad. He is capable of losing interest in a bull and in bullfighting more quickly than any matador I know of save Curro Romero, whose lack of interest is almost pathological. The late Rafael El Gallo would occasionally and in true Gypsy fashion decline to fight bulls because of some mystical aspect of their gaze, but Paula sometimes seems to have decided against performing any actual bullfighting from the moment he walks into the arena or even before, simply because the day doesn't feel right.

Astonishingly enough for a matador of his reputation, in twenty-five afternoons over thirteen years during the feria here, Paula has never cut an ear. Not once with fifty bulls. Yet there is great expectation whenever he comes to Sevilla because his capabilities are legendary. Among his staunchest supporters in town are John and Federico. Paula has known them for years and often dresses at John's house when he is on a cartel at the Maestranza.

The roll call of Gypsy matadors through the years is long and filled with *figuras de toreo*—Joselito and Rafael El Gallo, of course, and Cagancho and Gitanillo de Triana, and the mysterious Rafael Albaicín of Granada, and others. These days, Paula is the only one. "A typical Gypsy," says Federico, who at one time fancied himself the next great Gypsy bullfighter. We are sitting on the steps of his father's gallery a few hours before Paula will fight Jandilla bulls with Curro Romero and Litri, and Federico is as excited as I have seen him.

"Paula has an unmistakable art, he's afraid of the bull, and he doesn't like yellow," Federico explains. "You could spot him as a Gypsy from the moment you saw him in the ring." For one thing, Paula's cape isn't backed with yellow like that of every other bullfighter I have seen, but with a bright shade of blue. He has them made that way because there is a Gypsy superstition that yellow brings bad luck, and bad luck is one thing a matador can hardly afford.

I wonder why there are few young Gypsy bullfighters these days, no contemporary generation to carry on the legacy. There seems to be no easy answer. "Well, they really are afraid," Federico says eventually. He believes Gypsies somehow have more fear than other people, or are more susceptible to their fears, and that even those who become bullfighters do so without ever truly learning to conquer fear. "Hopefully, Paula's children will continue," he says. "He has two sons who want to be bullfighters, although they also are very, very scared. They are more scared than he is, I think, and Rafael de Paula is the most frightened matador I have ever seen."

■ ■ ■

La Maestranza is viewed at its best from across the water in Triana. At night the building is starkly illuminated, and the lights reflect off what used to be the Río Guadalquivir but is now a canal. (Like most places in Sevilla this canal is named after a saint or a monarch—in this case King Alfonso XIII, who was crowned at the age of sixteen in the beginning of this century, was displaced for most of the 1920s by the military dictatorship of Primo de Rivera, returned to power, and finally abdicated in 1931 when the military announced it would not support him. Following that, Sevilla became the center of Spanish Communist activity, which is one of the few times it was actually at the vanguard of any movement, political, social or artistic.)

In the daytime, especially on a hot day, La Maestranza shimmers. It is painted a seashell white with sand-colored trim and those who don't know figure it to be a cathedral or a museum. It is seen to good advantage too from midway across the Puente de Isabel II, which connects the mouth of Calle Reyes Católicos with the Plaza de Altozano on the Triana side. Middle-aged as far as Sevillano architecture goes, the bullring was inaugurated in 1762 with a series of corridas on April 22 and 24 and May 8 and 10. Three of the matadors involved were José Candido, Joaquín Rodríguez and Juan Romero, and they were reputedly some of the finest of the day. There is no record of whether any of them were Gypsies.

At the foot of the Puente de Isabel II on the Triana side is a black cast-iron statue of Juan Belmonte which looks very much like Picasso's Quixote. It exists to honor not just Belmonte, but all the matadors of the barrio. The list is extensive and mostly includes Gypsies, because Triana was where Sevilla's Gypsies lived—and its potters and tile-makers and seafarers, too. Rodrigo de Triana, a mercenary sailor, was the first of Columbus's seamen to sight the new world. For maybe three hundred years, the era of the great Spanish seaborne empire, shipping yourself off on a barkentine to explore and plunder beckoned as a means to escape the stifling, strictly codified life of poverty of the barrio, but there has been little empire left for some time now and no exploring to be done. These days Triana isn't too different from the rest of Sevilla, although many Gypsy families still live there.

If you were a young Gypsy boy in Triana at the beginning of this century and happened to gaze across the Guadalquivir at the bullring, a vista that has barely changed to the present day, except for the autos rushing past on the Paseo de Cristóbal Colón and the electric streetlights, nobody would need to tell you that a triumphant afternoon as a matador there would legitimize you in the eyes of this closed, conservative city in a way no business or other artistic success or anything else ever could. It probably wouldn't have occurred to you to think it strange that Sevilla's least respected citizens and this revered and exalted structure, so important to the social life of the upper crust of the city, should be thus intertwined—but then, many of the unquestioned ways of this place seem strange to an outsider.

Rafael de Paula was raised not in Triana but forty miles south in

Jérez, where sherry was invented and where these days the Formula I
Grand Prix of Spain is run on a state-of-the-art motor course. Paula
never endured a nomadic life such as Federico's; he spent his childhood
in a house. "He told me he always had enough to eat," Federico says,
"but you have to remember that stability doesn't make him any less a
Gypsy. Gypsies like to roam, but there are different kinds of roaming.
And you also have to say the life he has chosen, a bullfighter's life, keeps
him on the go."

I have been a fan of Paula's since that afternoon in Jérez, but I know
that when he is paired with Curro unpredictable things happen. They
have been terrific together, spurring each other on to transcendent toreo,
or, much more frequently, they have been disastrous, especially in Sevilla.
Couple those two with Litri, unsubtle even on a good day, and with
more than ever to prove to Sevilla, and the three of them comprise a
jarring cartel. What, we wonder, was Canorea thinking?

Curro is the senior matador by several years, and the first Jandilla
bull of the day belongs to him. My new theory on Curro is that at this
point he is physically incapable of performing well, and it is underscored
by this faena, which is the worst yet. He holds the muleta for perhaps
three minutes and doesn't even try to provoke a charge, much less pass
the bull. He takes four *estocadas* without even letting go of the sword,
and then needs seven tries with the *descabello* to end the travesty.

Paula's first bull is stocky and black, and his glittering purple *traje
de luz* looks splendid beside it. Paula is officially forty-nine years old,
yet nobody here believes that; it is said he is close to Curro's age. His
bearing is pure torero. He can lean against the barrera in street clothes
and look more like a bullfighter than Espartaco does while passing a
bull. No matter what Espartaco ever accomplishes with a bull, he will
never appear as much a matador as Rafael de Paula walking toward his
animal on the balls of his feet with the blue-backed cape outstretched,
moving it from side to side to attract the animal's attention, and a look
on his face that comes straight from Goya.

Paula has faced more bulls without cutting an ear at the Feria de
Abril than anyone else since the record keeping started in 1934, and the
only explanation I can come up with involves some destiny of his always
to fail here. This second bull of the day has plenty of steam—it has
already knocked the wooden planks from the bottom of the *burladero*—
and Paula lets it rush past a few times. He's standing still as a statue,
leading it with his cape, a perfect picture of a matador. In the *detalles*

de toreo, however, Paula is lacking. He needs several minutes to get the bull into position for the picadors, and when he does the bull is overpiced and comes into the second phase, or *tercio,* visibly sagging. Matadors often make a show of getting angry when they see a picador do this, but don't be fooled. Very little, if anything, is done by the members of the cuadrilla without the matador's unambiguous permission.

Paula sets up with the muleta along the barrera, directly underneath the president's box. He moves toward the bull with tiny steps, shaking the muleta, and finally gets the bull charging, but instead of passing it he parries it. Soon the bull starts to walk counterclockwise along the barrera. It finds a spot it likes and stops, turns its back to the wooden fence and proceeds to buck at Paula when he comes near. The bull then presses its side against the barrera, in its *querencia,* and appears to fall asleep on its feet. With little choice Paula profiles there and kills on his third try amidst silence. It is now fifty-one feria bulls for Paula over fourteen years—and not one trophy to show for it.

■■■

Litri's first bull, called Brevito, has a problem with its leg and is replaced, the president of the plaza signaling for the change by lowering the green handkerchief over the side of his balcony. Before the substitute bull can be released into the ring, the original one has to be removed. As always, this is accomplished with the aid of a group of castrated steers that are let loose into the ring with bells around their necks and the mandate to lead the marred bull out. That is the way it is supposed to work, but here at La Maestranza it rarely does. Time and again Brevito resists joining the herd, and each time the rest of them are led out of the ring and up the toril, Brevito remains. After some ten minutes of this, Montoliú, Litri's banderillero, flings his cape over the barrera from inside the *callejón* to catch the bull's attention, then runs toward the toril. The cape is just the right distance in front of the bull for it to follow, and soon the bull is back up the chute and we are ready to proceed.

The substitute bull is phlegmatic to start with, and later badly weakened by the picador. Nevertheless, Litri dedicates it to the crowd. His faena begins with four passes against the barrera, his feet for once wondrously still, and then he sends the bull away with a dramatic *pase de pecho,* and for the first time he is hearing "Olé!" in the Maestranza. Litri then runs the bull out to the center of the ring. He wants to bring it all the way over to the sun but loses it somewhere in the middle and decides to work there. Working the bull in the middle of the ring is risky because if the matador is gored there the banderilleros, who are not on the sand during the final *tercio* but behind the *burladeros,* have the longest possible distance to run to come to his aid. Everyone is aware of this and when a matador chooses to work a faena in the center of the ring it is greatly to his credit. However, if a matador ends up working a faena there because he is unable to lead the bull anywhere else, it is to his discredit, for it shows he is not in control of the animal.

Litri passes the bull well, linking his *derechazos,* and the band starts the music. Following that comes a bad series, problems with the *distancia,* then two strong right-handed passes—and then he nearly gets run over during an unexpected charge. He drops to his knees and works a series of right-handed passes from there, but after his profound work earlier in the faena the *tremendismo* looks cheap. His kill is off to the right, but there is some petition for an ear, and he takes a vuelta.

The afternoon's fourth bull is a travesty. It won't charge, Curro refuses to come out from behind the *burladero* until it works up some steam, and for several minutes we remain at a standstill. After the pic-ing the president of the bullring takes an unusual step: he drops the black handkerchief over the railing to signify that he wants black banderillas— *banderillas de castigar.* These are used to punish unusually recalcitrant bulls that have not been aptly pic-ed. There used to be firecrackers on the end of the sticks but these days the metal prongs are just longer than usual. They haven't been used in Sevilla in years.

During the placing of the banderillas the three matadors have specific places where they are supposed to stand. The matador who will be fighting the bull remains along the barrera, often sipping a cup of water. His job during this phase is to supervise the cuadrilla. The other two matadors are expected to be nearby, as Manili was yesterday when he saved Ecijano with his fortuitous *quite.* Instead, Paula is directly in front of my *tendido,* all the way across the ring from the action. It isn't the novelty of the black banderillas; he just wants to be as far away from the animal as possible. The only torero farther from the bull is Curro, who has disappeared behind the *burladero* into the *callejón.* He has not made one pass with the cape—has not, in fact, approached the bull in any manner.

Eventually, when forced to take the muleta, he does a cursory dozen passes, changes swords, and kills the bull with a *media estocada*. With Curro thus out of the way for another day we hope the last two bulls will somehow salvage the afternoon, but they don't. Paula is distracted and uninteresting with the fifth bull and earns an *aviso* for taking more than the requisite time to kill it. Litri's last bull is a little monster that gives the banderilleros fits, completing a difficult day for the Jandilla *ganadería:* not one of the bulls we've seen today could truly have been called a quality animal.

As Litri's frustrated peons run abortive arcs about the ring, I notice that the lights have been turned on. It is almost nine o'clock; the corrida has lasted two and a half hours. Litri's faena is rhythmless, full of stops and starts. "Very dangerous," says Enrique behind me. Enrique is hunched over in complete concentration, his mouth half open, even after two and a half dramaless hours, but everyone else is packing up to go. The bull rips away Litri's muleta, then, after Litri retrieves it, immediately does it again, causing Leonardo, to my right, to shake his head and unstop his inflatable cushion, a signal that for him the corrida has ended.

Suddenly Litri is caught on the back of his thigh, and for a sickening second he is riding high above the ground. He lands and scrambles to his feet, unbloodied somehow, recovers the muleta and continues to work the bull to show that he can do it. It is the typical response after a *cornada,* but not a smart one. The bull has learned too much in the process and will not play the game. *"No, hombre, no!"* Leonardo yells, attentive now. The bull almost catches Litri again, but he manages to fend off its bulk with his forearm. "Kill it!" someone yells from halfway around the arena. "Kill it before it kills you!"

Litri changes swords and disposes of the bull in one thrust, a fairly good kill. He leaves the arena with his head bowed.

■■■

The topic at the Bodegón before dinner is the identity of the next great bullfighter. Litri is not a nominee for the honor. Charles Patrick Scanlan, Michael Wigram and Noel Chandler are drinking white wine and taking part in the discussion, and Pleas Campbell and I and some others are drinking beer and taking it in. "We've got our eyes on several of them," says Wigram, who fancies himself the official spokesman for aficionados around the planet. "We like Joselito, Rafi Camino, Cepeda, Fernando

Lozano and a few others. I wouldn't say we've no hope for Litri, but he certainly doesn't have it yet, and from what he has shown so far the chances are he won't ever have it."

Wigram believes Litri should have maintained his *tremendista* style instead of trying to impress the difficult Sevilla crowd with classical toreo, especially since at this point in his career he is far more accomplished with the tricks than with anything else. "After all," he says, "El Cordobés is the least traditional torero of all time, and he cut a tail in Sevilla."

"Litri gambled and lost," says Chandler. "You see, the people of Sevilla don't like gorings. Just about everybody in the stands at La Maestranza either was a torero at one point or is the brother or the mother of a torero, or has some intimate connection to one. They don't want to see someone get tossed in the air. In Pamplona or Bilbao, they'd have given Litri an ear just for getting tossed and coming back to finish the faena. It's a different mentality here."

Everyone at the table has fond feelings for Litri, and several of them know his father well. But there is almost universal fear for what may become of him. Wigram reminds us that Litri doesn't need to be fighting bulls, as his family owned a large parcel of land that was coveted by the organizers of Expo '92. They eventually paid full price and then some for it and the children now have the equivalent of more than four million dollars tucked away in the bank.

"This is why I admire Litri," Wigram says. "He doesn't have to be as brave as he is, standing up there challenging the bulls. But he does it because he loves it. There's something to be said for that. Bravery beyond the call of duty."

"Something to be said for it?" Pleas asks. Count on him to disagree with Wigram. "I admire him, too, but he's playing with his life. He better figure out what he's doing or, I'll tell you something, that boy's gonna get himself killed."

Pleas is right: Litri may well be badly gored, and one day soon. But I have come to believe that it is his prerogative. Belmonte, possibly the greatest matador never to die in the bullring, lived for years a full life of consummate enjoyment, but he lived too long. At the end he was lonely and tragic. He could no longer cape his bulls or eat the foods he loved, or satisfy himself sexually, and therefore he killed himself. Many Spaniards consider the way he died as noble and fitting as the way he lived, and they say the same about Hemingway, who didn't want to exist if he couldn't exist in the fashion to which he had become accustomed.

Perhaps young Litri, handsome and wealthy, would rather die as a bullfighter, if it comes to that, than live a long life as another mortal. Is it our business to argue?

7

DEFENDING THE FAITH

LATER that night I have a discussion with some American students about the merits of bullfighting. Several who have never seen a bullfight disparage anyone who has.

This is at the Mesón Serranito, which is just off the Plaza del Museo on Calle Alfonso XII, a brief walk from my apartment. Typically it can be crowded late into the evening but it is nearly empty now because of the feria. The farther a bar or restaurant is located from the fairgrounds, the less chance it will be active during feria week. Life for most Sevillanos during feria includes only the *casetas,* a few hours each day at home and traveling between. Some restaurants around the city close all week and many shops are closed.

The Mesón Serranito is a hangout for some of the players on the Sevilla soccer team and I often see them having lunch or playing the World Cup video game across from the long wooden bar. But like most establishments in Sevilla, the main decorative motif is taurine. There is a vast photo of La Maestranza on the wall up front and elsewhere in the bar a full suit of lights in a frame with a set of real banderillas. A stuffed bull's head is mounted beside that, not as big as the one in Tres Reyes but big enough to make me pause before offering criticism of any matador.

The discussion starts when someone mentions visiting John Fulton's studio in the Plaza de la Alianza and seeing paintings done in bull's blood. Swiftly we divide into pro- and anti-bullfighting camps. The argument is long and debilitating and nobody's mind is changed. One girl from Texas insists on shouting. She says her distaste of the corrida is too strong for her to talk in a normal voice. "Y'all are butchers," she says, then plugs her ears with her fingers when we try to argue.

Any aficionado from outside the Spanish culture knows he must always have a defense for bullfighting handy, something to counter the inevitable opposition. It almost always comes from people who have never seen a bullfight, or have seen one but knew nothing about it. There are two ways in which people react when they hear you enjoy bullfighting, have made a study of it and travel to Spain often simply to watch it: with fascination or with disgust. Nobody I've met has reacted with boredom.

At lunch the next day I ask Pleas Campbell about his own taurine defenses. He's a good person to ask because he has few bullfighting pretensions and no interest in any of its academic justifications. There are books linking the intricacies of bullfighting to various tribal rites in Iberian prehistory, books detailing the sociological value bullfighting holds in modern-day Spanish culture, books with every kind of theory you can imagine. Pleas disdains them. He attends bullfights because he enjoys them; he appreciates the nobility inherent in both man and beast. Bullfighting gives him a kick, he says. And that's the best defense of all.

He tells a story about the local preacher in his hometown of Hickory, North Carolina, stopping by the family house to pay a condolence call following the death of Pleas's father. This was just a year or so ago. The preacher was there to see the mother because Pleas had moved out of Hickory as a teenager and has hardly been back since. He's lived in Barcelona and on the Costa del Sol and all over, and now he has a house in Miami, in Coconut Grove, and spends about four months of every year in Spain. But at that time Pleas was home for the funeral and met the preacher, and eventually the preacher asked what he did with his summers.

"I told him, Well, I go and see the bullfights," Pleas relates. The preacher reacted with horror, so Pleas trotted out his best defense. He has been using it for almost four decades now, since he first came to Spain in 1951 as an enlisted man in the Navy, although he has probably had relatively few such encounters with men of the cloth.

"I said, Whoa now, wait a minute," Pleas says. "I said, Don't judge lest you be judged. And then I started telling him a little something about bullfighting. I told him that it's not a sport, and there are rules to the game, and it only lasts about ten minutes because after that the bull starts feeling pain. And I told him to think about the meat he eats every day, and how the animal dies. Maybe they clubbed it to death, maybe they put it in the back of a van to suffocate it.

"Now, the bulls out there in a bullfight, I told him, they've had a hell of a life, they're tranquil. They've been out on the pasture doin' nothing. Nobody's bothered them with anything. Then the bull comes in and he gets his moment of glory. He dies, but sometimes he takes his tormenters with him. I think if I were an animal, by God, I'd like to be a fighting bull. At least my name might go down in history, and at the very least I know I'm going to end up on somebody's table like some old cow."

The preacher started to argue that the bull is being tortured in the ring, but Pleas interrupted. He told him that the bull is so distracted by the task of getting to the waving material in front of him that it barely feels anything. "Think about a time maybe you were in a fight, and you hit somebody and you got hit," Pleas told him. "Or you were having so much fun and you scraped your leg, but you didn't realize it until the next day. Wait a minute, you say, how did I get that bruise? You don't even remember. Now, what if the bull is fighting and he doesn't feel anything? See, it's all in hot blood!"

Pleas has videotaped every bullfight he has seen in the past ten years. He has the tapes lined up on a wall in his house and when he travels he brings a tiny five-inch television with him and a selection of tapes. Before long, he had that preacher watching bullfighting tapes. The preacher saw Rafael de Paula and Espartaco. He saw El Soro, the controversial *tremendista* for whom only Pleas, of everyone I know, has any affection. He saw Manzanares and the abstruse style of Paco Ojeda. "We watched a few of them," says Pleas. "After I talked it over with the guy, explained it to him and showed him some good faenas, why, damned if he wasn't looking at it in a different light."

The arguments against the bullfight are multiple, and they vary enormously in logic and coherence. Those who call themselves animal lovers often decry the inhumanity of the spectacle. Yet I know few people as keenly attuned to animals as those involved in bullfighting. A bullfighter or bull breeder or even a true bullfight aficionado understands the characteristics of the *toro bravo* in the same way that a racetrack trainer has an affinity for thoroughbred horses.

The traditional North American cowboy, who lives on a ranch surrounded by animals and depends on them for his living, has that same special attunement to the animal world, although he raises livestock for the marketplace. Because he relies on animals to survive, he's likely to have a far more accurate sense of their—and our—proper place in the universe than many animal lovers, who enjoy eating meat but are philosophically opposed to the slaughter. Some of them would prefer to wait until every animal died of natural causes, or was hit by a bus.

Some who would ban the bullfight say it is a misuse of prime agricultural land, and that is an argument more difficult to dispute. But on equal footing is the idea that the *toro bravo,* which has been on the earth thousands of years and according to cave drawings was interacting with man before the time of Christ, would cease to exist without the ranches. If a Spanish government ever came to power determined to stop bullfighting forever, it would be easy: strip the land from the *ganaderías.* Once the existing strains of these precisely bred animals die out it will be impossible to create others, and the wonderfully noble wild bull will go the way of the carrier pigeon.

There are also those who argue that the bullfight takes advantage of the underclass of Spanish society, dangling the alluring prospect of riches and fame before the poorest males as an incentive for them to risk their lives by providing entertainment for the wealthy. I agree, and I know that for every El Cordobés who gains financial security there are tens of thousands of aspirants who never see the inside of a bullring. Nobody keeps statistics on how many of these are seriously injured or even killed in some informal neighborhood bullfight, trying to cape some one-eyed six-year-old bull that has been fought a dozen times before, the local streets blocked off by makeshift barricades and everybody taking a turn with a single, torn capote—for that is often the only way a would-be torero with no money can afford to practice. It is horribly dangerous, something no established bullfighter would ever dare to do, and yet it happens all the time around the country. To hear the stories tears at the heart.

But is bullfighting so different as a means of escaping poverty from elective military service? Or professional boxing? Tossing off the shackles of a life of extreme poverty, in Spain or anywhere else, requires more than a dedicated work ethic. The economic inequality of generations isn't often overcome by scrubbing floors for eighteen hours a day. Risks must be taken, and those risks can take many forms, from dangerous sports to a life of violent crime, or even revolution. Outlawing the bullfight won't make the lives of those underfed urchins any better. All they would lose is an avenue of possible escape.

Among Spaniards, banning the bullfight has for years been the goal of a tiny number of activists, although in the years since Franco's death they have become increasingly zealous. And the ongoing European flux is currently polarizing opinion, pro- and anti-taurine. In 1992 a single economic entity will be created from the nations of Western Europe, and the anti-bullfight forces are using that milestone to rally their cause. There are those who sincerely believe bullfighting to be a throwback to the entertainments of the Roman Colosseum, a barbaric remnant in the modern age, and they don't want Spain to be considered the embarrassment of a united Europe.

The advancing shadow of 1992 has also energized those who support the corrida, serious aficionados and a surprising number of others. They envision a future Europe that is culturally homogenous, that being an unavoidable side effect of the demolition of trade barriers. After 1992, Mercedes-Benz autos will be built in Portugal and semisweet Swiss chocolate produced in Greece. Manufacturers will go where labor is cheapest and the average supermarket shelf in Sevilla will eventually be barely indistinguishable to that of one in Rotterdam, the argument goes. There will be one currency and, eventually and inevitably, a single pan-European culture. To prevent such absolute assimilation, that which is essentially Spanish must be cherished, not banned. Flamenco must be saved, and the afternoon siesta, and the *paseo* around the town plaza at night. And the bullfight—for nothing is more uniquely Spanish than that.

I have heard this from several Spaniards who themselves do not care for bullfighting. They are not arguing out of self-interest, but for their grandchildren. And their culture.

■■■

Like any aficionado, Pleas Campbell has his taurine likes and dislikes. If Michael Wigram is the guardian of tradition, Pleas, as would be expected, is the opposite, a bullfight student of simple tastes. He wants to see good value for his money, a noble effort, and honest passes.

"There are three bullfighters I don't care for at all," he tells me over a second bottle of wine. "Curro Romero, Rafael de Paula and Antoñete. The reason I don't care for them is that they're all over the hill. Curro Romero is afraid, and he's the first one to admit that he's afraid. He's also the first one to admit that he doesn't know why they pay him. He won't fight unless they pay him fifty million pesetas. He says, I don't know why they pay me, because I'm not going to do anything.

"Rafael de Paula's got no legs and he's looking for the perfect bull on rails. Yesterday, for instance, I was the only one of our whole group who sold my ticket because both of those guys were on the same cartel. There was no way in hell those guys were going to do anything. I'd rather take that money and put it down on double zero on the roulette wheel at a fixed casino. I'd have a better chance of coming out ahead than I would going to see Curro and Rafael on the same cartel. Might not have been true fifteen years ago, but it is today. That's the reality. But some of those others can't see it.

"Now, Antoñete, I've seen him run from a bull. Here's a man who had a nice career, he retired, he lost all his money gambling, his manager got him a fight and he came back because he had to. He had a following and he did a few good things, but now he's in his fifties and he's shitting in his pants because he's got big bulls in Pamplona. Well, what did he think? That's what Pamplona's about. They got the biggest goddamn bulls in the world. But Antoñete comes up there and he runs from the goddamn things! I mean, he runs. It's disgusting."

When he finishes his monologue it's almost bullfight time. We stop at the Laurel restaurant in the Barrio, where Wigram and Charles Patrick and some of the others are finishing their fifty-dollar-a-head lunch before walking to the Maestranza. Today's treat is Manili, Joselito and Rafi Camino, but there's a catch: they're fighting notoriously bad bulls, the El Torero bulls of Salvador Domecq. The one time I have seen these bulls before, it was like watching a bullfighter try to torear a bottom-of-the-line Japanese car, all tin and clatter—with someone at the wheel who barely knew how to drive.

Manili's first bull is too small for him, and torpid besides. The latter is a pity but the former is by design. Smallish bulls are a staple of the Feria de Abril. Sevilla doesn't mind them because the object here is artful toreo, which neatly complements the *alegría,* happiness, at the feria itself. Up north, in Madrid at the month-long feria of San Ysidro and at the ferias of Pamplona and Bilbao, the bulls are everything, virtual dinosaurs, and bullfighting is much more a matter of surviving with your honor intact than making pretty passes.

Joselito gets a 514-kilo bull called Formalito and immediately works his way into trouble. This is his last chance at this feria but almost nobody is even thinking about a rivalry anymore. It's funny how two weeks of bullfights change everything, the whole dynamic of the season. And by the time San Ysidro comes, in little more than a month, with Joselito in his home territory, it all could change again. Today Joselito is having trouble with his *temple;* the bull's horns are slapping against the waving muleta, and he also isn't linking his passes. There are murmurs of disapproval from the crowd, but not too many, for it is obvious the bull is terrible.

Then Joselito is caught. He is tossed in the air and lands on the bull's back and rides there for a moment like a rodeo cowboy, only upside-down—and then, in a flash, he has picked up the muleta and is ready to resume his work. I have been gifted with barrera seats for this fight, terrific seats in the shade, and Joselito is standing directly in front of me. I can see his hand actually shaking as he starts in on the bull, fighting off the fear. A moment later the animal stops in mid-pass and for a long instant it appears disaster will happen again. The bull considers its options as we wait and then takes the muleta with a quick swipe of its horns. Joselito changes swords.

Rafi Camino does nothing with his first bull, other than incite the crowd to jeer with a clumsy series of passes from his knees, and he hits a lung with his *estocada* and watches the blood spurt from the animal's mouth. And Manili, without much of an animal to work with, keeps his second faena brief and forgettable. He needs seven *descabellos* to kill the bull as the inevitable rain starts to fall. I have taken to calling this the Feria de Seattle.

Joselito then prepares to face his final bull of the feria. After all those posters, he is going to leave Sevilla virtually forgotten, having made almost no impact—unless he can triumph with this bull. Having seen the bulls that have come before it today, this will be virtually impossible. The finest torero in the world can't do anything of note with bulls such as these.

This bull is no better. But Joselito is too young and too proud, too much a born bullfighter, to dispose of it without effort. His faena begins well. He tucks the bull in and around his body, *cargando la suerte* by stepping across the bull's line of vision at the start of each pass, and sends it off with a *derechazo* to good applause. But several passes into the second series the bull swipes at the muleta with its horns and gets it and Joselito can't regain his rhythm. There is a gasp as the bull comes in for Joselito's thigh, a moment of terror, but at the last instant it catches sight of the muleta and veers away. The bull is stopping in the midst of nearly every pass, which is the way gorings happen. Given the choice between the muleta and the man in that situation the bull will usually choose the muleta but it will still sometimes choose the man, and when you are talking about a possible goring even odds of one in ten are not favorable. Joselito pushes the bull through with pure *valiente,* but there is an ominous feeling hanging in the air. I write these words in my notebook: *I think he will get caught again.*

It is painful to watch the next series. The bull's horn is at chest level and it seems ready to thrust through the suit of lights with every pass. What is Joselito doing? Is his pride this strong? Fusco, who had derided Litri for his foolhardiness, must be holding his head in his hands, up in his *grada* seat. And then, as if in slow motion, the bull hesitates and flicks its horns into Joselito's chest, knocking him down. He is up swiftly but with new blood under his arm. He takes the muleta and resumes the faena but the bull takes it from him once more, ripping it neatly in half. On his way to get a new one Joselito kicks angrily at the ground.

A goring or near-goring is a peculiar occurrence. Before the terrible moment, Joselito's total lack of dominance had earned him nothing but silence. He was fighting a bull the way many aficionados in the crowd believed they would do it if given the chance—knowing the passes but out of control, not communicating with the animal, trying to force a success like an *espontáneo,* and getting knocked about as a result. Then, for a moment, the crowd saw death. It happened with the first bull Joselito had today and again with the second. It doesn't matter that the wounds turned out to be minor, for the fear in such a situation is real for both the spectators and the bullfighter, no matter what the eventual result, and it adds meaning to even the least effective bullfighting.

Joselito, clearly, is trying. By the time he returns from the barrera with his new muleta, his bravery has won him the crowd. Perhaps sensing this, his last series is his best—cold but technically correct and forceful—and his *estocada,* on the second try, is the finest kill of the day. Joselito gets strong applause from the crowd, which is happy to see him alive.

He walks back into the ring and holds out his hat, thanking the aficionados for their support, and despite his bloodied suit of lights he is smiling. He is only twenty years old and has plenty of time left to win Sevilla, and he has done more for himself today with two earnest failures, and two gorings, than two weeks of pretension and posturing had accomplished for him before.

8

THE TRIUMPH OF
ESPARTACO

ESPARTACO, the son of an unsuccessful matador, was considered an unimportant bullfighter, immature and tending toward *tremendismo,* when he appeared in the Maestranza in April of 1985. With his first bull of the feria he cut an ear, and with his second bull he cut two, exiting out the big door on shoulders onto Avenida Cristóbal Colón, his extraordinary talent laid bare before all of Spain.

Before this year, in twenty-three afternoons at the Feria de Abril spanning nine seasons, Espartaco had earned twenty-two ears. Only one man has cut more since the record keeping started in 1936, and that was Francisco Rivera, Paquirri. He cut twenty-eight ears before his death in 1984, but needed sixteen years and some sixty bulls to do it.

With just a few days remaining in this year's feria, the visitors to Sevilla are beginning to depart. That includes the bullfighters. Each day, another matador or two finishes his work. Espartaco will fight his final corrida on Wednesday afternoon, with Sepulveda bulls and Rafael de Paula and Rafi Camino in rotation, and then he'll relax at his *finca* in Espartinas for a few days before appearing next in Jérez de la Frontera on the first Friday in May.

The prospect of not seeing Espartaco here again this year envelops me in melancholy as Wednesday approaches. It isn't just his impressive record in La Maestranza, but the aesthetic confluence of my tastes, this bullring and his style. Every aficionado has his own vision of what a perfect bullfight would look like, his own perfect bullfighter succeeding with his favorite bulls. I don't know what breed of bulls I'd have in my dream corrida, maybe Miuras or Victorinos, but I can easily conjure up the scene. Espartaco is the matador and the smooth white-and-golden Maestranza is the setting. The Giralda looms elegantly in the background, visible from my seat in the royal *palco* (this being my fantasy, I'll sit where I want). The faena seems to take place in slow motion and last forever. Espartaco passes his bull again and again, *naturales* mostly, but a few of the old maneuvers from Cossio that nobody's seen in years. The thumping music of the pasodoble accompanies the passes and adds to the intoxicating feeling. It is a dream sequence, as the best bullfights are. The moment arrives for the kill and Espartaco attempts it *recibiendo,* waiting a fraction of a second longer than prudence would dictate before rising over the horns with his sword and slaying the animal with a single perfect thrust.

It will be easy to see Espartaco fight plenty more this season. I'll see him in Madrid at San Ysidro at the end of May and also before that, in Córdoba if I can get there, in Jérez in three weeks, and probably in a pueblo or two along the way. If I want to, I can see Espartaco at Bilbao or Pamplona this summer, or at Salamanca or Logroño or any of the major ferias to come, for he fights everywhere. For the past four years, he has fought more bulls annually than any other matador. He fought 91 times in 1985, 88 times in 1986, 82 times in 1988, and an astounding 100 times in 1987, the most since El Cordobés crisscrossed Spain and the south of France in a frenzy in 1970, setting the all-time record of 121 corridas. He is both durable and in demand. If I wanted to follow Espartaco for the rest of the season, renting a car and following his Mercedes through the night on the six-, eight- and ten-hour drives between plazas, I could get a better tour of Spain than any travel agent could devise. I'd see pueblos without running water and cities full of sophisticated industry, from the farthest corners of Iberia to its center, Madrid.

But nothing he could do in any of those places would mean as much as a triumph in the Maestranza, with the unique audience here that is at once joyous and serious, the most earnest in Spain. Records exist tracing bullfighting in Sevilla back to 1405, and in 1479, thirteen years before Columbus embarked on his first voyage, there is documentation of a bullfight in the Alcázar celebrating the birth of a royal son. There was a singular enthusiasm for the spectacle then, and in the five centuries since it hasn't waned.

I wake Wednesday hoping for the impossible, the perfect corrida, and the day starts with a small but significant miracle: sun. Then we learn that the scheduled Sepulveda bulls did not pass veterinary inspection, and six Cebada Gagos have been supplied on short notice. This could mean that the Sepulvedas were without muscle or were underweight, not physically suitable for a first-class bullring, but bulls are also often rejected by bullring veterinarians because they are found to have been tampered with, their horns shaven.

Such shameful—and illegal—taurine disarmament may be the worst bullfighting development of this century. The insidious practice blossomed during the time of Manolete and continued to the point where El Cordobés admits to never having faced a bull that had its horns intact. Many who hear about horn shaving erroneously believe that the horns have been noticeably shortened or even blunted. Actually only a half-inch or less of the horn need be filed for the bull to be greatly affected, and the loss of a half-inch is all but undetectable to the naked eye from the distance of a barrera seat. There are aficionados who will tell you they can instantly detect a bull with shaved horns, and perhaps they can, but it is by studying the behavior of the bull—not from the horn itself. For a bull, losing a half-inch off its horns is equivalent to a person's losing the same off each of his fingers: everything is now farther from him than it seems. A bull with shaved horns is far less dangerous than one whose horns are unshaved because its sense of aim is off—and because its horns are tender. It doesn't *want* to catch anything with them.

You are far more likely to see altered bulls in a pueblo than at a major feria. Usually it is someone in the matador's camp who engineers the shaving of the bulls, or at least makes the demand. It happens in a small town because the matador knows he can be far more daring with the danger thus reduced and that few aficionados in the crowd will know the difference. However, if someone is discovered tampering with the bulls the matador will be shocked and dismayed and know nothing about it, even if the guilty party is his own brother.

We arrive at the bullring with the sun bright and hot above us, and after so many days of cloud cover it all but hurts the eyes. The corrida starts with Paula, and starts slowly. An interminable pic removes whatever fight his 534-kilo animal ever had, and we wait out the faena as he parries and fences. At the Maestranza there are two kinds of silences, a respectful one and a damning one, and after it becomes clear that Paula is doing nothing with this bull he gets the second kind for most of his faena, earning no applause as he finishes each series. He pinches his *estocada,* the sword going one way, the man another and the bull a third, then on his third try sinks a *bajonazo.* It is his fifty-third bull here without an ear.

Espartaco's first bull is tan flecked with white and quite handsome, but it limps its way through the faena, stopping and starting, not with malicious intent but with a lack of energy. Espartaco drives it through passes with sheer fundamentals. He can mesmerize a bull. This is a difficult one, with little *casta.* He works a series with his right hand, back and front, and then his left, back and front, ending with the *pase de pecho* and then posing in front of the horns, invulnerable.

Espartaco is holding the muleta inches away from the bull's head. That happens to be the optimum *distancia* for this bull, perhaps because its eyes are poor. The bull will charge only with the muleta dangling in its face, which leaves little room for art. Espartaco kills well on his second try and gets a standing ovation, but no ear. There just wasn't an ear in the animal.

Rafi Camino's first bull is black, with rippling muscle. Watching a bull like that strut around the ring it is easy to believe those stories one hears about bulls fighting lions in the early years of this century, and the fights ending in a matter of moments with the lion bleeding and dying and the bull, the true if uncrowned King of the Jungle, stabbing at its fallen enemy. Some of the bulls we've seen haven't seemed capable of killing any living thing, much less a lion, but this one has power and an intimidating way of trotting around the ring. It looks like a fighting bull. Unfortunately, it belongs to Camino, tall and awkward, who is doing a poor impersonation of a matador.

The bull quickly has Camino on the defensive. It takes Camino three series to realize that the bull has found itself a *querencia,* and then he makes an effort to lure it out. But the animal ignores him and the faena degenerates into a sleepwalk. Camino seems to have no feel for the bull, or for bullfighting in general. It is difficult to believe that this young man can be the son of Paco Camino, a true *figura,* and have so little innate knowledge of how to fight a bull; it is the flip side of Espartaco's genetic mystery. What produces a great matador, if not breeding? Nobody knows.

Rafael de Paula gets a big black second bull with white markings on its underbelly. He unveils some slow passes with the cape and hears "Olé!" for the first time here this year. Between the pics he constructs another emotional series with the cape, each verónica slow and graceful. It takes some energy for Paula to get the bull to the center of the ring with the muleta, but his good passes are as good as anyone's. He shows a good series with the right hand and then one a little choppier, because fright gets him backpedaling furiously.

Paula doesn't wait to see if he can work the bull on the other side but changes swords and puts a *media estocada* in a good spot. It is a shame because the bull was showing bravery and a willingness to charge and Paula aborted the faena when it was just gaining momentum. The bull takes an agonizingly slow walk along the barrera with the sword sticking out of its body. It stays on its feet for more than half a minute before dying beside a *burladero*.

We wait for the next bull to emerge, Espartaco's last of the feria, and the expectation and emotion are evident around the bullring. Already Espartaco has probably clinched the selection as the *gran triunfador* of this feria. He has turned away two so-called challenges, Joselito's and Litri's, and though there are five corridas remaining and a novillada he is not likely to be outclassed—not unless somebody gets lucky and cuts two ears off a Miura. He will probably be named the feria's best by the various committees no matter what he does here, and yet he still hasn't triumphed in grand fashion this year. He cut one ear on Easter Sunday, then had a fine day without earning a trophy with the *juanpedros* and cut an ear off a Cobaleda bull with a spectacular kill the following Sunday. If he doesn't triumph here with this last bull, he'll have two ears in four afternoons, which is admirable but well off his historic pace.

The bull is Alocado, 512 kilos. It emerges ponderously and stands in the center of the ring. Espartaco approaches with that rocking, upright walk of his, walking like he's happy to see the sun shining and he hasn't a care in the world, and soon he has the bull chasing the capote, although it is all he can do to get it to charge. There is absolutely no artistry in the capework but there is art in merely getting this bull to follow the cape. That is evident from the start. What a shame, we are all thinking. Camino's first bull and Paula's second were noble, worthwhile animals, and they were wasted. *Cuando hay toros . . .*

Alocado takes some time to get the courage to rush the picador but finally does. It is either too smart or too dumb for this game. Ecijano sprints past and pushes in one banderilla with his left hand, and the crowd whistles—but what can he do?

The faena begins and I watch Espartaco discover the *distancia* of this bull. The last one he worked by waving the muleta almost under its nose. This one, he learns through trial and error, needs to be cited from about four feet away. Once Espartaco deduces the *distancia,* it seems, he can get most any bull to charge. It takes two series for him to get the feel of this bull and then he lowers the muleta, bending his back slightly and passing from just above his knees, and that makes all the difference. Miraculously the bull is charging, and soon the music starts.

It's a fine feeling seeing Espartaco down there on the sand making a bull execute his wishes, with the plaza full and the band playing, and I try to capture it for all time, to fortify myself against the emptiness I know will come after the bullfight has ended. I try to memorize the emotion, to memorize the look of the bullfighter passing the bull so closely, the muleta in his right hand and the animal rushing by, to memorize the tune of the pasodoble coming from the band seated over my right shoulder. I try, but it's difficult, for bullfighting has an immediacy to it that doesn't lend itself well to memory. It's like trying to memorize the sensation of being in love.

Espartaco works a splendid series, all ins and outs. He has the bull on a leash now. His selection of passes is almost unvarying. He sends the bull up, around, and back with *derechazos* and *naturales* almost exclusively—for that, he has discerned, is the medium with which to create the most profound art with this bull. His *temple* is perfect, and the horns never brush against the muleta. When Espartaco finishes a series he turns on his heels and walks his stiff-legged strut away from the bull, his chin up, doing his best to look like a bullfighter, and to me much of his charm is that this is the only aspect of the corrida he can't quite pull off.

I watch a series looking for geometry, following the bull. It charges in graceful arcs, bending itself around the man with its lead eye fixed on the cape. The time needed for it to finish one charge and begin another is minimal because Espartaco is *cargando la suerte* this time, crossing in front of the bull to alter its path. He works a set with the more difficult left hand, *natural* after *natural,* sends it through with a *pase de pecho* and then stops it; turns, then walks off to a tumultuous ovation. It is not a perfect faena, a faena for all time. But it has turned into the faena of the feria.

Later, Zabala of *ABC* will rhapsodize. "It's been a long time since I have experienced convulsions that so jolted my soul of *afición*," he'll write. "Toreo of such overwhelming uniqueness, toreo born of the art of *temple,* produced by a young matador at the height of his career, a matador prodded by a formidable desire to reach beyond himself, and by an extraordinary pride in all that the word torero means." The other critics will not feel quite that rapture, but almost. For a quarter-hour, arguments about the quality of modern bulls today as opposed to those of previous epochs and criticism of modern bullfighting for overadorned toreo and toreo without validity, for the disgrace of tampered bulls and bulls bred smaller and too many tourists and too much commercialism and all that is wrong with the corrida in the present day, can be forgotten. There is unanimity in the plaza, an electric feeling, accessible to both veteran aficionado and unrefined neophyte. Each need do nothing more than watch the artistry unfold.

Espartaco changes swords to an even bigger ovation. It is exactly the right moment. This has been a triumph of technical bullfighting, Espartaco completely taming this wild bull. Now all that is left is the kill. He profiles and cites and on the way in he is caught slightly in the left thigh, just above the knee. There is a rip in his pants and he is limping stiffly and his banderillos rush to aid him but he waves them away. The kill is flawless and the bull succumbs quickly. There is one ear awarded and then clamorous petition for another and then the second is awarded, the first two-ear success of this feria, and Espartaco takes his vuelta with a stiff limp and a wide-faced smile, holding an ear in each hand all the way around.

9

WAITING FOR THE
MIRACLE

MY FRIEND FUSCO is faced with an agonizing decision. For weeks he's been telling me about what Curro Romero did last year and how it was worth all the waiting. It wasn't an entire faena of quality like anyone else might perform, just six slow-motion verónicas, but to Fusco even that made up for the disappointments. He has been pontificating about how sinful it would be to miss a chance to see Curro in Sevilla, because the next time he's good could well be the last time. But now that the feria is down to its final weekend, Fusco is almost out of money, and he's considering skipping Friday's corrida, Curro's last here. It may come down to Curro Friday or the Miuras Sunday, and Fusco has always loved the Miuras.

He counts the negatives and positives of the situation over lunch. Curro will be fighting with Litri, the third time that unlikely pair has appeared together here this year, and Fusco has grown to despise the little *tremendista*. The third matador on the cartel, Fernando Cepeda, cut an ear last year in his only feria appearance and is usually quite good with the cape. The bulls are Torrestrellas, a high-quality breed. But money is money, and what are the odds?

We stop at a *reventa* and learn tickets are going for fifty dollars for *grada* seats in the sun. You might think that after what Curro has done his first three times out this year the people here would finally wise up, but it has been that way now for fifteen years and still he sells out every time. I'm almost ready to give Fusco my seat but in the interest of research I decide I can't miss Curro's last try, just in case something does happen, and anyway I'm eager to see Cepeda and Litri. Half an hour before the fight I leave Fusco in misery at the Bodegón with no idea what he'll do.

Fusco is the latest in a long line of aficionados to be put in a quandary by Curro Romero. Curro first appeared at the Maestranza as a novillero in 1957, took his alternativa in Valencia in 1959 and has fought in the Feria de Abril every year since. His ninety-seven appearances over thirty years are by far the highest total extant and in ears cut he is behind only Paquirri and Espartaco and Ordóñez, but he has been uneven from the beginning and the older he gets the less often he shows his magic. It has been a bad feria for Fusco, what with the rainy weather and Joselito's failure, but the feria has been even worse for Curro, terrible press and cushions thrown at him in the bullring and not even a hint of proper toreo, although Curro has earned hundreds of thousands of dollars here to help salve his wounds while Fusco has nearly gone broke watching him.

A glimmer of something from Curro today would save the feria for Fusco, but not if he isn't there to see it. If he isn't inside the Maestranza this afternoon, it's much better that nothing happens. If Curro decides to fight and gets the Maestranza crowd that idolizes him going and the music playing and all that, Fusco will never forgive himself for missing it.

With his first bull Curro does nothing and reinforces my opinion that Fusco doesn't have to worry. It's a quality animal, not too large, aggressive enough—but, again, somehow not to Curro's liking. After a cursory attempt at fighting, he stabs twice with the sword, then picks up the *descabello*. He pokes the bull and prods it but he can't hit the right spot and it won't die. Four times he tries, five, six, seven times, nine times . . . and again the crowd is chanting. Ten! Eleven! His twelfth *descabello* finally kills the bull.

A lifeless faena by Cepeda follows and then Litri gets the third bull. He dedicates it to the crowd and starts his first three series with *litrazos,* the baroque pass made famous by his father. Holding the muleta behind his body with both hands, he cites the bull from across the ring by jumping in the air. At the last moment, with the bull charging at top speed, Litri lifts an arm and swings the muleta away from his body like a sail that has picked up a gust of wind.

The pass is quite a thing to look at, the bull coming hard from the other side of the ring, but there is a dispute about whether it is meaningful toreo. John Fulton disdains it, saying a bull's charge is so much show until it lowers its head, for it can't gore anything with its horns held high. It's true that the bull, which arrives at full speed and intent on mayhem, nearly always chooses to rush the muleta, which is moving, and not the matador. But there is quite a lot of valor needed to stand there and watch a bull charge toward you at that speed, from that distance, without flinching or moving. And in contrast to a conventional pass, Litri has cited the bull by moving his body, not the muleta. The body is the first thing the bull sees from whatever distance away it starts and the last thing it sees as it lowers its head, and there is always the danger that it won't notice the cloth appearing from behind Litri's back and will instead head straight on in. The *litrazo* alters the movement of the bull and demonstrates the control of the matador, who is risking a goring while exhibiting his bravery. That sounds like valid toreo to me.

The *litrazos* are successful, but they can't save the faena. Litri, trying all sorts of *tremendismo,* is citing the bull from all the way across the ring even on conventional passes. That's fine as long as he can maintain control of the animal, but he can't. The faena is lacking one of the elements of good bullfighting, *mandar:* the ability to make the bull go where you want it to. "Save it for the small towns!" someone yells when Litri drops to his knees. His kill punctures a lung and the bull dies drooling blood.

■ ■ ■

Curro's last bull is dark brown with a cream-colored back and nose. It is called Buenasuerte: Good Fortune. There is complete silence in the plaza. The bull takes a tour of the ring, circling twice, then starts to charge as Curro steps out from behind the *burladero*. What happens next happens quickly. Curro bunches his cape so that it is about half normal size and then works seven verónicas like those I have heard about. They take me by surprise because they come so suddenly, yet each one by itself floats by incomparably slowly. The cape moves as if it is underwater and the bull follows at the same speed.

Curro is standing right on top of the bull. When passed this way the bull's charges are made from a standing start and it doesn't have any space with which to work up momentum, and this means the verónicas can be even slower. There is no way for Curro to know yet if the bull has bad intentions or even bad eyesight, which can be equally dangerous. He just somehow senses that it doesn't.

As the preliminary work with the cape ends, the crowd is in an uproar. So much for the Sevilla silence. People are shouting to each other and backslapping and even hugging. Having doubted Curro vocally for the last two weeks, I am accosted from all sides. "That's toreo!" says Enrique, pounding my back. "Completely distinct from what any other torero can do," says Leonardo. Rafael cuffs me on the arm. "Don't you get it? That's art!"

How great was it? The verónicas were exceptionally good, and certainly unlike any I'd seen, but I'm not yet ready to rate Curro, the 1989 version, as a taurine immortal. I believe my neighbors cheer so ardently for Curro because they remember what it was like when he was truly good, good like that for a whole faena, pass after pass. A hint of that prowess rekindles the memory, and that memory fills in the rest. It's a reverberation of his youth, and of their youth, too.

I'm trying to judge his success based only on what I see now. To me it doesn't approach what we saw Wednesday, when Espartaco cut two ears off a very difficult bull with a complete faena, but in Spain the volume of the art produced and the consistency of it are immaterial. A man is judged by the best thing he does, his masterpiece, not by the bits and sums of all his work. In terms of pure emotion, Curro's succeeding with a cape can rank with anything. But this was still just seven verónicas, nothing more, and we have all three *tercios* to go. It was astonishing, but he still hasn't fought the bull.

It comes in on Curro's fists and he is forced to fend it off. The picadors arrive and the bull digs in under the horse and stays there a nice long time. Then Curro reels off four more slow verónicas, one of which is the slowest I have ever seen. The cape moves so slowly and it appears so effortless, you wonder why he can't always do it. Fernando Cepeda comes out to take a *quite* and shows two soft verónicas, artful but no comparison with what we have been seeing. Next to what Curro has just done, the work seems childish, and Cepeda a youth masquerading at bullfighting.

The banderillas are placed and the bull chases a peon to the barrera,

Litri being unable to stop it with a *quite*. It is a fine bull, that is obvious. And as Curro takes the muleta and adjusts his suit of lights, a single question is being asked everywhere in the bullring. Will he fight it?

His first series is quite good, and with the penultimate pass he crosses the bull and guides it around his body, *cargando la suerte,* then sends it away. Everyone is standing and shouting Olés; it's infectious. For Curro's next four passes he stands stone still as the bull approaches, then waves the muleta with a shake of the wrist to make the bull drift past. The music starts. The bull is terrific, and Curro is doing well.

He has some problems getting the bull to charge in the next sequence and is in danger of losing it, but he forces it past on the right side and makes the return pass on one knee, then hops up and stares for a while. During the following series the bull stops and seems to have a moment of enlightenment, as if suddenly realizing how stupid it has been to chase after the red cloth all this time. Curro doesn't back down but completes the pass and the faena, showing uncommon courage for him. He changes swords for the kill, misses twice, trades for the *descabello* but never gets a chance to use it. The bull, weakened and wounded, collapses and dies, Curro never having landed a sword thrust of any kind.

Despite the marvelous capework, the faena was not good enough for an ear and the kill was nonexistent. Instead, he gets a standing ovation. He considers whether a vuelta is appropriate and finally takes it. *"Vuelta con protestas,"* the result box in *Toros '92* will record, but the vast majority of aficionados in the bullring are thrilled to see him do it. They can finally say they saw Curro perform well enough to take a vuelta, for he hasn't cut an ear in years and even his vueltas are rare. Somebody later tells me Curro hasn't taken one in a first-class ring in three years.

Leonardo turns to me, very solemn, as if he is about to impart great wisdom. "What you have just seen is completely different from anything you will see by any other torero," he says. He shakes a finger. "By any other!"

When I emerge from the portal onto the street I immediately see Fusco. He has a look of absolute dejection on his face. "I heard the cheering," he says. He is close to tears. "I heard the cheering and I knew what was happening and there was absolutely nothing I could do about it. I stood as close as I could to the doorway and heard the Olés. It made me sick to know that it was happening again and I was right there but I wasn't seeing it."

I start to tell him what it was like but he stops me with a raised hand "Don't tell me," he says. "I don't even want to know about it."

At first Fusco says he's too distraught even to go to the Bodegón, but then he decides he wants to hear what everyone has to say. "A couple of passes do not a faena make," pronounces Pleas Campbell, but the cadre of *curristas,* Wigram and Joe Distler and some others, are enraptured. People are telling their war stories, how long they had to wait to see Curro perform well. "For me it was seven years," says Mike Bottino, the white-bearded aficionado from New York. "I had been watching him two years before I finally saw him get a bull he liked at a festival down in Puerto de Santa María, and we all said, This is it! But he tripped and had to go to the infirmary and never got to fight it. I had to wait five more years before I saw him do anything, and then he cut an ear."

Distler wants Wigram's opinion about Cepeda's *quite.* "I think it was bad judgment on Cepeda's part to come out and take a *quite* at that time," Distler says. "I mean, he has twenty-five years to go and he'll probably be a major *figura* of toreo in his time, and here's Curro, and how many more days like this does he have left? He should have seen what Curro was doing and respected it. What do these four passes mean to him?"

"I agree, and it didn't do him any good, did it?" Wigram says. "All it showed was that he doesn't have the impact of Curro. Oscar Wilde said it best: It was worse than a crime. It was a mistake."

I look at Fusco, who seems to be drinking up all the money he saved today in glasses of *fino,* but he is lost in a reverie about his own bad judgment. He tried to apply logic to an inherently Spanish decision, and he should have known better. In Spain it doesn't follow that because Curro has been dreadful for three corridas or even for thirty, you should behave as though he won't triumph the next time out.

The thing to do, if you really admire what the man can evoke when he's on, is to spend the time and the money. Likely as not he'll fail again—but then again, perhaps he won't. It is the gesture of faith that counts, for innate faith and symbolic gestures seem to have an extraordinary power here, in religion and also in bullfighting.

■■■

The next morning the discussion continues above *tendido* 3, in *grada* seats high in the sombra section. There is a morning novillada, a Feria de Abril tradition, and the tickets aren't included in the *abono,* so the whole crowd sits together. We're all tired and hung over but we've come here on little sleep because two of the best young bullfighters in Spain, Julio Aparicio and Pepe Luis Martín, are on the cartel. Either or both could emerge as *figuras* in the years to come, although the way bull-fighting works it's also entirely possible neither will ever fulfill his potential.

Aparicio is the son of the matador of the same name, who was a contemporary of Paco Camino, Litri *padre,* El Viti, Ordóñez, Diego Puerta and the rest. Julio Aparicio *padre* took his alternativa following a highly successful 1949 season as a novillero, and for the 1951 season was one of the best matadors in Spain, a revelation, but somehow never became as important a bullfighter as it seemed he would. Fighting only occasionally in the years that followed, he'd succeed from time to time in Madrid or another of the major ferias, but he also was capable of looking inept with the muleta, emotionless and unfeeling.

His son, Julito, has been brought along slowly—pampered, many believe. This is a danger inherent in a successful matador's guiding his own son's career. The temptation to make things easy is difficult to resist.

There have been plenty of sons of famous matadors who have tried to become bullfighters in the latter part of this century, Pepe Luis Váz-quez *hijo* being the best known because of that famous name, and by the time Julito Aparicio came along his father knew all the tricks. In pueblos, Aparicio *padre* would arrange to rig the *sorteo* and handpick his son's bulls, taking the smallest and most docile of the lot. When this wasn't possible, such as at the major ferias, he would often schedule Julito to fight in a *corrida mixta* as the only novillero on a cartel with two matadors. This meant that the full matadors would be dividing two lots of two bulls each, and Julito would be left with the two novillos. Aparicio could virtually pick the animals straight from the *ganadería* since no *sorteo* was necessary. And there was also the assurance in a *corrida mixta* that no other novillero could upstage Julito on the cartel.

Pepe Luis Vázquez did the same thing in 1980, making a triumphant romp through Spain with Curro Romero and other matadors while still a novillero. This afforded aficionados the opportunity to see two well-publicized bullfighters at a time but in the end it did great damage. Vázquez, deprived of the opportunity to face a variety of bulls and hone his skills, had an initial period of success but never really developed as a matador. A Sevilla native and a great favorite of the aficionados here, over seven seasons he appeared on the feria carteles thirteen times without cutting an ear. He was contracted for only eight corridas in the whole of 1988 because it has come to the point where nobody else in Spain will pay to see him, and this year, for the first time, he was not chosen to compete here in the feria. It was a blow to Vázquez and to the *afición* of Sevilla, but everyone understood the reasoning. "He just never got any better," Federico Fulton said.

If Julio Aparicio isn't careful, the same thing may happen to Julito. In a short time, a matter of months, his parentage and his publicity have combined to make Julito Aparicio the best-known novillero in Spain, much as Litri and Rafi Camino were before him. But he has made a name for himself largely on facile novillos, little animals that hardly teach him anything. Julio hasn't hesitated to obtain a medical certificate on several occasions to pull his son out of corridas at the last minute when the bulls didn't seem propitious or the terms weren't to his liking. He may have thought he was preempting a probable failure, but in reality what he was doing was depriving Julito of a rare opportunity to learn. However, those who have seen Julito Aparicio torear have returned to report that he has undeniable talent. He is said to fight somewhat like the young Paula.

Pepe Luis Martín has also received plenty of attention. He is from Ronda, a majestic hill town perched on a precipice southeast of here in the provence of Málaga. It's where the immortal Pedro Romero was from and Cayetano Sanz, one of the first great artistic bullfighters, and also Cayetano Ordóñez, Niño de la Palma, the father of Antonio. Seeing the elder Ordóñez triumph for the first time, Gregorio Corrochano wrote the famous line *"Es de Ronda y se llama Cayetano,"* meaning he's from Ronda, and he's serendipitously named Cayetano, the same as Cayetano Sanz.

Ronda, where Antonio Ordóñez is now the impresario at the wonderful antique bullring, is so starved for a taurine hero that recently another critic mimicked Corrochano and wrote this: *"Es de Ronda y se llama Pepe Luis."* The meaning is there, if not the poetry, and it gives you an idea of the pressure Martín is up against.

Still a teenager, Martín is the hero of a town—and not just any town but one of the most important in all of bullfighting—yet he remains open and engaging. Last year there was a corrida to mark the end of the season in Ronda and John Fulton and his girlfriend Judy Cotter attended. The director of the Ronda taurine museum, an old friend of

John's, told them to stop by the Martín household because there was a celebration going on.

"I had some friends in from Hawaii," Judy told me later, "and Pepe Luis came out, which he didn't have to do, and he invited the whole carload of us in and it was the most marvelous time. His mother sang sevillanas about him. He struck me as the sweetest, nicest kid."

Judy has come today to see Martín triumph. The rest of us are curious to see both of the well-publicized novilleros, but we're also here to soak up the warm weather and to continue talking about Curro, and what it all meant. Already the debate has started here in the *grada,* and I have a feeling it will be a long time before anyone will be discussing much else, to the great discomfort of Fusco. Sitting a row above me, wearing his blue windbreaker despite the comfortable temperature and complete absence of wind, I see him cringe each time the man is mentioned.

10

THE END OF
SOMETHING

THE BULLFIGHTERS are paying
their respects to the president of the bullring as Wigram and Pleas resume
their argument. Wigram brandishes a copy of the day's *ABC* with Curro
adorning the cover and holds it with his arm extended, as if it were
some holy artifact. "What he gave us is a glimpse of what he used to
be," Wigram says. "That's what all the excitement was about, you see.
Because there never was anyone else quite like him."

"I think you used exactly the right word," says Pleas. "A glimpse."

Some years ago there was a corrida held at the Houston Astrodome.
The crowd there understood nothing about bullfighting, and after a
deserving pass someone with a working knowledge of it would push a
button and a mighty "Olé!" would appear in lights on the scoreboard
to cue the cheers. This story is well known among foreign aficionados,
and Wigram invokes it now. "Curro happens to have that button for
Madrid and Sevilla," Wigram says. "Those Olés we heard yesterday
were unlike any others we've heard all feria."

Pleas is hardly convinced. In fact, in the past two weeks I have yet
to see anyone in this group convince anyone else of anything. They'll
argue at the slightest provocation, about the fastest route from here to
there or the quality of a certain white wine. I marvel at what opposites
these two men are. The aristocratic Wigram, done up in tweed, quotes

Oscar Wilde and Andalusian poets to underscore his points, while Pleas, the North Carolinian with a beer paunch and wearing a Members Only windbreaker with epaulets, holds his own with good ol' boy logic that sounds like it came from a Jerry Jeff Walker song. If not for toreo I can't imagine what they would ever have to talk about.

The novillada in front of us begins, temporarily ending the discussion. Julio Aparicio is the second novillero on the cartel, and once he establishes a rhythm with his animal he is superb. The toreo is standard and elegant and he uses his feet correctly, crossing over to make the bull go around the body. He works the *derechazo,* changes hands to a *natural,* then sends the bull away with a chest pass, the music playing. The three of us, sitting in a row, agree on something: it is fine work.

Aparicio's kill is marvelous and he knows instantly he has triumphed. He raises his arms in what seems like honest exultation, not a pose. Even though we know all about his father's machinations, it is difficult not to embrace Julito as a bullfighter. For certain he has won the Maestranza crowd. There is strong petition for an ear, and it is obvious he is going to get one, but the *presidente* waits until the last moment to award it so there isn't time for the masses to petition for another.

Sometimes it's tempting to see bullfighting and bullfighters in moral terms. Ever since I saw this novillada on the cartel some months ago, I've been thinking of it as a struggle between good and evil, Martín representing sincerity and innocence and Aparicio the forces of depravity and destruction, a subscriber to a code of taurine behavior that, if wide-spread, eventually would bring down the spectacle. (The third novillero, José Luis Peralta, is mediocre and largely ignored except by Wigram, who is trying to discern his exact relationship to a *rejoneador,* a bullfighter on horseback, who has the same last name. At one point he appears to be sketching the Peralta family tree on the back of his program.) Perhaps some of us secretly hoped to see Aparicio flounder here in the big plaza and his reputation prove fraudulent. Now, after a single faena, there are people in the row behind me invoking him as a challenger to Espartaco.

Pepe Luis Martín places his own banderillas and dedicates his animal to the crowd. His faena is jittery and I am unnerved; he hardly seems like the bullfighter I've heard so much about. It isn't the bull, which is easily workable. Martín is just somehow off today. After some syncopated passes and an utter lack of *temple,* Martin pinches his first *estocada* and does the same with his second, then goes in directly over the horns with his third.

At the crucial moment, just as Martín is landing his sword thrust, the bull lifts its head and spears him in the thigh. Martín falls to the sand and then staggers to his feet, dragging himself toward the barrera and away from the bull with a sickening limp as the capes flash around him. This is happening across the ring from where we are sitting, but even from here the wound appears grave. There are few worse places a bullfighter can be gored than the thigh—the chest is one, and that's about it. Within seconds his banderilleros have lifted Martín and passed him over the barrera. He is rushed down the *callejón* and out the door to the infirmary.

As the senior novillero, Peralta will kill Martín's other bull. He would have disposed of this one, but it isn't necessary. The last sword thrust has stuck and the bull dies even as Martín is heading for the operating table, so the banderilleros take the vuelta in their torero's honor.

This is the first major goring of the feria, and, though still a novillero, he's the first significant bullfighter to be badly hurt this season. Martín was supposed to fight next month in Ronda with Aparicio and Finito de Córdoba, a well-advertised novillada that had already sold out. Now he won't.

After a major goring it is common for the other toreros to work the remaining bulls with dispatch, then depart as quickly as possible. However, Aparicio doesn't appear to be affected by Martín's accident. He starts his second bull with a wonderful series with the cape, full of *revoleras,* and gets terrific applause. And his second faena is even better than his first one, slow and dignified toreo with no wasted effort. With these small novillos, at least, he is the real thing. His work has distracted the crowd from the vivid goring it has just witnessed—an admirable feat. But he botches his kill, hitting bone twice, and then can't get the bull to stand still for another try. He finally kills off the mark, a foot or so low.

Despite the poor *estocada* Aparicio should earn an ear. The faena and capework deserved one, but more to the point, a majority of the plaza is clearly petitioning for it. But the *presidente* refuses to comply, although it's not his place to deny it. Aparicio waits as the bull is dragged off, but nothing happens. So he takes a slow vuelta to the accompaniment of a tumult of cheers, and then, with the noise even louder now, he continues around the bullring again for another lap.

In a different situation the reaction here would be outrage—some teenage novillero showing up the president of the bullring. But because nearly everybody in the plaza thought the ear was deserved, and because they've already fallen in love with this bullfighter and the things he can do with the cape and the cloth, the second vuelta serves only to focus the outrage on the president. Aparicio is no ordinary novillero, of course; his father has instilled that in him from the beginning.

■■■

The afternoon corrida features the Sevilla debut of El Soro, the most shameless of the current *tremendistas*. Everyone is curious to see if he tries the vulgar stuff here or plays it relatively straight and tries to win over the crowd on its own terms. Soro has been waiting eight years to fight in La Maestranza and he said in a newspaper interview earlier this week that triumphing here would mean much more to him than going out the Puerta Grande in Madrid. It's an easy thing for him to say right now, as he isn't scheduled to fight at San Ysidro this year and has done nothing at Las Ventas since debuting there just months after taking his alternativa in 1982, but *tremendista* had best be of the highest order to have a chance at an ear in Sevilla.

Pleas Campbell is the only person I know who admires the work of El Soro. The worst news we have all heard in some time is that Soro's brother, who is called Soro II and fights in the same style but with even less ability, is preparing to take the alternativa. Joselito was going to give it to him last month but a fortuitous rainstorm canceled the corrida and now he has to wait. If anything El Soro or his brother does in the bullring bears any relation to classic toreo, it is a happy accident.

El Soro does own a place in taurine history. When Paquirri was fatally gored at Pozoblanco in 1984, Soro was the third matador on the cartel. He was alternating with Paquirri and José Cubero, El Yiyo, who was also fatally gored the following year. It is bullfighting legend that when a bull fatally wounds a matador, whoever ends up killing that bull will also die in a plaza. It happened with Ignacio Sánchez Mejías, who finished fighting the bull that ended Joselito's life and was himself killed when he attempted a comeback years later, and then it happened with Yiyo, who was killed in 1985, almost a year to the day after he stepped in to dispose of Paquirri's bull.

Who killed the bull that killed Yiyo? Yiyo did. He had already landed the *estocada* and had turned to acknowledge the cheering of the crowd when the fallen bull, in its death throes, rose on wobbling legs, lurched forward for one final charge and stabbed Yiyo in the back. The matador never saw it coming.

Yiyo was the last full matador to be killed in the Spanish bullring, about three-and-a-half years ago, and the way Soro fights it sometimes seems he's bidding to be the next. He greets his first bull on his knees at the end of the toril, waving the cape over his head. This is called the *faro de rodillas,* the kneeling lighthouse, and it is the very maneuver that landed Pepe Luis Vargas in the hospital here last year. Two days after that goring, Espartaco tried a *faro de rodillas* as homage to Vargas and the bull sliced him in the side of the head. "It's the only time in history a bull almost cut its own ear," said Joe Distler—a terrific line, but the *faro de rodillas,* however absurd it looks, is not a laughing matter. It is the most dangerous way I know to begin fighting a bull.

The bull comes out of the toril with some speed and El Soro twirls his cape over his head. The bull charges directly for him and we all stop breathing for a moment but when it approaches it springs for the cape and actually leaps over the kneeling matador, something I have never seen. There is an audible gasp from the crowd but El Soro has quickly scrambled to his feet and is making a dizzying series of passes of all sorts, seemingly inventing them as he goes along. The bull is never more than a few feet away from him and he seems in constant danger of a goring. Soro winds the cape over his head, flings it to the sand, and has the bull bucking and hopping and at one point nearly standing on its hind legs to reach the cape. It is all happening at the mouth of the toril, for the bull hasn't yet advanced any farther into the ring. The crowd is awestruck by this display, its aversion to this sort of bullfighting momentarily forgotten, and the Olés are coming one after another. Soro's miracle passes are happening so quickly that one Olé is hardly finished before the next begins. I haven't decided if this is valid bullfighting, but it is certainly dangerous and exciting. Finally Soro throws his arms in the air and grins and gets a standing ovation, twenty seconds into his first bull in the Maestranza.

Those twenty seconds are the highlight of the day. Soro's first faena is odd and not nearly as exciting as that first series with the cape. He insists on flinging the muleta about with his wrists, which simply isn't an aesthetic movement, and many of his passes are jarring. But he knows what he's doing, at least, and after a bloody kill he gets fine applause.

His second faena is more adorned, full of useless spins and twirls, and less interesting.

The Portuguese matador Victor Mendes places his own sticks and as usual he places them well, but sharing the spotlight with Soro's pyrotechnics seems to bother him. He seems continually frustrated in his zeal to turn ordinary bulls into memorable toreo. Mendes is a marvelously intelligent man, a student of law who speaks five languages and a student of toreo too, but his work with the muleta never quite fulfills the expectation created by his artistry with the banderillos. I have been warned against getting too attached to him. Michael Bottino said it happens to everyone as soon as they learn about his background, for who can resist the idea of a bullfighting lawyer? Everyone can, it turns out, once they start to see him regularly with the muleta. "Don't try to be a Mendes fan," Bottino said. "He'll break your heart." I am beginning to see what he means.

■■■

The last Sunday of the feria is the last day for many of the *extranjeros,* who see the corrida and the lights extinguished out at the fairgrounds across the river and the fireworks, and then head to the airport in the morning. It's also the traditional setting for the Miura corrida, which places Spain's most famous and honored bulls in its most famous and honored bullring.

It is difficult to explain what makes the Miuras so different from every other breed of bull. It all goes back to science, basic genetics. When a *ganadería* has been around as long as a hundred years, the bulls it breeds, generation after generation, develop specific characteristics. It happens with people after a certain number of generations and you can see how it would happen even more conclusively with animals bred in a controlled environment.

Seeing Miura bulls for the first time you are reminded of the old bullfight films from the turn of the century. The animals looked different then, with tight, barrel-shaped bodies and big, wide horns, and that is what these bulls look like, only in living color. They are not as compact as the rest of today's bulls but long and muscular. Miuras look wilder and more dangerous—and they are. They also are smarter than other bulls and if you let one in on the big secret, that the cape and muleta mean nothing and that the matador is the real enemy, they will not ignore that or forget it. You cannot afford to make a single mistake with a Miura because it will capitalize on it. If you get sloppy with the muleta and lose control of the faena, the bull will refuse to continue the fight—if you are lucky. If you are unlucky, it will kill you.

That intelligence sets the Miuras apart. Tricks that work with other breeds simply won't work with them. And this is the watered-down breed. Hemingway gives them special mention in *Death in the Afternoon*, which was published in 1932, but bemoans the loss of the purer breed from a decade or two before that. Surely today's Miuras cannot compare with the massive bulls Frascuelo and Lagartijo fought, bulls with "ferocious and prescient intelligence which made them the curse of all bullfighters," as Hemingway described them. If they were like that now, it is safe to say that nobody would fight them.

Hardly anyone does, anyway. Very few bullfighters in recent years have triumphed with the Miuras. Rafael Ortega did, and Limeño, and John Fulton on that Christmas Day corrida, and Ruiz Miguel. Espartaco once fought six Miuras in an afternoon and didn't cut a single ear. Most matadors don't even try. There is just too much risk involved, both physical and professional. This year three of the regulars have been contracted: Ruiz Miguel, Manili and Tomás Campuzano. Since Ruiz Miguel is retiring, this will likely be his last appearance in the Maestranza unless he is booked for one of the September corridas, so there is even more interest than usual. It's a nice touch that this well-respected matador would end his Maestranza career by fighting the bulls that made him famous.

The afternoon's weather has fulfilled the promise of the morning—not always the case in Sevilla in the spring. It's hot at my seat in the sun, and a marvelous air of expectation fills the plaza. There is probably nobody in attendance who doesn't know that several true *figuras* have been killed by Miuras over the years, El Espartero and Manolete and others. There are very few foreigners in evidence, for tickets to the Miura corrida are the most difficult to get each season, and since most foreigners don't know the difference they'll usually choose to pay a scalper less money for some other corrida.

Last year, the 1988 season, was an especially good one for fighting Miuras. In a memorable corrida here, both Manili and Espartaco cut ears off a Miura, and then in Madrid during San Ysidro, in the faena Fusco swears is the best he has ever seen, Manili cut two ears. Victor

Mendes and Manili and Tomás Campuzano later all had three-ear after-noons with the Miuras, and in substantial places. Mendes cut his in Nimes, Manili in Pamplona and Campuzano in Bilbao. So it can be done. But it usually isn't. It is very hard for a matador to look good with a Miura. Luis Miguel Domínguín once said that toreo is the art of making a bull go where it doesn't want to go, and as slowly as you can. It is more difficult to do that with a Miura, on a consistent basis, than with bulls from any other breeder.

■■■

Ruiz Miguel's first bull is large and ink-black, with wonderfully wide horns. He coaxes it into position for the pic with six *chicuelinas,* the difficult maneuver introduced into serious toreo by Manuel Jiménez, Chicuelo, in which the matador wraps himself in the cape as the bull charges past. (Chicuelo didn't actually invent the pass. A taurine co-median called Llapisera was using it in his Harlem Globetrotter-type act when Chicuelo saw it and brought it to the real corrida. When you see it done well, it is as close as bullfighting comes to ballet and there's nothing humorous about it.)

This bull takes two hard pics and then the picador allows it to get to the horse. The first banderillero misses the bull completely and the second tries to stick just a single shaft in the bull's hide and can't. They are blatantly terrified and don't want to be anywhere near this bull. It is long and sleek and fearsome to look at, the way the bulls of old used to be. In those days, nobody needed to use tricks or adornments. There was enough emotion generated by simply passing the gigantic bull with a small piece of red cloth. As a spectator you were scared to see it and relieved to see the bull killed.

Ruiz Miguel, in lilac and gold, dedicates the bull to someone in a dark suit in a *palco* seat. He then brings it all the way across the ring, from sun to shade. He works a series from the right side and the bull reveals a tendency to chop its horns in that direction. He devotes another series to experimenting with the bull and by the time he is ready to assert his domination the bull is not to be dominated. This, too, is a Miura characteristic: if the torero doesn't take control swiftly, he loses the opportunity to do so. These bulls learn. "This one speaks Latin," Leonardo whispers. After the second series the bull starts to hesitate before charging and before long Ruiz Miguel has lost control. He changes swords and then it takes some time for him to get the bull in position for a kill. It is wise to him and incorrigible. He misses his first four *estocadas* without even releasing the sword, and he may be working on an *aviso* if he doesn't hurry. On the fifth try he kills in a good spot with a *media estocada*. Farewell performance or not, the crowd reacts with silence.

Manili's toreo is always full of bravura and he likes bulls as big as possible. His first is 529 kilos, brown and black, with plenty of muscle and horns set apart. The picador entices it to charge from a long way off but pics badly, giving it a glancing blow. On its second charge the bull is allowed to get under the horse. Tomás Campuzano takes a *quite* and has problems, too. The first banderillero misses with both sticks. The next banderillero runs past without even trying, circles back to try again, and then pushes one in as he scoots past. This is the tone of the corrida—extreme wariness. Nobody wants to jeopardize a year's earnings by getting foolhardy with a Miura. The bull steals a cape and bucks its way across the ring. The banderilleros are trying to place one more pair, but the president has seen enough and the trumpet sounds for the next *tercio*. That is as ignominious as banderilla placing can get.

The bull has returned to the Puerta del Principe, under the president's box, so Manili sets up there. But the bull doesn't stay there. Two passes later, it's all the way over in front of me, digging in. It has found a *querencia* and Manili has to coax it out. He works the bull into the middle but tries to *cargar la suerte* and bring it around his body, and he loses it out the front door. They're making a tour of the ring now, pass by pass. They return to the sun over on the far side. It is like a couple waltzing all the way around the dance floor.

Manili finally gets the bull in the center for what amounts to his first series, but even that is fractured. Each pass is a challenge and he can't get any kind of rhythm going. Soon he changes swords and kills nicely, having accomplished little earlier. Tomás Campuzano, the younger of the two Campuzano brothers from Écija, near Sevilla, does a little better. His capework earns him Olés and he gets the music going during his faena. And then he can't get the bull to charge and the bull starts cutting in on him, ominously. It soon becomes obvious that he's lost his faena, and the bull has another victory on points. His kill is *bajonazo*.

Ruiz Miguel's last bull is ornery and weak-kneed, and nothing can be done with it. Again he gets silence from the crowd, not even an acknowledgment for all the fine work he has done here over the years. The fifth bull hurts its foot and has to be replaced, and the substitute, from the Santamaría López *ganadería,* is a coward. It paws the ground and refuses to charge, and Manili finally has to do away with it. We have now seen seventy-seven bulls here this season, not counting novillos, and only eight ears awarded: four to Espartaco, two to Robles and one each to Parada and Manili.

Campuzano has the last chance to show us something. His banderillero, Luis Mariscal, places the first artful pair of sticks we've seen all day, but on his second try he lingers over the horns and is gored. He is knocked to the ground, and this creates chaos in the ring. The bull is distracted, everyone who has a cape is running around flapping at it, and Mariscal tries to struggle to his feet but can't. It is horrible to see. Finally Mariscal drags himself to the barrera and is lifted over and carried out.

Campuzano dedicates his faena to the crowd and takes the muleta with added fortitude. He is going to fight the bull for his fallen peon and succeed with it. You can see it in his demeanor, the way he walks, and when he comes over to my side I can see it in his eyes. This is the attitude you have to have with a Miura. The music starts after the first series because it is evident that he is going to do well. The second series earns him four Olés, and at the end of the third series he guides the bull all the way around his body, switches hands and sends it out to strong applause.

Later, the bull stops in mid-charge. Campuzano keeps his body still and forces the bull through by shaking the muleta, then commands it back the other way. Then the bull stands inert and cocks its head so that it is looking behind Campuzano's back. Campuzano moves the muleta from the front of his body to behind and then pivots, passes the bull backhand, stills it with a *remate* and struts off to an ovation.

Campuzano is one of the very few matadors who carries the heavy killing sword with him at all times so he doesn't have to interrupt his rhythm by changing. He's big and strong enough to do this. The vast majority carry a false aluminum sword, used for show and to extend the muleta when held in the right hand, and then they change for the *estocada.* Sometimes it's enjoyable to see the matador add to the drama by changing swords, but Campuzano is to be commended for doing it this way, the old-fashioned way. In bullfighting, and in Spain in general, anything done the traditional way is usually commended.

He lands his *estocada* in a good spot and seems to have won a trophy. But the bull doesn't die, and he botches the first two *descabellos,* killing with his third. The emotion dissipated, there is some petition for an ear but not enough, so he takes a vuelta and manages to look both arrogant and relieved. After that he leaves the sand for the infirmary to check on the condition of his banderillero.

11

THE MORNING AFTER

ONLY in Sevilla could a day have a name like this—*la resaca,* the hangover. And only in Sevilla would a day like this be a holiday.

The feria has officially ended, but Monday is nevertheless another day off from work for Sevillanos, who don't seem to have worked much since I arrived here in January. The official reason for this one is to recover from the revelry. There is a bullfight scheduled for the afternoon, one more, and traditionally it is for the locals. The tourists have gone home, and many of the foreign aficionados have left, too.

It is a beautifully clear, hot morning with no wind. Fusco and I walk to the Macarena district up near the cemetery, a distance of several miles, for lunch at the bar Río de la Plata and to see the insignias of defunct *ganaderías* hand-painted on the wall tile. We make predictions about the awards of the feria. Espartaco will again be the *gran triunfador,* that is agreed. Fusco insists the best faena will be Parada's, but I think it has to be Espartaco's. You don't cut two ears without winning best faena. The best *quite peligro,* taking someone out of danger with your cape, will be Manili's for saving El Ecijano. (Last year that prize was awarded to a spectator who flung her purse from the barrera to distract a bull that was on its way to goring a banderillero—the only evidence I have found that the bullfight politicians of Sevilla are not wholly without humor.)

The prize for best overall capework may well go to Curro, and the best *estocada* to Espartaco. We disagree on the best banderillero. I say it will be Mendes and Fusco says Montoliú, as a symbolic reward for Litri's entire cuadrilla.

After lunch we walk until we hit the river—and La Cartuja, the site of the 1992 Expo. There is a bridge there that is being built slowly and another one farther down for pedestrians that seems almost completed. Otherwise there is little evidence that any work has been done. Sevilla also hosted the Ibero-American Exposition of 1929, and for that the construction was started ten years ahead of time. But nobody here seems to be concerned that the opening is less than three years away. "My only worry about the Expo," my friend at the newspaper kiosk told me, "is this: Will Curro still be around to participate in the bullfighting exhibition they're going to have? If not, how will the rest of the world learn about real toreo?"

■■■

The María Luisa Domínguez bulls are some of the best in Spain, and two of today's matadors, Jose Antonio Campuzano and Emilio Oliva, have triumphed with them before. The third is El Soro. Fusco, a confirmed Soro hater, is sitting above me in a *grada* seat. He calls from there, and I see he is wedged in beside an entire Soro peña and a banner unfurled in the matador's honor. A photo of the moment would symbolize the entire feria for him.

Jose Antonio Campuzano, the older brother of Tomás, was on the verge of retirement in 1982 when he cut three ears off Domínguez bulls and was carried out the Puerta del Principe here, his career revived. His first bull today charges well and attacks the picador eagerly. Fusco has hopped the metal fence that separates the *gradas* from the *tendidos* and moved down beside me, for today's corrida is not nearly sold out. "Espartaco would be dancing the waltz with this bull," he says, when Campuzano falters during the faena.

El Soro gets the second bull and opens with traditional capework. He places his own banderillas and the music starts. He goes into a little dance, stops, places the first pair cleanly and then is chased by the bull all the way to the barrera. There is nobody in the ring to make a *quite* and Soro hops up on the *estribo* and vaults over the wall headfirst. He does not reappear. In a moment we see him hoisted up and hustled off to the infirmary, something evidently broken. All of a sudden this has become a *mano a mano* between José Antonio Campuzano and Emilio Oliva, which is not the most enticing prospect in the world. Not after thirteen days of bullfights.

In a way, I'm glad the daily corridas are ending. It has become a grind, the two hours a day here and the lengthy discussions at the Bodegón, and I look forward to doing something else with my afternoons. I know I'll be back here to see Julio Aparicio in a novillada next Sunday and there will be a full corrida here at the end of May, Corpus Christi. The word is that Pepe Luis Vázquez will be fighting, which interests me. Even if his career has stagnated, he's still the son of his famous father.

So Fusco and I loll in the sun and pay only slight attention. Campuzano gets applause and then Oliva's first bull is a noble one and charges the picador from a long way off, practically the center of the ring. Oliva gets music and Olés early but loses his bull. At the end only a handful of people are clapping—probably his relations.

In a fit of generosity, Fusco buys beer for just about everyone in our row—with what money, I don't know—and we turn our attention back to the ring just in time to see Campuzano land a nice *estocada*. Oliva works the fifth bull well, the bull that should have belonged to El Soro, and he actually has a chance at an ear, but he has trouble with the kill and takes so long profiling that an *aviso* sounds. In the end he needs seven *descabellos*.

The last bull of the feria is also Oliva's and it is another good one, but Oliva seems to have become aware that nobody is paying attention. As he plays out his faena I suggest an all-boring cartel to Fusco: Manolo Cortés, Franco Cadena and Oliva. He counters with José Luis Galloso, Álvaro Amores and Rafi Camino. It would be a close call.

Oliva stabs the bull and I say my goodbyes to Enrique, Rafael, Leonardo and the others around me, although we'll all be back next weekend. After handshakes all around I turn back toward the sand and am stunned to see that the bull is still alive, wandering around with the sword in its back. An *aviso* sounds, making Oliva one of the few matadors in history to hear *avisos* on successive bulls in the same corrida. You don't usually fight consecutive bulls unless there has been a goring or you have been contracted to kill all six of them, and you won't often be contracted to kill six bulls yourself unless you habitually manage to dispose of them in the allotted time. And that, it occurs to me, would be the retort to Fusco's all-boring cartel: six bulls for Emilio Oliva, *como única espada*.

■■■

Even though Distler and Charles Patrick and some of the others have gone, there are still plenty of people left at the Bodegón. I find myself getting emotional about the end of the feria, until I'm reminded of something Michael Wigram's driver once said. Watching a reunion of some of the aficionados outside a hotel somewhere, he shook his head. "These people travel together from one feria to the next," he said, "and when they meet in some hotel lobby or outside a bullring they hug and yell, just as if they hadn't actually seen each other that morning someplace else."

It is not until nearly noon the following day, after I have been awake several hours, that I realize there will not be a bullfight in the afternoon. There is mail for the first time in a week, because Sevilla's mailmen stop delivery during the feria even though they are federal, not local, employees. They simply refuse to work and nobody notices to complain. Today I have plenty of mail and the time to sit on my terrace in the sun and read it, and my afternoon free for a nap or for exercise—but it is not enough.

After two weeks of corridas every day I have a bullfight hangover, my own personal taurine *resaca*. There is a bad taste in my mouth from Oliva and Campuzano and some of the others, and yet just like with the cognac or the Cruzcampo beer, I long for a hair of the dog that bit me. All I want is one more faena in the Maestranza, the music going and the sun beating down, and somebody working some good passes as the excitement builds. Then I'll feel better.

PART · THREE

THIS

DANGEROUS

SUMMER

1

OF ART AND LIFE

USING logic that defied explanation, the directors of the Real Maestranza decreed that their inaugural exhibition of bullfight art would be open to the public at a local gallery only from six to nine in the evening each day of the feria. This was precisely when many of the potential viewers were busy attending bullfights—and at the Maestranza bullring, which is run by the same people! I was enraged by this incongruity, then amused. I resigned myself to missing the exhibition. But several days before the end of the feria the Maestranza abruptly announced a one-week extension for the show, because almost nobody had seen it. With the city having again settled into the languid rhythms of Andalusian commerce, I can now choose to visit any day I like.

This is the competition John Fulton entered in February with his painting of the Gypsy girl. Several weeks ago we learned that he didn't win the grand prize; in fact, he wasn't even named as one of the three finalists. At the time I credited the snub to Maestranza politics, the same politics that have kept John out a suit of lights in this city for twenty-one years. When I finally see the paintings I'm forced to admit that the verdict was justified: there are perhaps half a dozen others I'd rather hang in my house.

The exhibition is hidden deep in the labyrinth of narrow streets that fills the Barrio de Santa Cruz, in a crumbling three-story stone building of substantial bulk and presence which is difficult to find, hundreds of years old, in disrepair and yet not without a certain stateliness: a Romanesque ruin in formal dress. Inside is a courtyard and a typically Andalusian patio. Up a set of steps you emerge, overlooking orange trees. The building is set in the middle of the busiest quarter of all Andalusia but the ambience once you are inside is almost rural, which is the way the best Spanish buildings are. From the outside, fronting a busy street, they may look common and uncomfortable, but sitting on a balcony above a verdant courtyard, magically insulated from the city's hum, you have the impression you are in the country, with acres of pastureland beyond the front door.

The exhibition is situated in two rooms to the right of the staircase. Some of the paintings are simple, portraits or action scenes, in the tradition of Spanish art, Velázquez and Zurbarán and Murillo and Goya. One I stare at against my will is a vision of a devilish-looking Rafael de Paula. Others show various views of La Maestranza, with the blue sky above it and the water beyond. Some of the more representational use a glimpse of the Maestranza together with images of bullfighters or bullfight paraphernalia, as John's does.

His painting hangs to nice effect along a side wall, and the Gypsy girl wrapped in the colorful matador's cloak is a unique image. A painting nearby shows a ghostly revolera performed over the entrance to the Maestranza's *tendido* 12, including the two wooden doors with the iron lamp above them. And there is another unusual work, called "La Última Tarde," which shows the cutting of a bullfighter's *coleta,* the symbolic end of his career. In the background, dozens of bulls of various types and colors, presumably victims of that matador's toreo, look on from a vale of mist that can only be the afterworld.

To my eye the best of these are the most abstract. My favorite is a work by Rafael Villanueva Casales called *"Para un Viejo Esquema de la Fiesta;"* or, "For an Old Sketch of the Fiesta." Villanueva has created a montage from some of the better-known works of Spanish art, altering them as he goes. It is a cut-and-paste masterpiece. The face of Don Juan of Austria, as painted by Velázquez, is visible in one corner, and Goya's Queen María Luisa on horseback fills the right half of the canvas— except this María Luisa is not merely on horseback, she's a picador carrying a lance. Behind her is an open window, the shutters flung back

Sevilla-style, and far below the bullring and the neighborhood behind it, as if the vista was seen from the tower of the Giralda.

This is the first year of the Maestranza's competition, but taurine art dates back tens of centuries. Bulls can be traced through most of history's known aesthetic movements, and several thousand years after the first known taurine representations, bullfighters begin to appear. Probably the best-known bullfight work, both because of its graphic content and its prominent display in the Prado in Madrid, is Goya's "The Picador." Goya is believed to have traveled with a bullfight cuadrilla during his youth and toreo is a recurring subject in his work. His paintings and prints include portraits of Pedro Romero and José Romero of the Ronda dynasty, and of Costillares, who was from Sevilla; and a *tauromaquia* series that includes the goring and death of another Sevillano, the legendary Pepe-Hillo, in 1801. His art provides such a precisely detailed depiction of the bullfighting of the era that today corridas are occasionally held using only the costumes and techniques evident in those works. Such corridas, popular in Ronda and elsewhere, are called *goyescas*. Goya's use of the bullfight as a study in physicality and motion can be compared to the way Degas used ballet, and for Goya the fascination endured until the end of his life; his last series of four lithographic bullfighting prints were made at the age of seventy-nine.

In the twentieth century the most famous bullfight art has been done by Picasso, who attended corridas as a youth in Málaga. Sketches of his drawn at age nine survive depicting bulls tossing matadors; and as his career advanced he utilized the bullfight in his works, both with verisimilitude and as a thematic prop. (In one painting, Christ is shown sweeping a loincloth in front of a bull as if it were a cape.) In the 1950s Picasso returned to the subject with ink drawings, lithographs and pottery, and he even designed several *trajes de luz* for Luis Miguel Dominguín.

After an hour at the exhibition I take a walk around the balcony overlooking the patio. There are busts and paintings scattered throughout, vases and other sculptures and small wooden benches. A man in a side office is typing on a manual typewriter and the sound of striking keys echoes off the marble. There is sunlight slanting through the open roof—another perfect spring afternoon. I sit on one of the benches, surrounded by the art, and leaf through the catalogue until the sun goes down.

■■■

The Maestranza would do well to keep the exhibition open even longer, through the summer if possible, because there won't be much else for the bullfight-obsessed to do here other than argue and reminisce. The 1989 *temporada* has just begun in Spain, with the major ferias in Madrid, Pamplona and Bilbao to come, as they do every year, in the late spring and summer. Yet in Sevilla, the city of the bull, the season is all but over. From now through the autumn there will be occasional Sunday novilladas, the first one this weekend, and a corrida on Corpus Cristi in late May, and another in August, two more in September and two in October, but the important ones have gone. Despite the passionate interest in bullfighting here, the discussion and debate all twelve months of the year, there is hardly ever any significant activity in the Maestranza after the two frenetic weeks of corridas at the start of each season.

The 1989 season will eventually consist of nineteen full corridas at La Maestranza and an additional fourteen novilladas, with all but six of the former having taken place by mid-April. The distraction of a bullfight exhibition during the hot weeks of summer would be welcome.

Many of the foreign aficionados have already moved on to Madrid, where San Ysidro begins soon, and they probably won't have occasion to return here until next April. There are locals I know here with easy transportation, John Fulton and Navarrito and others, and they'll be traveling to El Puerto de Santa María and Jérez and elsewhere in the coming weeks, nearby towns with bullrings that are charming enough, if not as stately or as storied as the Maestranza. These small cities stage a limited number of corridas each year, and they'll usually schedule Espartaco or Litri or another of the more popular bullfighters to alternate with some second-echelon matador they can get cheaply, and a local product, fighting bulls of marginal quality. It's a formula that all but guarantees a good crowd and a profit.

I'll be attending some of those, but the average Sevillano won't. For Enrique, Antonio and Leonardo, my Maestranza neighbors, bullfighting means bullfighting in Sevilla. Perhaps they'll watch the televised corridas and they doubtless will read the chronicles in the papers, but it would never occur to them to leave the city to see a corrida. If something important is happening in the fiesta, some taurine breakthrough or the emergence of a new *figura,* the feeling is that it will arrive in Sevilla eventually and prove its worth. If it doesn't, they haven't missed anything.

As always the bullfight talk continues in the bars and the cafés of Sevilla, and at the newspaper kiosk and at Fulton's gallery, but with the feria completed there is time for other interests now. A Yugoslav dance troupe performed yesterday and a new burlesque show is opening at the theater on Calle Sierpes. McCoy Tyner and Al Stewart are booked at a local amphitheater in the coming weeks, and the movie *Tequila Sunrise* has arrived in its dubbed Spanish version as *Conexión Tequila.* The center page of the Andalusian edition of *ABC,* which gave us a double-truck dose of Vicente Zabala on the toros every day for the past two weeks, was filled today with a feature on the hundredth anniversary of the birth of Charlie Chaplin. The mascot of Sevilla's Expo '92, aptly named Curro, was unveiled in Madrid. And everyone is talking about going to the beach.

■■■

Bullfighting continues to appear prominently in the local paper, *El Correo,* although nothing like the way it dominated that publication during the feria. One day they print an absurd paean to La Maestranza on the editorial page. A few days later a twenty-nine-year-old man announces that he is Curro Romero's illegitimate son. And on the following Wednesday, the feria awards are announced.

As expected, Espartaco is named the *gran triunfador* for the fifth consecutive year, and he also receives the awards for the best faena and the best kill. This, everyone is quick to point out, is only the second time that a single matador has won the three major prizes in the same year since they started awarding them in 1965. Only Paquirri had accomplished this previously, in 1981, but I have a feeling he was up against better bullfighting than what we saw from Espartaco's rivals this year.

Espartaco's athletic peon, El Ecijano, is given the prize for best banderillero, eclipsing Montoliú of Litri's cuadrilla. Francisco Martín Sanz is named the best picador. Curro Romero and Jose Luis Parada share the prize for capework, El Mangui is the best peon on foot, and the best animal of the feria is Varino, the Palha bull that was worked in disappointing fashion by Ruiz Migual. The prize for best *ganadería* is left vacant. Two special prizes are also awarded: to Ruiz Miguel, because he is retiring this year, and to Julito Aparicio, for his promise of future contributions to the art of toreo. I can imagine how Michael Wigram will react upon hearing that news, for if anything is guaranteed to offend him it is an award given in advance of taurine accomplishment. *Future contributions?* he'd say. *I would imagine we'll have to wait and see, won't we?*

But the pro-Aparicio sentiment seems almost unanimous, as starved for a new hero as Sevilla's aficionados are. Julito will be fighting in the novillada this Sunday, which is reason enough to make me postpone an out-of-town trip, and the buildup for the event has started by midweek. By the time the weekend comes there will have been a full-page interview in *ABC* and a large picture in the front, a three-quarter-page story in *Diario 16*, and another substantial one in *El Correo*. More than that, the Maestranza seems to have already contracted the boy to fight again on Corpus Cristi, in a mixed corrida with Parada and Pepe Luis Vázquez. It isn't yet official, but that's the rumor.

One night I call Fusco in Madrid because I know he has seen Aparicio in Aranjuez with difficult novillos, and I hear what I was expecting: that the revelation of the season was distinctly ordinary there.

■ ■ ■

Aside from the prizes, I have been following the other tangible results of this year's feria. Three injured bullfighters—a matador, a novillero and a banderillo—are currently recuperating in hospital beds, their ferias having ended not in triumph but in blood.

Three is about an average take for two weeks of bulls, six of them every day fighting for their lives against top-quality bullfighters. Contrary to what those ignorant of the corrida might think, no aficionado goes to a bullfight to see such tragedy, but gorings are an unavoidable side effect. Every bullfighter gets caught occasionally, to more or less serious degree. It is uncommon for a matador to fight an entire season without suffering at least a small *cornada,* and every two or three years it is almost guaranteed that each matador, no matter how skilled, will be hurt seriously.

The idea of returning after a serious goring is largely a phenomenon of the second half of this century, for prior to that a major wound was liable to be fatal. But medicine has advanced to such a degree that now it is rare that a matador is killed because of wounds incurred in the ring. Toward that end, there is a statue of a man wearing a long coat incongruously placed outside the Las Ventas bullring in Madrid. It is of Sir Alexander Fleming, the inventor of penicillin, and the statue is as big as any honoring bullfighters, for Fleming is something of a lay deity of the fiesta. There are few toreros of today who have fought for any substantial length of time who don't owe their lives to Fleming. It is safe to say the rest of them will, eventually.

None of the bullfighters hurt during the feria was hurt badly. Pepe Luis Martín, gored during his *estocada,* is quoted in the newspaper saying that the mental hurts are greater than the physical. More than anything, he's disappointed he wasn't able to triumph in Sevilla. El Soro, injured in almost comic fashion leaping over the barrera into the *callejón* while placing banderillas, is to be operated on in Madrid for a broken ankle and is expected to miss four months. Banderillero Luis Mariscal says "It was a miracle that what happened wasn't more serious," but he, too, is expected to return later this season.

Yet it is far too soon to tell what the eventual results of the *cornadas* will be. Each time a bullfighter is badly gored, his life threatened, the experience inevitably changes him and his art. This is especially true after the first time. He will emerge from the ordeal a harder person or a softer one; more determined to succeed or less so. He will almost never be as he was.

Julio Aparicio doesn't have much to prove in the Maestranza on Sunday. He already won the public during the feria, and now it will forgive him several worthless afternoons if it has to. The idea that Aparicio is the next Paula has taken hold, and if we are to accept that literally it may be some time before he is good again. Yet many of us who have *abonos* have returned after a week away, to see this bullfight, because the afternoon is bright and warm and we miss the ritual: drinks beforehand, buying the cushion, hunting down a program, making our way to the seat. Leonardo, Antonio and Enrique are already seated when I arrive and there are also some new faces. Doubtless some Sevillanos have headed to the sea for the weekend or to houses in the mountains, and their places are filled by friends. Wigram is not here, nor are Charles Patrick, Fusco, Pleas and the rest, and there is no meeting at the Bodegón beforehand nor *pringás* after. There is just a bullfight, six novillos from the Domecq ranch for Espartaco Chico, Aparicio and Martín Pareja Obregón.

Pareja Obregón is a twenty-two-year-old from Sevilla whose well-known family lives outside of town and has a reputation for lunacy. I have heard several stories about the Pareja Obregóns this week, one about a donkey placed atop the roof of a house for no reason other than experimentation, and another about Martín firing a rifle during an indoor dinner party as some sort of demonstration. Pareja Obregón has only recently decided to devote his energies to bullfighting full time, but because he is Sevilla-born and his family has connections he was able to get a fight in the Maestranza.

This kind of story lifts John Fulton and Navarrito to new levels of frustration, for Manolito has been trying for several years to get a fight here and the Maestranza people won't even look at him. But what do they expect? He's a Mexican import with no connections other than John, and even though he has lived here for several years nobody knows who he is. I have to admit I would rather be here watching Pareja Obregón than Manolito. If nothing else, I was able to learn the story of the donkey.

This afternoon is Pareja Obregón's debut with picadors, and his debut in Sevilla. He gets a good first bull, a bull that must have set Julio Aparicio *padre* to wondering how he could have better fixed the *sorteo*. Pareja Obregón capes the small animal well and works with his feet pressed tightly together. His bearing is stylized—he walks the way somebody might have told him matadors are supposed to walk—but there is something likable about him.

There is absolute silence for the start of his first faena, Sevilla again watching one of its own. When you trace the line of Sevillano matadors down through the years—Costillares and Pepe-Hillo and Espartero and Belmonte and Joselito, through Pepe Luis Vázquez *padre* and *hijo* and Emilio Muñoz—the debut of Pareja Obregón acquires some meaning. The odds are hugely against his ever becoming a bullfighter of note, as they are with any bullfighter, but at some point someone will emerge as the next great Sevillano. Maybe it will be him.

At twenty-two he is the oldest of the three novilleros fighting today but by far the least experienced, and the only one who didn't grow up with a matador for a father. His work with the muleta is clean and classical, and the bull is solid and dependable, and he gets Olés and a standing ovation and music. The Sevilla school of bullfighting traditionally depends on an extroverted grace, the matador performing a repertoire of passes with some kind of flourish. By contrast, the Ronda school is more austere and introverted, a man alone with his art, and the crowd looking on is almost incidental. Pareja Obregón is very much of the Sevilla school, a performer in the bullring.

Pareja Obregón kills his first bull with a low *media estocada* and gets an ear. His second bull he dedicates to Canorea, the Maestranza's impresario and the man who has given him this first opportunity. He then loses his animal into a *querencia* and can't get it out. The bull is not difficult but Pareja Obregón's inexperience makes it difficult and he finally lands an *estocada* just seconds short of an *aviso*.

Pareja Obregón gets good response for his work, leaving the plaza at the end of the day to a nice ovation, and Espartaco Chico gets silence after two *avisos*, but Aparicio is the one everyone has come to see. His first animal is 430 kilos, about average for the day and about 100 kilos smaller than a good-sized four-year-old. Its coat is a shiny black with a white-mottled underbelly and it comes out with enthusiasm and runs all over the ring. This is a difficult novillo that wants nothing more than to spend time in its *querencia*, not charging but moving from side to side, and Aparicio doesn't see difficult animals often. The faena is brief and insubstantial because the bull has become purely defensive, and when Aparicio tries to kill he pinches four times because it won't lower its head.

His second bull gives him material to work with. It's a 439-kilo animal named Egipcio with a nice swell of neck muscle and good tendencies, and the faena starts well, with Aparicio passing the bull low. The music begins and he shows an accomplished series against the barrera before coaxing the bull to the middle of the ring. There he pulls the bull around himself, *cargando la suerte,* and gets a standing ovation. "Look at his feet," says Enrique, and they are perfect, the back foot a step forward of the front foot to force the bull to alter its charge. The bull is ready to be killed but Aparicio is working it well and wants to continue. And there is great temptation to hope he does, even though the moment for the kill has arrived. This is the torero we have been promised, the work of a *figura*-in-waiting.

He ends his faena with a short series of three passes, the last one a *trincherazo,* a backhanded pass that is similar to flipping a door closed behind you without looking at it. He changes swords but is back to work again, four nice low passes. This gets us anxious. We don't want him to spoil what he has accomplished. Finally he cites to kill and, as we feared, it won't comply. But eventually he profiles and lands a beautiful *estocada,* finishes with a *descabello* and gets an ear. Circumnavigating the ring he does seem to resemble a young Paula, and as he passes I see a glint in his eye not unlike the mischievous look of Paula's in the painting in the exhibition.

That was bullfight art in still life, but this was bullfight art in actual life: a matador who can pull a bull around his body and kill the way bulls are supposed to be killed. Paintings can convey the ambience and the fervor of the bullring, but they can't convey this, and photographs and television can't convey it either, not really. To see what Aparicio did, or something similar, you have to be at a plaza, and then you need the luck to see a good bullfighter with a good bull on a good day. It is probably better for Sevilla that the art exhibit has ended today because having those paintings around would tantalize the aficionados here. They would only yearn for more of this, the real thing.

2

NEWS OF
A GORING

WORD has come from Mexico that Joselito was gored yesterday in Aguascalientes; he is seriously but not mortally wounded. That it happened in Mexico and not Spain is fate's humorless joke, because the famous nickname this talented matador has adopted carries far fewer morbid connotations there.

Upon hearing the name Joselito in whatever context, a Spaniard immediately conjures an image of the original: José Gómez Ortega. Anyone who has come to bullfighting in this century knows the name and in Spain he remains a part of the national consciousness. This is primarily because of his death, which was violent and unexpected—as much as any bullfighter's death can be unexpected. To think of Joselito El Gallo for even a fleeting moment is to be reminded of the May afternoon in Talavera de la Reina. It can happen with a mere glimpse of the name of that town on a roadmap.

Joselito symbolizes death in the bullring to many Spaniards, a death that even transcendent talent couldn't prevent. Entire books have been written about Joselito's death, with abundant chapters about the life of the bull, Bailaor, son of Canastillo and Bailaora. It is why so many Spanish aficionados, keenly attuned to the past as they are, have feared for the life of this boy, this Joselito, since he arrived five years ago. He who would choose that nickname puts himself at the mercy of its bloody legacy. Joselito himself understands the risks he takes. "I did not choose the nickname," he has said. "It chose me."

The bullrings of Mexico are haunted by different ghosts. There, if you talk of Joselito, it is assumed you are referring to the current one, José Arroyo. The story of the original Joselito is universally known in Mexico, but it doesn't weigh on bullfighting there. Like most historical tragedies, it is distant enough to be benign.

It's relatively unusual for a Spanish matador to be fighting in Mexico during the spring or summer. Once the season starts here Spanish bullfighters usually stay here. They are loath to miss potentially profitable dates while traveling, and any triumphs off the continent will be barely reported here and of little use when the time comes to negotiate contracts. It is during the winter hiatus that many of the better Spanish bullfighters work a shortened season in the New World and earn supplemental income.

So a bullfight in Mexico between March and September will nearly always feature Mexican or other Latin American matadors. But each year there are exceptions. This spring, Joselito—who was a huge success in Mexico in the off-season—returned for Aguascalientes, which is one of the better ferias there in the hot-weather months. He is a draw there, so perhaps he was paid extremely well.

Bullfighting is also different in Mexico. The most important reason is that the bulls are different. They tend to start slowly and get stronger as a faena progresses. They are stereotypically turgid but have plenty of stamina, and knowing precisely when to kill them is difficult for someone accustomed to bulls from Spanish *ganaderías*. Fighting Mexican bulls when you have been fighting Spanish bulls for many weeks is courting trouble if you plan to fight them well.

I heard the news about Joselito at the gallery. Federico had received it by phone from one of John's friends in Mexico. Today the newspapers have it. The details are sketchy, but he is said to be in serious condition in a hospital there. They do say that the goring came at the end of a triumphant faena.

The newspaper report says the horn wound almost tore Joselito in two from behind, but it appears as though he is no longer in mortal danger. The feeling is that if he was going to die it already would have happened. His worry is that he will not return in time for San Ysidro, a month away; to him, a Madrileño, it is the highlight of his season.

Coincidentally, his only previous goring of this gravity happened during San Ysidro—on May 15, 1987. He was extremely lucky then, too, and only missed two months. He now believes that accident may have been fortuitous because it forced him to cancel his first scheduled appearance in the fateful town of Talavera de la Reina, where he is convinced his life would be endangered. He has been signed to fight there once since then but missed that corrida, too, because of illness and now says he will not try again—and for good measure neither will he fight in Colmenar, where Yiyo died. "I'm not generally a superstitious person," he has said, "but I admit I'm handcuffed by some strange ideas."

When you hear about a serious goring, you take time out of your day to reflect on why matadors do what they do—and why we watch it. But the business of bullfighting continues. Every bullfighter is aware of the odds, but each reacts differently to that knowledge at different times in his life, which is why the trajectory of a career is so difficult to predict. And so we read that an entrepreneur has guaranteed Paco Ojeda nearly $3 million to fight twenty corridas and, yes, he is considering the offer. Palomo Linares, once described by *Toros '92* as the Ringo Starr of toreo, is making a comeback beginning in June. And Julito Aparicio, still pristine and all but immortal, is on the cover of that magazine this week.

■■■

Most of the prominent bullfight critics live in Madrid, because it is centrally located and close to most of the major ferias. Many of the rest live in Sevilla, because this is their taurine orientation. One of them is my acquaintance Borbujos, whom I see from time to time. He always nods hello, although I don't believe he remembers who I am. It hardly matters because we can't communicate. I have lived in Spain for months now and still can't understand his accent.

Toros '92 is based in Sevilla, in a crowded office in the Barrio de Santa Cruz. Soon after I arrived here I met José Antonio Del Moral, who is the most respected of their writers. He is balding, well-dressed, almost scholarly in his demeanor, in his late forties or early fifties, sober but not oppressively so. Talking with him you get the impression he could have written about anything, not just bullfighting, and it is true: he is well educated and studied architecture with the intention of making that his profession. He was raised in Madrid, where Antonio Ordóñez was a childhood friend, and his first published writings were letters to bullfight critics. They were so well composed and thoughtful that he was given a job and never returned to architecture. The corrida is his passion and this work, he says now, all he ever wanted to do.

I saw plenty of Del Moral during the feria. He was always rushing past in his immaculate suit talking to some bullfight dignitary. When it ended we made a plan to meet for lunch. It's his habit to take a walk in the early afternoon, so I arrive at his office at two o'clock on a warm Tuesday. We set out toward the Giralda and the plaza in front with the fountain and end up in the alfresco restaurant beside the stately Hotel Doña María.

Del Moral rolls up his shirtsleeves and orders ice water. He tells me he had lately been depressed about the state of bullfighting but the feria has raised his spirits. He doesn't believe the next generation of matadors is ready, but he is convinced it is talented. "In five years or so, the toreros who are youngsters now will be at their peak," he says. "I'm not predicting it will necessarily rival the sixties, the epoch of great *figuras,* but look at what you'll have: Litri, Rafi Camino, Joselito, Cepeda, Lozano. I'd say those five. Niño de la Taurina is good, but not in the same class. And Aparicio, well, we just don't know yet. If he can do with toros what he does with novillos, he'll be a monster. But it's a different thing entirely, and people don't understand that.

"But those five will form a sensational core for the nineties," he says, sipping his water. "Remember that the aficionado is always looking backward, because everything seems better when you were young. You'd see a Manolete or an Ordóñez, have five beers afterward, make love to a woman all night. Now you have these people in their seventies, old men, they can't drink five beers at all, they can't make love to a woman, naturally they remember everything about the old days as better—and that goes for the toreo, too. But that doesn't necessarily mean it *was* better, or that it can't be just as good again. Just when things seem the most hopeless, there is a ray of light."

I ask him what first drew him to bullfighting—and why he remains drawn to it.

"Bullfighting is an uncertain art, uncertain because it depends on an animal," he says. "It happens in some minutes or even seconds, and then it is gone forever. That's the attraction for me, the fascinating thing about it. It's the same as if Beethoven wrote the Fifth Symphony and it was played as he was writing it and then never again. And toreo is also the most difficult of the arts when it's done right, because there is risk.

It is impermanent, a mixture of painting, music, dance, writing and everything else. And it is never a sure thing. It is only when you get that perfect combination of artist and bull that it happens."

We discuss my book, and which matadors I should write about to give a foreign audience a clear picture of bullfighting today. It is a difficult problem to Del Moral, because he doesn't believe the corrida can be taught, or even truly described, in a book—and certainly not by an outsider. To write about bullfighting one must undergo an apprenticeship nearly as rigorous as learning to actually fight the bulls. "It's not like cinema, where you can go once or twice and talk with great authority about what you've seen," he says. "You need to go to a great deal to appreciate it. When you are about thirty years old, perhaps you begin to be a true aficionado.

"If I have any advice to give, it is this: Don't become the kind of aficionado who only likes one style, especially if you plan to write," he says. "That's very bad, because you close yourself off. You must understand that you can like all different types. Just as you can like El Greco, Goya, and Picasso, you should be able to appreciate a faena of Litri's, of Aparicio's and of Parada's—provided that each one is done well. Never forget that art is art. That's the only truth I can offer." And all, he might have said, ye need to know.

■■■

At a novillada at the Maestranza my bullring neighbor Enrique extends an invitation for me to visit him, and several days later I do. As much as Del Moral is an intellectual, and relates to bullfighting from that perspective, Enrique is the typical Spanish aficionado. He is maybe fifteen years older than Del Moral, has worked as an engineer's assistant, and lives in a high-rise in Rochelambert, a barrio of Sevilla out past Nervión that has only existed for a decade. Before that it was farmland.

Rochelambert is at the end of the number 25 bus line that begins at the Plaza Nueva. Everything is modern and antiseptic. The apartment houses could be anywhere. Enrique meets me at the bus stop. He is barely more than half my height, with a huge belly and blotchy skin, a mouth perpetually half-open and an easy manner. We walk toward his building and he points out every detail, naming each street as we pass and making sure I understand what each name means, discussing the merits of each store. We arrive at the fifth floor of a cheerless brown concrete building. However, his apartment is comfortable and well furnished. There is art on the walls and every modern convenience: VCR, color television, deluxe refrigerator with an ice-maker.

He tells me that his life is much easier now than it ever was. "I'm a pensioner and I make five thousand pesetas a day," he says. "My wife makes some, too, although not as much. That's a big difference from how it used to be." He says he routinely worked fourteen hours a day, not for furniture or clothes, but merely for money to eat. Everything else was purchased on credit. "I have an *abono* for the bullfights now, but that's a recent thing," he says. "I never used to have one. I don't think the change has all that much to do with politics, the socialists and all that. I think it's just progress. Man is getting better at living."

Growing up, he could afford to go to the feria only one day every year. "I'd bring a sandwich wrapped in paper," he says. "I kept it in the pocket of my pants. I would dance in the streeet and clap my hands, but I wouldn't be able to enter any *casetas*. Then I'd walk to the Plaza de España and eat my sandwich there.

"I was poor my whole life. Now I have this." He waves a hand around the room at his things. "And I say, now that I have it I don't want to lose it. I'll fight for it. I don't have any politics. All I want is peace, and for my family to live well."

Enrique has been following bullfighting for many years through the newspapers and television and, later, when he could afford to, at the plaza. He believes that not only has the quality of the bullfighting declined, but also the quality of the *afición*. "The people in the old days were such fanatics that they used to pawn watches at the pawnshop to get enough money to see Belmonte fight," he says. "I can remember people taking the pillows off their beds and going down to the pawnshop and pawning their pillows to get money to go to a big corrida. That's the way Sevilla was. If the corrida was important enough, the people would rather see that than have their pillows. You don't see something like that now, and you don't see the kids playing at bullfighting in the streets. Now its *futbol* and basketball."

Enrique brings out framed prints, sixteenth- and seventeenth-century maps of Sevilla as seen from Triana, and he shows me where the old Plaza de Toros used to be and where it would be today. He puts a tape of pasodobles on a cassette player. It is a routine he has, he says—the prints, the music, bullfight talk. Around here, life is made up of many routines. Sevillanos prefer it that way.

"If I want to have a beer in this barrio, there are fourteen bars to do it in," he says. "But there is one that is mine. The reason is that they know me there by now. Why go anywhere else? And I don't. Every time I want a beer I go to the same place. And I can't understand doing it any other way." We watch bullfight highlights on a big color television he has. We see the corrida from Easter Sunday, highlights from "Tendido Cero," and at one point he stops the tape—and we're on it, sitting in the stands. Antonio is standing and applauding, and so is Leonardo. Enrique is sitting and applauding, and Rafael is just sitting. I am taking notes. "For the book!" Enrique says. He is a great supporter of my project.

He serves me a tapa of ham and cheese and a beer and walks me to the bus stop. On the way we stop at the butcher's. "This is my American friend I told you about," Enrique says to the butcher, who is much younger. "He is a big aficionado of the toros."

"Really?" the butcher says. He turns to me. "What do you think of the toros?"

"I love bullfighting," I tell him.

"Really?" he says. He cannot comprehend this. He turns back to Enrique. "And he is an American? Like Hemingway?" Slowly it dawns on him. "Hemingway was American!"

The bus is rounding the corner and we say goodbye. "You have a brother in Spain," Enrique tells me. "Forget the nationalities. I'm your brother. Well, a much older brother." We shake hands. I pause on the steps of the bus to write in my notepad and he waves me on. When he sees me aboard, he turns back toward his apartment.

■ ■ ■

A bullfighter's schedule is plotted by his agent before each season, and additional corridas are added as the summer progresses. For an aficionado who wants to maximize his time and see as many quality bullfights as possible, plotting a schedule is an art of its own. The feria in Córdoba overlaps with San Ysidro in Madrid, and with Granada, and there is always a fine corrida in Aranjuez in late May, but that is when the plazas are active in the south. Pamplona begins in July but Alicante and Badajoz come in between. And many of the better fights in the weeks after that are in southern France.

Of course, if it is a single matador you want to follow, it is that much less complicated, although the driving will verge on the impossible. The *apoderado* has already made the schedule—you just have to find a car that won't break down and a driving partner and set out, provided you have the money. For most people, the time and expense involved make it nearly impossible anyway. "Let's not kid ourselves," the American matador Sidney Franklin said when Hemingway suggested following him around Spain. He recorded the conversation in his book, *Bullfighter From Brooklyn:* "In the first place, the travel part would cost you an arm and a leg. Then, when you got to a town where I was to appear, and since it would be right in the middle of the fair dates, unless you had reserved some accommodations from six months to a year in advance, you'd never be able to find a place to sleep standing up, much less a bed! . . .

"Let's say, for argument's sake, that you managed by hook or by crook to get to these towns. It wouldn't be possible, but let's say you were also able to find some hole-in-the-wall where you could stay so you wouldn't have to spend each twenty-four hours on the street. You may not know this, but since my first appearance in Sevilla, the moment my name appears on a card you can't find a ticket. If I didn't have it stipulated in my contract, even I couldn't get tickets to my own fights. Now how do you suppose you'd get in to see these fights after all the expense and trouble of getting to the places where they are held? Can you answer that?"

Hemingway, already renowned as the author of *The Sun Also Rises* and *A Farewell to Arms,* was sufficiently famous to manage. The rest of us do what we can. Each week I buy the new magazines and take them back to my terrace and try to figure out where I want to be and when. Then I pull out the bus schedules and figure out how to get there. Usually it's a one-day trip, since most of the early season takes place here in Andalusia, where it's far more likely to be warm. When I have to stay somewhere I find a cheap *hostal.* And tickets are just a question of how much I'm willing to pay.

Last weekend I traveled to Ronda to see Aparicio with Finito de Córdoba and, the surprise of the afternoon, a teenage novillero named Jesulín de Ubrique. The highlight of the trip was nothing that happened on the sand but a glimpse I caught of Antonio Ordóñez, chunky and balding, standing inside the ticket window of the old bullring there. Beside Ordóñez was his grandson, Francisco Rivera, the son Paquirri had with Carmen Ordóñez before their divorce. Antonio Ordóñez's wife—the boy's grandmother—is the sister of Luis Miguel Dominguín, so this teenager has perhaps the best taurine bloodlines in Spain, directly related as he is to at least four true *figuras:* Antonio Ordóñez (his grand-father), Niño de la Palma (his great-grandfather), Dominguín (his great-uncle) and Paquirri (his father). This is not to mention Domingo Dominguín and Pepe Dominguín, Luis Miguel's brothers and fine bullfighters, too, or Riverito, Paquirri's brother, who by all accounts had more natural ability than Paquirri but lacked the desire to make himself a *figura.* Seeing Francisco beside his grandfather, a whole century of taurine history in two men and with the boy's taurine career still to come (for there is little doubt he will be a bullfighter) was a moment that made the entire two-day trip worthwhile. Discovering Jesulín de Ubrique was a bonus.

My plan now is to go to Jérez this weekend to see Paula with Espartaco and Litri. The bullring in Jérez is one of my favorites, and the bullfight is the highlight of the three-day feria there. Jérez is the birthplace of sherry and of *fino,* and its feria, a miniature version of Sevilla's, is known for superb drinks in large quantities and majestic horses bearing men and women in traditional costume. And there is always something special about seeing Paula at his home bullring. The way he fought in Sevilla this year, so bad as to be embarrassing, I don't know how many more chances there will be to see him anywhere.

Del Moral agrees that Jérez is the place to be this Friday, but for different reasons. He's eager to see how Litri will do in his next two tries, on Friday in Jérez and the following afternoon in the town of Écija. Both days he will be performing head-to-head with Espartaco, and he will be looking to rectify his unmitigated disaster in Sevilla. The days to come are important ones for Litri's career, because what happened in Sevilla was so visible. He runs the risk of being typecast as a matador who has nothing more than bloodlines, a matador not to be taken seriously, which would be unfair: at twenty, he has hardly had the chance to mature into a full-fledged bullfighter. But that is the danger of overhype and underfulfillment.

It will be easy to chart his progress, for he's fighting with Espartaco on carteles all spring. There are at least this many scheduled already: Jérez, Écija, Nimes on May 15, Puerto de Santa María on May 21, Madrid on May 23, Aranjuez on May 30, Haro on June 3, Floriac on June 4. My plan is to get to at least four or five and to see what develops. It will be especially interesting to see Litri on May 23, with San Ysidro as the backdrop—his debut in Madrid, and the confirmation of his alternativa—but only interesting if Litri has managed to triumph and resurrect his reputation between now and then. If not, I wouldn't be surprised to see him pull out of San Ysidro with an injury. A *fracaso* in Madrid after what has already happened would be a professional death knell.

"Litri has a whole season to spend with Espartaco," Del Moral says. We are in his office and he has his pad in front of him indicating all the bullfights he is planning to attend. "I think they're going to end up fighting together forty afternoons. So the boy had better do better than he did in Sevilla. Espartaco, of course, is a given. You know that he's going to be good, and that puts the pressure on anyone who's with him."

John Fulton has said he's heading to Jérez, too, and if Rosa can get enough of her work done during the week she may have an interest in going. I take a handful of coins from my jar and head to the pay phone in the plaza, looking to make inquiries about a car.

3

FOLLOWING
THE CONTENDERS

THE TOLL HIGHWAY from
Sevilla to Jérez costs nearly six dollars but the road is perfect and at that
price almost nobody else is driving it. In a friend's rental car the trip
takes an hour and a half. We arrive to find streets closed off because of
the feria so we take a circuitous route to the bullring. The traffic flow
in Jérez is notoriously absurd, one-way streets changing to two-way
streets and back again with regularity.

The day is hot, but far from ideal bullfight weather. Jérez is a dusty
place to begin with and today a strong wind is swirling, collecting the
grit into clouds, stinging eyes. Walking against the wind from the car
to the plaza is difficult enough; I can only imagine what it would be
like to fight a bull today.

Women in feria dress are circulating and men are riding horseback.
John Fulton is here with a picador from Mexico who is part of a dynasty
of picadors. Everyone is looking for tickets. I have already bought mine:
a seat in the *gradas* for twenty-three hundred pesetas, five hundred over
list price, the cheapest in the place. John is headed for a *reventa* booth
around the corner. Earlier he stopped by to see Paula dress. "He didn't
even have any tickets," John says. "He was so pissed off about the wind,
he didn't even want to see me."

Paula also has other worries. Four years ago, in March of 1985, he reportedly hired a friend to murder a man who had become his wife's lover. The man was a soccer player for the Cádiz club named José Gómez Carrillo, and in the end the murder attempt was farcical and nobody was hurt. A week after this Paula was arrested walking out of a corrida in El Puerto de Santa María and he actually spent some days in prison. The day after his release he fought in the Easter Sunday corrida in Sevilla.

It was all supposedly taken care of then but now the case has resurfaced and the prosecution wants seven years. The trial is scheduled to begin May 22, which is the day after Paula fights in Pamplona with John. "That's either very good news for me or very bad," John said when he heard. "He'll either be so distracted that he'll let me do some capework and maybe even a series with the muleta, or he'll just want to get the thing over with and hurry through it." However, Federico believes the impending trial may not affect Paula at all. "He worries all the time, but not about those kinds of things," he says. "I wonder sometimes if the man knows what's going on around him."

The bullring here is made of faded brown brick, and from the outside it seems ordinary, even ugly. Up a flight of steps, you find yourself on a walkway looking down on where you just came from. Through a passageway you go inside, where the thin metal posts have been painted a bright ballpark green. It is a tidy, small plaza with excellent sightlines. Up in the *grada* the wooden seats are comfortable and no cushion is necessary.

These bulls are Jandillas. From the weights that have been posted we know they'll be small. The crowd waits with rhythmic flamenco clapping, the stress on every third beat. From the beginning Paula has trouble. The wind is gusting and he clearly doesn't want to be out there, and on top of that the bull is troublesome. It circles around the horse and charges from behind, confounding the picador. A peon trips but the bull chops and misses and someone makes a *quite* and the man is up and gone. Paula's faena is the usual mess and the whistles come—even here. He is backing away from the bull, blatantly scared of it. Paula's feet shuffle on his passes and he misses his first three *estocadas* because he won't stay still.

Espartaco's first bull, called Destilado, is tiny, dark brown, 460 kilos. He brings it out of its *querencia* and into the sun, where his blue suit of lights glitters. For his first series he uses his left hand and doesn't get much. The bull, weak but willing, stumbles into the sand. By his third series Espartaco has it charging. With the music playing he has the bull circling around him as if it is on a rope, passing it in the style of Paco Ojeda, working the angles with one foot motionless. He switches to the right hand and the bull cuts inside and ponders mayhem but Espartaco will have no part of that. He falls to one knee and passes it through, and the crowd understands exactly what has happened—that Espartaco has reasserted the dominion of his will with a single pass—and responds with a thunderous Olé!

The wind is so strong that napkins have blown into the ring, and with each gust they run along the sand like crabs. Espartaco continually glances over that way because the napkins are dangerous. If their movement catches the bull's eye, it is liable to charge through Espartaco to get to them. He finishes his faena with *derechazos,* then a slow backhanded pass, through to the chest pass and out; changes swords, profiles with the wind rustling his hair, and kills the slightest bit *bajonazo.* It is done so gracefully that nobody much cares about the imperfection and the requisite ear is awarded. Once again Espartaco's work has set a standard for Litri to meet, and he can either respond in kind or look bad by comparison. Such is the price he must pay to compete with the best.

Litri's bull is fearful. It paws the ground instead of charging. The picador Saavedra is sent off after a single, firm pic. Montoliú places a set of banderillas artfully. El Mangui then drags the bull all the way across the ring, allowing Litri, his back turned, to pay his respects to the president.

His first series seems overly complex, bullfighting from the textbook and not the heart, but then Litri slides toward the bull, tap-tap-tapping his front foot as he advances, the muleta in his left hand and the sword in his right, and begins a good, tough set. He stands between the muleta and the bull, then shows the cloth and passes the bull very close four times in succession. That is the way to use bravery, not through tricks. The passes are emotional because they are so close. He is not *cargando la suerte* at all but standing with his feet together, letting the bull exit through the back of the pass each time. There is no linking, and the bull never heads around his body, but that's fine—there is emotion enough. You enjoy different faenas for different reasons, and the enticement of this one is watching the domination, the passes closer than normal because the bull is loath to charge.

Litri swaggers around and gets very good applause. This is a confident Litri and the swagger doesn't look false on him as he did in Sevilla, when he was strutting around the ring like a boy dressed in his father's clothes. But he isn't all the way there yet. It is at this point in the faena that he often manages to lose his bulls and now suddenly he can't find the *distancia.* This time he does a smart thing, the smartest thing a bullfighter can ever do: he adapts. Instead of forcing his simple *derechazo* he shows the bull the backhand, gets it going, then rolls it past with a *pase cambiado* and struts off, a nice recovery.

He pours the sword straight in with the kill, then stands and watches, waiting for the bull to die. Everyone is motionless. The bull is standing straight, perfectly still, the sword inside it. It remains there for a long time, standing. Litri watches, his right arm outstretched, ready to signal the bull dead. The bull remains erect. It is clearly dying and a *descabello* won't be necessary, but it won't go down. It starts to walk slowly forward and lurches, but still it won't fall. Two minutes have elapsed since the *estocada.* The crowd is standing too, all eyes on this brave bull. Litri is behind it now and the bull senses that and turns to face its tormentor. Finally it kicks and falls dead. Litri leans over and pats it on the side. The crowd applauds for the noble animal.

■■■

The fourth bull is the only truly unmanageable one of the day, and Paula, who loses more capes and muletas to bulls than any matador I've seen, spends most of his time retrieving them. The fifth bull, Espartaco's second, is bigger and better and allows for some interesting capework: in rapid succession a *chicuelina,* a *media verónica* and a *revolera.* Six more passes put the bull in position for a pic, but the bull gets too close and the pic is made too far back, at the rear of the swell of muscle—and, of course, bullfight terminology has a phrase for exactly this kind of mishap: a *puyazo trasero.* Espartaco calls off the picadors and Ecijano comes on to place two perfect pairs of sticks. He gets a standing ovation and tips his hat.

Espartaco dedicates to the crowd, placing his hat face down on the sand. He starts with two low passes, then steps back and takes a long moment to consider a strategy. The bull is noble and willing but it chops upward with its horns. The wind is whipping up the muleta but Espartaco keeps the problem to a minimum by working low, right hand to left hand, passes linked, and this restrains the bull from bucking, too. The faena ends with a *molinete,* Espartaco wrapping himself in the muleta as the music plays.

He kills almost perfectly, putting the sword four-fifths of the way down in the killing spot, then administers a single *descabello*. He gets an ear and there is strong petition for another. During his vuelta he gets a hat, a sweater, another hat, the usual flowers. He dutifully tosses back everything, never losing that huge grin. Somebody jumps out and hugs him, then jumps back into the stands, and the crowd is chanting: "To–re–ro! To–re–ro!"

The final bull is small but feisty. Litri is fine with the cape. Sanz the picador is artful and gets an ovation, and then good banderilla work all around earns a standing ovation for the cuadrilla as a whole. This crowd is knowledgeable and appreciates the details, and Litri's cuadrilla has had an outstanding day, considering the conditions. With everything humming along Litri starts his faena, but he quickly grinds the momentum to a stop with two bad series, his footwork all wrong. He recovers with help from this eager bull. Two very good right-handed passes that open his third series start the music and lead to a set of linked passes, and then another. Later the bull comes in on his hands and forces him to stumble backward and this breaks his rhythm. It is a long faena, too long now, and the bull is learning fast and won't move. Then Litri gives his best exit pass of the day, leaning in as the bull rushes by, every inch a matador, using body control to avoid falling onto the bull, then turning it right around and out with the *pase de pecho*. He kills slightly low on his second try, ending a successful afternoon.

The road show continues the next day, Saturday, May 6, Litri fighting with Espartaco in the town of Écija. It is on the Córdoba highway in the province of Sevilla, a half-hour beyond Carmona and the well-regarded parador there. Anyone who saw the corrida in Jérez and wanted to see another could have returned to Sevilla for the evening meal and started out for Écija after lunch the following day, or else spent the night in Carmona and headed east after checkout and a meal there.

The impresario in Écija usually schedules one full corrida a year, and at the last one, on May 7 of last year, Espartaco cut four ears and a tail. Ears are not hard to come by here, a typical third-class ring, but four ears and a tail means an impressive performance anywhere. El Ecijano, Espartaco's peon, is from Écija, as is the retired *figura* Jaime Ostos, and so are the Campuzanos, Tomás and José Antonio, although they live in Sevilla. José Antonio Campuzano, who is in the midst of a trying and unsuccessful season, is the third matador on the cartel today.

We see seven ears awarded during the afternoon, and several of them are deserved. Espartaco cuts two ears off his first bull and an ear off his second. With the latter he doesn't dominate, can't get his momentum going, kills badly—and gets an ear for his name alone. But the afternoon belongs to Litri. It is the best I have ever seen him, and Del Moral would later write that the faenas were his two best since his alternativa. He gets two ears with his first bull, mixing classical toreo with *tremendismo* and killing well, and on his second responds to a fine animal with inspired work. His capework is marvelous, for once, feet set and the cape floating. He starts his faena from his knees, back and forth, then segues into five quality minutes of classic toreo devoid of *tremendista* riffs. Four times in succession he pulls the bull around himself, back foot forward, the proper way. He ends with a series of slow passes, looking more like Manzanares than an eager twenty-year-old. It's a fine faena, worthy of an ear anywhere. His killing is off—third try, and quite low. But he gets his third ear of the afternoon—the first time he has done that since cutting four ears and a tail in a pueblo near Almeria last October, and he and Espartaco depart from the bullring on shoulders, each then heading to his chauffered Mercedes and roaring off into the night.

■■■

It has been getting hotter every day in Sevilla, the approaching summer blowing its dragon's breath into the stillness of every afternoon. Sunday hits ninety degrees by lunchtime and Monday is up into the nineties early. But the heat is not oppressive and it's worth some perspiration to see the city shimmer. The bright light makes the white buildings sparkle and the glare hides the dirt of the river and the sky is a brilliant blue behind the bullring, just like in Fulton's posters.

From the Triana Bridge I can see the sun reflecting off the white two- and three-story apartments across the river, the old Gypsy quarters, a high-rent district now. Half a block down the street I see Navarrito in his usual place outside the Tres Reyes, wearing a polo shirt and sipping coffee. He tells me Paula's benefit in Pamplona has been announced in the papers and John is officially listed as *sobresaliente,* and that Manolito has fought near the Portuguese border during the weekend without much success. Inside the bar I notice some new bullfight posters on the wall. The Córdoba feria is approaching and will have a full week of fights. Granada, less of a bullfight town than Córdoba or Sevilla, runs a feria concurrently with Córdoba's, and they have Roberto Domínguez there on the 25th with Mari Carmen Camacho bulls and Espartaco and

Manili fighting Torrealtas on the 27th. There is a novillada without picadors about fifteen minutes from here in Santiponce next weekend, and a corrida on the 28th in Sanlucar de Barrameda with Parada, Cepeda and Litri.

The huge Las Ventas cartel is there with the lineups for all twenty-four corridas during San Ysidro. I have heard that Joselito is back in Spain and that he is improving and might possibly make Madrid. One of the bartenders assures me this is so but a patron, who claims to be a doctor, disagrees strongly and says the boy would have to be a masochist to attempt a comeback so soon. *"Hombre,"* the bartender replies, "don't you agree that every bullfighter is a little masochistic?"

After a beer I cut through the back streets to the bullring. A bullfight museum has recently opened, and even though I have heard it isn't much, I want to see it. The idea of a bullfight museum in La Maestranza may seem like a natural one, for there is a fine museum attached to Las Ventas in Madrid and another good one in Córdoba, but in Sevilla every bar is a taurine museum, so why create another? For a long time the people who run the Maestranza resisted the idea, but so many people were coming by asking to see the most beautiful bullring in Spain that finally a small museum was opened with a tour included.

The tour starts in an anteroom. It costs two hundred pesetas and begins on the half-hour or the hour. The anteroom has scale models of two old bullrings, antecedents of the Maestranza. It has a couple of carteles from recent ferias, a huge bull's head and some drawings; on the whole, much less to see than just about anywhere I could have chosen to have lunch.

Ten of us are led out a door and through a dark hallway, paved in stone, but with smooth earthen walls that are cool to the touch. We emerge in the *callejón,* beneath the president's box, beside the Puerta de Príncipe. Our guide, a young woman, gives a short historical talk studded with names and dates. I believe I am the only American in the group, but there are two Japanese with cameras around their necks who seem not to understand anything she says, and may not understand Spanish at all.

Next we're taken to the infirmary. Through a window we can see an operating table, an IV unit and various other medical devices. The guide is silent, letting the sterile solemnity of medicine speak for itself.

The museum is located in four interconnected rooms in the bowels of the bullring. The first section looks more like a museum of medieval costumes than toreo. There are lances and spears and 18th-century wool breeches and red military-looking coats. Then some carteles: Lagartijo in Madrid in 1893 and Frascuelo in Sevilla in 1885; Espartero and Guerrita fighting Miuras here in 1892. There is the original cartel from Talavera in 1920 the day Joselito died, accompanied by a bust of him and a suit of lights he wore when he was fourteen. The suit of lights he had on in Talavera has long ago been claimed by the museum in Madrid. There is a cartel from 1919 that shows Chicuelo taking the alternativa with Belmonte as the padrino, and also Manolete's alternativa from 1939 with Chicuelo as padrino. From 1916 there is a hand-painted tapestry cartel. It is at least ten feet high and shows all six carteles of the feria that year. Joselito and Belmonte are in every one, two of them *mano a mano*.

Farther on there are some swords of Luis Fuentes Bejarano, a Jean Cocteau watercolor, and a Picasso painting, done with black ink on a violet cape, of a bullfight scene. Curro Romero's suit of lights hangs in the far room and Manolo Vázquez's too, but our half-hour is up. I cast a last, lingering glance at the far room, which seems to be full of *trajes de luz*.

The guide tells me I can stay longer but I decline. There is sunshine waiting outside—and the lure of a bright blue sky that reminds me more of a good corrida than all the musty fabric hanging on those walls.

4

FEARS FOR FULTON

FOR MOST of last week John Fulton was out at Santiponce training with a mechanical bull. We're all worried about him. He goes to Pamplona on Thursday, and he's out of practice and out of shape. Yesterday Martín Pareja Obregón was there working with him but I'm not sure who was supposed to be teaching whom.

The contraption at Santiponce looks like a shopping cart gone amok. It's designed to simulate the charge of a bull but it's no substitute for work with live animals. Fortunately one of John's *ganadero* friends has arranged for a last-minute *tienta,* so John won't be completely cold. The breeder, Manuel García Fernández Palacios, is one of the richest men in Jérez. He calls in the morning to say that the *tienta* is set.

Manolito refuses to come because Fernández Palacios hasn't asked for him specifically. He gets in strange moods sometimes. Last year he almost didn't go to a party for John in Jérez celebrating his twenty-fifth year of alternativa. "Why should I go?" he asked. "John will get all the good cows." In the end Judy Cotter talked him into it, since he does owe whatever professional standing he has and virtually his entire existence for the last three years to John. He went, but he didn't dress to fight and he pouted the whole way. When he said he was staying home this time nobody argued.

Instead, Antonio Vázquez is with us. He's another novillero John has helped. I keep hearing he has less potential than Manolito but he does get fights in Sevilla sometimes. He's in his early twenties, about five years younger than Manolito, and overwhelmingly polite. It is all I can do to convince him to drop the formal *usted* and talk to me in the second person familiar.

We arrive in Jérez in the middle of the afternoon. The house is directly downtown, behind a huge iron gate. It's large, breezy and wonderfully furnished, all oak, glass and marble inside. Don Manuel's money was made in rice and other commodities, and his wife is an heiress to the González Byass sherry fortune. He receives us in his living room and serves coffee, cognac, and licorice-tasting *anís,* a tamer version of the dangerously potent absinthe Hemingway used to drink in the 1920s. He tells me his hobby is long-distance horseback riding and that he has been to Virginia several times for competitions. He's in his sixties now but still wakes up early every morning to ride, and it shows: he seems youthful and vigorous.

Finito de Córdoba arrives with Zurito, his manager. A former matador, Zurito will be seriously gored later in the season when a bull jumps the barrera and charges through the *callejón.* Finito has an important fight Sunday, the first in this year's Córdoba feria. He's on a mixed cartel with Curro Romero and Julio Aparicio, a combination that will attract more notice than he's previously had. He's only seventeen and made his debut with picadors just this year, but already he's being touted as the best hope Córdoba has had for a *figura* since El Cordobés. They're expecting him to triumph Sunday and then fill the plaza for his novillada Wednesday.

Finito seems restless and asks to see the copy of *Toros '92* I have rolled up beside me. He immediately turns to see how many ears he has cut this season and finds the number is fourteen, which is more than any other novillero. He doesn't seem overjoyed or impressed by this news— if it is news to him. He returns the magazine, thanks me, and sits back down in his chair, more restless than before.

We drive half an hour to the *finca,* which is outside the town of Arcos de la Frontera. Finito has a white van with his name painted on the side, and it is a good thing Manolito isn't here to see that. In the car, John seems preoccupied. He knows that he is ill prepared for Pamplona. He hasn't worn a suit of lights in Spain since 1974, nor in Mexico since 1986, which shows how little activity he's had recently outside of festivals and *tientas,* and there haven't even been many of those. In Pamplona he won't be wearing a suit of lights, either—not because he's merely the *sobresaliente,* but because Paula will be killing novillos (with shaved horns, no doubt) instead of full-grown four-year-old bulls. When a matador fights novillos he must wear *traje corto* in place of *traje de luz* so everyone knows it is not a true corrida.

John hasn't been told how much he'll be allowed to do, but he has to be prepared for everything. If something happens to Paula, John will be called upon to kill for the first time in three years. I ask if he's planning to work on any technique in particular this afternoon. "Getting out alive," he says.

The *plaza de tienta* is in a valley surrounded by green hills. Finito's van rolls up beside us and a series of handlers emerges. Finito stands in the back and changes into *traje corto.* John and Antonio are wearing jeans and sneakers.

On the platform perched above the ring there is only room enough to stand, not like the spacious viewing area at Alonso Moreno's ranch. We can see the cows milling in the pens below us. We look down at them and they look up at us. Each cow must be isolated in a different pen so when the gate is lifted it will readily charge into the ring, and this division of the herd takes some time. The picador arrives, straps on his padding and mounts the horse, and the *tienta* starts. We jump down and watch from behind the *burladeros* inside the makeshift ring.

John uses the cape with the first cow. He's stiff but his passes are effective. The cow is energetic and strong and spills the picador off the horse. Antonio comes in with the cape and impresses me with his smoothness. John has to hustle to get in position each time and the labor in his movement is evident, while Antonio, so much younger and more agile, is already where he needs to be and can concentrate on grace and form. Of course, he's trying hard to impress. John merely wants to get the work in.

The cow takes four pics and still shows interest, meaning it's a worthy fighting animal and will likely be used for breeding. John picks up the muleta and starts a faena. He has fine technique but gets winded easily. After a few series his shirt is soaked with sweat. Panting, John motions Antonio in and rests behind a *burladero* across from where we're standing.

It is nearly 7:30 but there is plenty of light and even sun. The green humps of hills in the distance are so lush they look African, and in truth Africa is not so very far from here. Tarifa is little more than an hour down the highway, and from there you can see not just the mountains of Morocco but the white houses nestled in their foothills. In the ring Antonio is doing well with the muleta and Fernández Palacios is visibly impressed. "Antonio is one of the best campo bullfighters I've seen," Judy whispers. "But he's had about twelve opportunities in the Maestranza and each time he just falls apart."

We watch Finito take a turn and then Antonio with the next cow and then John again. He's moving a little better but he still isn't nimble. "I'm worried about John and Rafael because neither of them has good legs," Judy says. "Which one is going to help the other?" John and Finito alternate series with the cape. The cow keeps taking pics and going right back to the horse. Finito takes the muleta and grunts and furrows his brow, and his concentration pays off with a splendid series. We watch intently now because the passes are so exciting, and I have never seen good toreo from quite this close: behind the *burladero* in a tiny bullring.

A young aficionado watches with us, junior high school age, some friend of somebody's, and after Finito is finished the boy is allowed to take the muleta and try some passes. The first three are not so bad, although they look like nothing after what we've seen from Finito, and then the kid gets a little cocky, thinking, hey, this isn't so hard. He prances a step too close, showing the muleta with a bit of his body behind it, and the cow, which has been learning all this time, steps in and almost catches him. The muleta ends up draped over the head of the animal like a tablecloth and Antonio and Finito and John hurry in flashing their capes. Since there is no infirmary on the grounds as there is at a bullring, and since a *finca* is almost by definition a long way from civilization, even a simple gash here can turn into a serious problem. This kid was never in any real danger, but with an amateur you can't be too careful.

When the excitement has died down, John takes the next bull and at once Judy and I notice he is having some difficulty with his leg, as if he has pulled a muscle. He hobbles over. "It's my tendon," he pants. "This has happened to me before." John and Antonio share the bull and John passes it well but it is evident he has lost mobility, and it's not as though he had any to spare. The teenager wants to redeem himself and is given another chance, and on his first pass the cow catches him. He stumbles and falls and again everybody runs in with capes waving. The cow steps over and around the boy but not on him. Antonio distracts it with a *quite* and the boy stands up and limps away. His pants are ripped almost the length of the inseam, but fortunately he's still ambulatory.

It is 9:30 now and chilly; the moon is high in the sky and the hills are pink. Finito is working the last cow. John is beside me in the *burladero* and he's impressed by Finito's artistry. *"Bien!"* he calls. *"Muy bien!"* He tells me he thinks Finito has more talent than Jesulín de Ubrique, Chiquilín, even Pareja Obregón. Finito asks if John wants to finish the last animal, but John declines; he can hardly walk. This is a bad portent for Sunday. "It always happens to me before a fight," he says. "I mean, it's about the fourth time. I think it's psychologically induced."

Even before this injury John had the body of a man pushing sixty, not a bullfighter in his prime. He didn't want to wear boots today because he has bone spurs in his heel and he knows the surface of a *tienta* ring is frequently hard and dry. "So I wore these low sneakers, and instead I hurt my tendon," he says. The same thing happened some years ago in Tijuana two days before a fight and a friend arranged an appointment with the team physician of the San Diego Chargers football team, a man accustomed to treating leg injuries. The doctor advised John to stay off the leg for two weeks and then begin a rigorous calisthenic program. When he said he had to fight a bull in two days the doctor threw up his hands and said he couldn't be responsible. "If you were a player, I'd bench you," he said.

Against all advice John fought, because he had worked hard to get the booking and didn't know when he'd get another. During the corrida the bull rammed his kneecap and when he arrived at the infirmary the doctors told him they would never have let him fight if they'd seen his leg. He tells the story dispassionately, as if we were talking about someone else, but as he talks he is sitting with his leg elevated and somebody has driven off for ice—and there are only three days remaining before Pamplona.

We emerge from the bullring to find a folding table loaded with cheese, two kinds of salami, bread, shiny black olives and plenty of sherry, beer and Coca-Cola. We stand under the darkening sky and eat and drink and talk. There are some friends of the Fernández Palacios family there, women in their twenties or even younger, and after everyone has eaten and had plenty to drink, one of the women starts to clap and another starts to sing and soon all of them are clapping in rhythm and singing in tune. John limps forward and starts a graceful sevillana. One of the women joins him and their bodies are fluid, moving and turning to the beat of the handclapping and the flow of the singing. I'm telling Judy that it seems unwise for John to be dancing on an injured leg when someone interrupts with a raised glass of *fino*. "There is the complete *Norteamericano,*" he says. "He's more Spanish than we Spaniards. The man fights bulls in the daytime and dances sevillanas at night."

Antonio steps forward. "All my life I've wanted to dance sevillanas and I've never done it," he says shyly. There is an uproar. He must dance! The moon is almost full overhead, so bright that I can take notes by its light. The clapping and singing start again and soon everyone is dancing, some expertly and others stumbling around, and it strikes me how extraordinary the scene is. There we are, a dozen of us, sipping sherry not thirty miles from where it was invented with a full sky of stars and a benevolent moon above, dancing sevillanas beside a bullring with toreros and dark-eyed women from Jérez. It is so archetypically Spanish as to be a cliché, an idealized scene from some bad opera. Only John's limp is a concession to reality. That wouldn't be in the script.

Later we decide to wander around in the bullring. The moon is so bright we can see perfectly. "You hear all the stories about Belmonte caping bulls by moonlight and you scoff," John says, "but tonight it's evident that they're all true. Look at that light! You could have had the whole *tienta* now. If I had gotten rich and bought a *finca,* the first thing I would have done was to have *tientas* by moonlight."

He smiles. "I guess it's a good thing I never really did get big in the business," he says. "Can you imagine? They wouldn't have been able to handle me."

■■■

John leaves for Pamplona the next afternoon in the station wagon and I decide not to accompany him. It's a twelve-hour drive each way, a long trip to see someone serve as *sobresaliente*. The only reason to have a *sobresaliente* is in case the featured matadors are gored or otherwise injured and unable to proceed. This way there will be someone there capable of fighting, and killing, the remaining bulls. In a typical corrida of three matadors there is no *sobresaliente* because the odds of all three being put out of action are minute. One is on hand only when two matadors fight *mano a mano,* or when a matador kills six bulls for charity *como única espada,* as a single swordsman. And while the tradition is to let the *sobresaliente* do some capework, the matador seldom permits much more because the crowd would be displeased. They have paid to see a *figura,* not a stand-in.

John says that if he wasn't involved he wouldn't go, and limping the way he is it's probably better that I don't see him. Judy is staying home and so is Navarrito. Only Federico is going; he'll drive while John rests. "It doesn't matter, because I probably won't get to do anything," John said. "Rafael doesn't get close enough to the bull to ever get gored."

On Saturday, while John is in Pamplona preparing for his fight, I'm in the whitewalled town of Osuna watching Manzanares, Espartaco and Pedro Castillo. The bullring there is tiny, with uncomfortable seats of cut stone. The prices are too expensive for the people of Osuna and the ring is half full. My twenty-five-dollar seat is the cheapest there is and doesn't offer much of a view, but I move down until I'm in the fourth row.

Castillo, whose style of *tremendismo* is even more vulgar than El Soro's, is gored by the last bull of the day and he shuffles to the infirmary bleeding from his lower leg. Manzanares has done nothing all day with his own two bulls but with Castillo's bull, which has hardly been fought, he creates a splendid faena, kills well and gets two ears. Espartaco cuts an ear off his first bull and an ear off his second, his usual steady performance.

The next day I'm off again, to El Puerto de Santa María, twenty minutes past Jérez on the Atlantic coast. There are plenty of bullfights to choose from now, every Saturday and Sunday in Spain; if you wanted to, you could see two every weekend without much effort. Originally Espartaco was scheduled to fight here with Litri and José Luis Galloso, but in the morning I read that Litri has fallen ill and Julio Robles, popular but wildly inconsistent, will replace him on the cartel.

The trip to Puerto takes me through small towns, whitewashed and quiet. Puerto has palm trees and a wide plaza overlooking the harbor, but few tourist amenities. The foreigners there are mostly Americans from the nearby military base at Rota. Most have been in the area for at least a year and behave as locals. The restaurants are good here and not overly crowded. I eat at the Romerijo, where they have shrimp and lobsters and crayfish and fried fish of all kinds. You buy them at the counter, freshly cooked, and they give you your order wrapped in paper. Then you take the bundle out to the plastic tables, order a beverage from the passing waiters and eat under a canopy, watching the harbor. The beers come in huge mugs and cost a dollar and a half. I have shrimp and *percebes,* which are barnacles, and succulent fried squid and tiny baby clams and beer.

The bullring at El Puerto is a huge, triple-decked place, one of the largest in Spain, so big that there is a fire station, unrelated to the bullfight, tucked away in the plaza. There are more than a dozen different classifications of ticket you can buy. Along the top of the plaza are alternating flags, the yellow and red of Spain and the green and white of Andalusia. A *tendido sol* seat for twenty-five hundred pesetas gets me in the fourth row with a perfect view. The sand is meticulously manicured and the seats, though stone, are not uncomfortable. There are a fair number of Americans here because of the nearby base—probably more blacks than at all the other bullrings in Spain put together. Many of the servicemen are here every weekend there is a bullfight during the summer and have become quite knowledgeable.

As the corrida begins I know that Paula is already fighting his novillos in Pamplona with John standing by, Curro is in Córdoba with Finito and Aparicio, El Pere and two others are fighting in a novillada in Sevilla, Victor Mendes is the headliner in Barcelona, and Parada, Oliva and José Antonio Campuzano are in Madrid in one of the early San Ysidro fights. I would not mind being in any of those places, in any of those bullrings. I'm also perfectly content where I am—sitting in the fourth row of a grand plaza after a seafood meal, watching Espartaco as he walks stiffly across the sand, trailed by his cuadrilla, to pay his respects to the president.

Yet, as Galloso prepares to meet the first Sepulveda I find myself thinking of John. I'm so concerned that I actually take a moment to mumble a prayer. This is probably one prayer more than he will say for himself, for John is the least religious bullfighter I know. Most toreros make a big show about religion, and I think I would, too, in their place. Theirs is a culture that believes in superstition and portents and symbolism even at the best of times, and when you go out knowingly to face death it would seem to be a case of any port in a storm.

There are stories of matadors traveling with a veritable cathedral's worth of virgins, crosses, relics and altarpieces. Paula has a suitcase full of virgins he carries with him, all different kinds. "Gypsies believe very strongly in the Virgen de los Gitanos," says Federico, "but he doesn't just have that one, he has all of them—Marcarena, Rocio, Fatima and the rest. He wants to make sure."

Almost every bullfighter is Catholic, but some are more nominally Catholic than others. Navarrito used to wear a bull-shaped pendant around his neck and once a woman asked him why he was wearing it and not a traditional religious medallion such as a cross or a virgin.

"Who puts food on my table," he asked her, "the Macarena or this guy?" Every plaza de toros has a chapel where toreros can go for a final prayer; some of them are, in effect, small churches. The one in Sevilla is adorned with virgins of all kinds—statues and medals and paintings. It is done in blue-and-white tile with a simple stone floor.

"It may seem a long way from the cathedral to the bullring," Havelock Ellis wrote in 1908 in *The Soul of Spain*. "In Seville one feels it is not so." He, too, believes that the disparate worlds of toreo and religion are actually intertwined: "In the church," he writes, "the ceremonies of every divine office gain their solemnity by association with the highest conceptions of the Christian faith; in the plaza the sense of solemnity is gained by the possible imminence of death. But in both cases, ceremony and a poignantly emotional background furnish the deepest element of fascination."

The corrida in El Puerto is a disappointment. Galloso is renowned for his capework and some of his *verónicas* are technically superb, but they don't transmit much emotion. He does get two ears with his second bull, a 605-kilo animal the size of a small tractor that he kills *recibiendo* on his second try. Robles has one nice faena with a difficult bull and takes a vuelta. Espartaco gets two absolutely unfightable bulls which even he can't elevate, earns a vuelta with the first for his effort and kills the second swiftly, knowing that he has no chance with it and everyone wants to get to the feria.

Sometime after midnight I meet people in one of the *casetas* who know John. Sons of one or another of the *ganaderos,* they're in their early twenties and covered in expensive clothing. They've heard that John would be with Paula in Pamplona today. Like me, they don't trust Paula and have a queasy feeling about the corrida. "It's not because he's a Gypsy—I'm not prejudiced in that way," says one. "But Paula is just no good. When I heard John Fulton was going up there I was sure it was a bad idea. I even said that to my father."

I arrive home at seven in the morning. By the time I fall asleep, an hour or so later, after typing up my notes and reading the early edition of *El Correo,* John and Federico are already on the outskirts of town, rolling toward home in the station wagon, having cursed Paula's name through many hundreds of miles of the long, dark night.

5

THIRTY YEARS OF
FRUSTRATION

JOHN Fulton didn't get gored in Pamplona. He didn't do anything. Paula refused to let him take one *quite*. John never made it onto the sand.

As soon as I'm awake I head to the gallery. Federico is there and he tells me Paula was astonishing with the six novillos. "The best I've ever seen him," he says. But that's hardly consolation for the trip. John had the best spot in the plaza to watch from, inside the *callejón,* but he didn't get any closer. And Paula didn't pay anything, not even expenses.

We know that Paula is temperamental, so his behavior wasn't entirely unexpected. He seems to have had a fear of being overshadowed by John, who has fought often in Pamplona and is popular there with the aficionados. Paula, very much a bullfighter of Andalusia, hasn't seen Pamplona since 1960, when he was a novillero, and he seldom feels comfortable north of Sevilla. After taking his alternativa during a *goyesca* in Ronda in September of 1960, Paula didn't confirm it in Madrid for fourteen years. In Pamplona the bullfight people were calling John "Maestro" and telling him to consider the place his second home, which must have made Paula feel all the more threatened. Then, at a dinner party the night before the corrida, a group of aficionados from England approached the two matadors. Ignoring Paula, they told John they had flown in from London just to see him fight. "It's not every day we get this chance," they said to John. That sealed his fate.

Paula left immediately after the corrida for Cádiz, where his trial begins today. He didn't thank John or even tell him goodbye. John and Federico drove home, venting their anger during the ride, but toward the end, with morning approaching, laughing about the absurdity of the situation. By the time he arrived in Sevilla, John says, he wasn't angry anymore, just disappointed. "It's the last time I ever do something like that," he says. "I've learned my lesson."

John, Judy Cotter, and I join friends for lunch at an inexpensive chicken restaurant hidden down an alley off Calle Sierpes. "I had a new *quite* I was dying to show," John says. "Out of all the bulls I've ever had an opportunity to fight, the one that would have been ideal for this maneuver was out there. I should have just said, I'm going to take my *quite* on this one, and done it. That's what anybody else would have done. And if Rafael had stopped me, he'd have heard it from the crowd."

There's a bullfight in the Maestranza this Thursday, Corpus Cristi. Last week's rumors were two-thirds right: the cartel will include Parada and Pepe Luis Vázquez as part of a corrida mixta. Instead of Aparicio, Martín Pareja Obregón has been contracted to fight the novillos. He's hotter at the Maestranza right now and probably came cheaper. Mention of the corrida leads John to announce he will no longer purchase bullfight tickets. He has had enough of paying his money, difficult enough to come by, and getting nothing in return. "I only come out of there angry," he says.

Judy and I linger after everyone else has gone. She tells me John has been saying this about the tickets for a couple of weeks now, but that he'll go to a bullfight if someone else buys the ticket. "I can't imagine him turning it down," she says, and it is clear she is going to buy his ticket to this one.

Judy is relieved that John returned from Pamplona in one piece. She even thinks Paula may have done him a favor because John clearly wasn't in shape to fight, and may never be again—which is no shame for a man approaching sixty years old. She'd love to see him cut his *coleta* and officially retire, but she's also certain he'll find it exceedingly hard to live without toreo. "I don't mean being peripherally involved, I mean doing it," she says. It scares her to see his intensity when he talks about bullfighting, and to imagine what he'll be like when he can't get into a ring and pass a bull anymore.

More than anything she fears John will decide to end his life before such a condition comes to pass. It would seem to be the ultimate Spanish act, which is enticing for John, who could never be Spanish enough for the Spaniards, and the precedent is there in Belmonte—and Hemingway. "I thought there was a chance of him just throwing himself on the horns of a bull in Pamplona," she said. "Or, more likely, just fighting it without a care, figuring if he happened to get gored, he'd get gored. I can very easily see him just going out in a blaze of glory, figuring at least he'd be remembered for that. I mean, you know the way he talks and the way he acts. I've never seen anyone as obsessed with anything as John is with bullfighting."

In Pamplona he never had the chance. But there will be more *tientas* and one day another opportunity for John to fight a bull in a real plaza de toros. He has always said he wants to succeed once more in a major bullring before he stops fighting for good. Until today I never realized that could mean something other than cutting his *coleta* in triumph, withdrawing in peace.

■ ■ ■

John and I take a ride in the station wagon. We're transporting a painting from his gallery. We wonder how Paula's trial is proceeding and if Joselito will return in time for Madrid. John is taking an interest in Joselito's goring, although he doesn't have great respect for him as a bullfighter. He tells me he often senses a certain matador is going to get gored before it happens. He spots a superficiality that reveals the matador doesn't truly understand what he's doing. He knew it would happen with Vargas in Sevilla two years ago and he had a feeling Pepe Luis Martín was headed for trouble last month.

John believes the way a bullfighter reacts to a goring often depends on how much he understands why it happened. "If you understand why you get gored, there's no mystery about it," he says. "A kid will start out, he's got this wonderful thing going for him, he thinks he's invincible, and all of a sudden he gets a bull that somehow he doesn't understand. Maybe it gores the shit out of him. Well, he may really be in trouble to get it back again unless he can figure out why it happened. I believe the later a goring comes in your career, the more chance you have of taking it in stride and using it. You're much more likely to say, I got gored for this reason. I made this particular mistake."

"Like Joselito in Mexico?" I ask.

"We'll have to wait and see. That may be the stabilizing factor of his entire career. He may suddenly say, oh, that's what it's all about, and turn into another Joselito El Gallo. Right now, the way he was fighting, I don't think there's any real substance there, not to produce the caliber of bullfighter that Joselito's publicity is trying to make him out to be. It's almost irreverent, with that name. Of course, I don't wish anybody bad luck. Everybody should have the best possible luck. The more *figuras,* the better. I hope I'm wrong, and Joselito does become an important bullfighter. I just don't feel there's any basis for believing he will.

"Now, Rafi Camino and Litri are a whole other story," John says. "I have a gut reaction toward all of these bullfighters' kids who have had all of the advantages. I think for their age and their capability, this is all very heady and top-heavy stuff. Like the child prodigy that everybody fawns over, and then when he starts going into puberty he doesn't play as well or act as well and he can't understand why everyone isn't flocking around anymore. The equilibrium for these guys is so delicate.

"I had a real aversion to Rafi Camino and Litri. I've seen them now several times. Rafi has been coasting on all the advantages of his name, his father's influence and the money behind him, and has never picked up the ball and run with it. Litri has. Litri has had all the advantages, as Rafi did, his father and the publicity and all that, except he has gone on to justify himself as himself, while Rafi hasn't. For better or worse, he puts his ass on the line. I've seen him do it a couple of times now. You saw it in Jérez. It wasn't beautiful and it wasn't soul-churning or anything like that, but it was meritorious. And you can't say people applauded him because of anyone else's help."

I ask about Espartaco, who has never been to John's taste. He appreciates the valor and the technical merit inherent in Espartaco's toreo, but John came of age as a bullfighter and an aficionado watching Ordóñez, Camino, Pepe Luis Vázquez *padre,* and the rest of the *figuras* of the early sixties. He studied their bullfighting and patterned parts of his own after what he saw. He would love to be able to enjoy today's somewhat barren toreo as he did that age of intense artistry, but he can't.

"Espartaco's a *figura,* no question about it," John says. "But his work, even at its best, does not generate profound emotional reaction. I don't think that his makeup, his cosmic projection, is at that level. That bull in Jérez the other day—if there had been any great depth in his work, we would have seen it. We saw the best of his stuff. He had an animal with which he could have created something really important, if he had the depth of a Paula, that kind of communication."

"There aren't that many people around who have that."

"No, there aren't, and that's why the Paulas and Curro Romeros go on for years and years, because every once in a while there's a tiny little spark of communication. It's not much, but it's more than you'll get from anyone else these days."

We drive for a few minutes in silence. I'm tempted to raise the subject of Judy's fears about the future, if only to reassure myself that what she believes is preposterous. If I present the idea as my own, that he will have a difficult time finding happiness when he can no longer fight bulls, he need never know that Judy is terrified he'll respond with a self-destructive bravado when that day comes. He could laugh, assure me that he has no such intentions, and that would be the end of it. Yet the idea of asking such a question makes me profoundly uncomfortable, probably because at heart I believe her fears are sensible. I have seen the depths of John's obsession, too.

I decide to ask. A fraction of a second before I do, he starts to talk again.

"You know, in every other kind of thing, two and two is always four," he says, looking straight ahead at the road. "In bullfighting, it never is. Once in a while it might be. But it could be twenty-two. Or anything. There's no logic."

He pauses, then continues.

"I mean, if you study law and go to law school and you have the right kind of personality, you can become a very, very successful lawyer," he says. "If you don't, you can still be a good lawyer. But you can learn all the rules of bullfighting that anyone will teach you or that you can pick up, and you might still never become a good bullfighter or a wealthy bullfighter. You probably won't. And then, someone else can know none of the rules and become a star. Maybe that inconsistency, that unknown factor, is part of the excitement of all this. I don't know. I can tell you one thing: it's certainly part of the frustration."

We continue down the road in silence, John alone with his thoughts, me alone with mine.

■■■

Thirty years ago today Hemingway's Dangerous Summer of 1959 was just beginning. Hemingway crossed the ocean on the *S.S. Constitution,* and by the time he arrived, at the beginning of May, the feria of Sevilla had already ended. Ordóñez and Dominguín hadn't yet fought together. In fact, Dominguín hadn't fought in Spain at all yet that year.

Ordóñez fought in Jérez on the third of May and Dominguín didn't begin his season until May 7, in Oviedo. He didn't fight again for nine days, then appeared in Talavera de la Reina on the 16th, at the same time Ordóñez was fighting in Madrid. Ordóñez was gored and wounded on May 30 in Aranjuez after earning two ears, a tail, and a hoof, and he subsequently missed some days. It was June before he and Dominguín finally appeared in the ring together. That happened in Zaragoza.

There is no Dangerous Summer this year. Instead we have Espartaco versus Litri or Joselito, depending on what week it is, and already, by mid-May, those rivalries appear to be fading, if indeed they ever truly existed. The last word we had on Litri is that he was ill, and Joselito is in his bed recovering. Nobody is waiting breathlessly for either one to return. In Sevilla, with all three matadors at full strength, the feria provided less a rivalry than a coronation for Espartaco. There is nobody fighting bulls right now who is his equal.

Whom else do we have? There is the continued shamelessness of Curro and the fear of Paula. There are maybe a dozen other matadors who are good enough to watch but not good enough to follow anywhere, and then a few better ones, including Manzanares and Ortega Cano and Roberto Domínguez; interesting bullfighters who are capable of highly emotional toreo but are somehow not particularly relevant right now. It may be that none of them fought in Sevilla. We have Paco Ojeda, but he is intransigently retired. And there are the novilleros, Julio Aparicio and Martín Pareja Obregón and Finito de Córdoba and Pepe Luis Martín, but who knows what they will become?

There's no Hemingway celebrating a birthday with a pool party in Málaga, only Michael Wigram and Charles Patrick Scanlan waiting in Madrid, Pleas Campbell back home in Miami, and Joe Distler traveling somewhere. There's no Matt Carney to incite a brawl in a bar and emerge from the chaos grinning. The only constant is John Fulton.

Fulton met Hemingway during that summer of 1959 and saw him

again the following year. The summer after that one, Hemingway died. The two got along well and John believes it is because he reminded Hemingway of Sidney Franklin. When Hemingway was in Spain in the 1930s, he traveled with Franklin. When he returned in 1959, there was John in Sidney's place, young and vigorous, another American bullfighter to remind him of the glorious days of his youth. That's Fulton's theory, anyway.

Fulton and Hemingway spent several days together in Málaga when they first met. They were with Mary Hemingway and Pepe Dominguín, Luis Miguel's brother, and Robert Vavra and several others. Waiting for their car to be brought around outside a restaurant they had a contest to see who could piss highest on a telephone pole, and Hemingway won. John swears there was a trick involved. John was in his mid-twenties, healthy and virile, and thinks he should have beaten Hemingway, but he didn't. Later, when Hemingway was leaving, he shoved some folded-up paper into John's shirt pocket: a cartel for the feria of Málaga with something else inside.

"I thought it was some kind of *recuerdo,* a souvenir," John says. "We said goodbye and when we got out of there I pulled it out. I opened it up and there was a traveler's check for one hundred dollars in there. A hundred dollars, man! I could eat for four months on that in those days. He never said anything about it, he just decided to do something for me which at that time was a tremendous gesture.

Hemingway asked Fulton if there was anything he could do to help his bullfighting career and Fulton told him there was. "Domínguín and Ordóñez are fighting these *mano a manos* all over the place, and every time they fight they need a *sobresaliente,*" John told him. "Maybe Antonio could put me on somewhere." Fulton suggested Ciudad Real, where he was hardly known and had never fought. In the end, Ordóñez and Domínguín did put an American on as *sobresaliente* there, but not Fulton. They chose Ed Hotchner, Hemingway's friend and later his biographer of sorts. Hotchner not only wasn't a full matador, he had never passed a bull in his life; but Ordóñez dressed him in *traje de luz* and readied him for action as a grand joke. They called him El Pecas, meaning "The Freckles," which was Hotchner's nickname. The idea was to let Hotchner think he was the *sobresaliente,* although there was another matador in attendence to actually handle the bulls if that became necessary. "It was absolutely illegal and I do not know how grave the penalties would have been if anyone had spotted Hotch," Hemingway wrote.

It was a wonderful joke for everyone who was in on it, but it wasn't wonderful for John. Thirty years later he is still angry. "Hemingway asked this favor of Ordóñez, and Ordóñez's warped sense of humor was such that, knowing how important it was to me, he would choose a poofy television playwright from New York as *sobresaliente,* not me," he says. "That's the kind of shit Ordóñez was. And Hemingway worshiped him. I saw Hemingway in Ordóñez's room after a great fight in Ronda just like a whimpering little kid. He was sitting next to him, saying, You know, my car is in the garage, I don't know how I'm going to get to your next fight, do you think I could go with the cuadrilla? And Ordóñez is in the bed naked. After the fight he had torn off his clothes and gotten in bed under the sheet and now he was holding court with all of his admirers and Hemingway was sitting there just like a little puppy dog, a whipped puppy dog, waiting for Ordóñez to make arrangements. It was pathetic."

It is impossible to travel through Spain writing a book about bullfighting and not encounter the ghost of Hemingway. He is everywhere. If you can somehow manage to forget that you are following in his footsteps, that he has already written the best book in English on the corrida, that his unadorned style is ideally suited for this matter of death and life and art—even if you do put it out of your mind and try to do your own work you own way—some Spaniard is sure to step up and remind you.

I know now that 1989 will not be another 1959 but will instead be something else. Each season tells a different story, with different heroes in a different style. We don't have Ordóñez and Dominguín fighting but we have others acting out their own dramas, and we'll take from them whatever meaning and emotion we can. My plan now is to see Espartaco with Litri as many times as possible. I want to watch them in small towns and in big cities, fighting the *tremendismo* of Litri's bloodline and the classical toreo of the Maestranza, with the big bulls of Madrid and the pliable animals of the south. I want to see if Litri learns from Espartaco and emerges a better bullfighter, or if, more often than not, he merely manages to look inept by comparison.

The two are supposed to be fighting together in Madrid next week and I plan to be there, and then they will be just outside the capital in Aranjuez with Curro on May 30, the thirtieth anniversary to the day of Ordóñez's goring in that plaza. That is a corrida I have to see, if only for the historical comparison. There are ghosts to follow and ghosts to avoid when you are doing this kind of thing, and you have to know how to pick your spots.

■■■

The bad news comes on the day Litri is supposed to confirm his alternativa in Madrid. The front page of *El Correo* has the story and it makes me fling the paper across the room in disgust: "The matador de toros Miguel Baez Litri will be inactive for at least a month after being diagnosed yesterday in Madrid as having acute hepatitis."

The doctor has prescribed bed rest for four weeks, meaning Litri will miss his fights in San Ysidro and plenty more. He will return, most likely, at the beginning of July, slow and rusty, and maybe get himself back in form by August. But he has already failed in Sevilla, and he will have missed Madrid; anything he does in August or September will be nothing more than preamble for next year. Later there will be talk that Litri's father concocted the illness because he knew his son wasn't ready to fight in Madrid. One of the critics will visit the sickbed just to verify that the hepatitis is real. I don't even consider that now, only that the season has taken another unexpected turn. Just when I figured two and two had finally made four.

Inside the same edition of the newspaper there is a note that Joselito will attempt to keep his Madrid carteles, although his doctors are strongly advising him not to. He and Espartaco are fighting at Las Ventas with Ortega Cano and Cobaleda bulls on June 2. With halfhearted enthusiasm I circle that date in *Toros '92* as a corrida I will likely be attending. I hardly suspect it will turn out to be the bullfight of the year.

6

TO CÓRDOBA
AND MADRID

I'M PLANNING my itinerary for the coming few weeks: here to Madrid, with something along the way. Córdoba is a sensible stop. It has a relatively major feria that starts tomorrow, and I see from *Toros '92* that two of this year's carteles look especially promising: Friday's and Saturday's. From Córdoba I can get to Madrid overnight to see Ruiz Miguel on Sunday, if the railroad strike has been settled. If not, there's always the bus, and I can include a bullfight in Granada. I want to be in Madrid by Monday at the latest to see Manzanares, Manili and Joselito. Such are the machinations of a taurine junkie.

First I have a ticket to the Corpus Cristi corrida Thursday in the Maestranza, a benefit run by the Association of the Press that isn't included in my *abono.* When there is a holiday on a Thursday in Sevilla the next day is called a *puente,* meaning bridge, Friday being the bridge to the weekend. Work ceases for four days and everyone stays out late drinking in the streets.

Thursday afternoon John, Judy and I are sitting together. As expected, she bought him a ticket. He's looking forward to seeing Parada, whose classical style he admires, though most of the talk here has been about the novice Pareja Obregón. For me the primary attraction is Vázquez, whom I haven't seen fight. It isn't surprising, for he doesn't do it much.

215

He only worked eight times last year and hasn't fought at all this year.

Pepe Luis Vázquez, son of the bullfighter, stands at the crossroads of his own troubled and enigmatic career. He is Sevilla's most important and best-known matador, at least until Aparicio takes the alternativa, but that's only because of his ancestry. He's a local celebrity in the bars and at the grocery stores, but few Sevillanos have much expectation for his toreo anymore. For the first time since he took the alternativa in 1981 Vázquez was left off the feria cartels this year, which is ignominious enough, and what's worse, nobody made much of a fuss about it. He was hardly mentioned when the important absences were detailed. His toreo has declined steadily over the course of the decade and it has been a long time since he has shown much of anything at the Maestranza.

There isn't any hostility toward Vázquez; everyone is just mystified as to what happened to him. Plenty of the people in the stands today will know him personally and nearly everyone will at least know someone who does. Judy is buying an apartment in Sevilla after several decades of teaching in California, and the real estate agent happens to be Vázquez's first cousin. He looks just like the matador, the same perfect hair and watery eyes.

It has been clear since the beginning of his career that Pepe Luis will never be the matador his father was. During the 1960s, Pepe Luis Vázquez *padre* performed at a level above Litri *padre* and Julio Aparicio *padre* and even Paco Camino, up there with Ordóñez and Dominguín as *figuras*. Once you get that rarified, it is impossible to say which was the better or more important torero, for it depends on personal taste, but Vázquez was as successful as anybody. He was Sevillano by heritage but also by sensibility, the embodiment of that classically stylish school of toreo. He was skilled at every aspect of the corrida—the cape, the muleta and the sword—and did everything impeccably and with the utmost grace, a taurine Joe DiMaggio.

Now his son is in danger of letting the career—the family business, as it were—slip away. After eight years as a matador, his honeymoon as the son of Pepe Luis Vázquez is over. When he first started, young Pepe Luis had some good afternoons. He wasn't a disaster from the beginning, as was Rafi Camino, or he wouldn't have lasted eight years. The talent seems to have been there but it hasn't surfaced in a while now. Today will be the most visibility he's had since last year's feria here, and it seems incumbent upon him to make the most of it.

Unless, of course, Pepe Luis Vázquez doesn't want to be a bullfighter—and that's a popular theory, too. At the time he took the alternativa there was talk that because he was the son of Pepe Luis and nephew of Manolo, Antonio, Juan and Rafael Vázquez, all bullfighters, he felt the pressure to make his living that way. He didn't have the fortitude to say no; in this case, becoming a matador was the easier route. It doesn't seem to be a profession he felt drawn to on his own, with the determination a bullfighter must have if he is to endure.

Perhaps his way out was to try it, fail, and move on. Perhaps he has become fearful of a goring, a phobia which can arise gradually or suddenly. It happened to Paco Ojeda one afternoon last July, and he walked away from a scheduled bullfight and hasn't fought since. There's also a chance, however slight, that Vázquez has conquered whatever has been ailing him and will re-emerge as a talented bullfighter today. Fulton scoffs at that idea, but I have an open mind.

The bulls are from the Gabriel Rojas ranch, and the novillos, for Pareja Obregón, are Juan Pedro Domecq's. Parada begins with graceful capework and during the pic-ing of the first bull Vázquez comes out to take a *quite* but does nothing. "When Pepe Luis gets a bull that's at all difficult, that isn't exactly the perfect bull he wants, he gets a look like a hurt puppy on his face," says John, frustrated already. "Look at him! I mean, he doesn't exactly inspire confidence."

Parada has a difficult time beginning each series with the muleta because he seems to keep losing the *distancia,* but each time he gets one going he shows his artistry. The music starts in the fourth series and the exit pass that follows is exquisite, the best single pass I've seen him make. He runs into trouble after that but builds a strong sixth series around two terrific passes and in the seventh he shows his *aguantar,* his ability to stay with a bull and bring it past the cloth with sheer willpower. It has slowed up, is barely charging, is just about *aplombado* now and ready to be killed. But he remains in front of it with the muleta, not moving his feet, waiting, waiting, his chest just inches from the horn. He finally incites the charge and then has to repeat the scene again, and then another time, and each time, showing maturity and patience, Parada stays right where he is and succeeds. It is a wonderful thing to see.

■■■

Vázquez waits to meet his first bull under the president's *palco* in the shade, near where we are sitting. He shows the cape twice to the bull and it rushes past without incident, and then he makes an elemental bullfighting error, the mistake of an utter novice. Vázquez somehow gets his body between the bull and the cape, and the bull notices the cape's movement and it charges. The goring is the worst I have ever seen. The bull catches Vázquez in the left leg, lifts him high with the horn, and spills him onto the sand. Much later we learn that the horn had penetrated into the abdomen, causing hemorrhage and shock, but for now all we know is that the wound is grave. Vázquez lies unconscious on the sand and as soon as the bull is distracted he is lifted up and carried directly to the infirmary. From there, he is taken to the hospital for an operation that takes two hours and saves his life.

Every serious goring is a tragic experience, and the feeling you get is like seeing a wreck on the highway. When someone you know is involved it must be immeasurably worse. Nobody in the bullring is paying any attention to Parada, who now has to fight this bull and two more, and they won't remember much of Pareja Obregón and the novillos, either. They are trying to register what they have just seen and first there is silence and then the hum of discussion fills the plaza.

For some reason Pepe Luis *padre* never attends his son's corridas, and his mother, apprehensive about the profession to begin with, is at home in Nervión. But somebody nearby spots Vázquez's brother in the stands and a man to my left points him out. This man knows Pepe Luis, too, and is convinced he was coerced into risking his life for a living. "I know him well," he says. "He never should have been a torero, take it from me. All he ever had was the name, and the name was his curse. He didn't want to be one. It's as if he had to."

I can see several people near me with watery eyes and John has fallen completely silent. But, as always, the bullfight proceeds. Nobody knows if Vázquez is dying or recovering but the four bulls and two novillos must be killed no matter what and Parada and Pareja Obregón are obligated to do it. It happened that way when Paquirri was gored and Yiyo and Manolete and the rest. The ritual must continue until all the bulls are dead.

Outside afterward the talk is only about Vázquez. We stand in front of the main door facing the river and let the streams of people come out of the bullring and we hear that name again and again. We go to the Bodegón and Charles Patrick is there, in town for the corrida. We make plans to meet in Madrid and then I leave, to wander the city and get my mind off bullfighting.

I walk away from the water toward the center of town, the Puerta de Jérez, and then outside the walls of the Alcázar gardens, skirting the Barrio de Santa Cruz and up Menéndez Pelayo, and eventually end up at the Plaza de la Encarnación. Nearby is Sopa de Ganso, a bohemian bar with good music and a clientele that spills out into the streets, but I don't feel like company. I still have my bullfight program with me and my notebook, and when I leaf through the pages I come across something John Fulton had told me a few weeks ago.

"What happens in the bullring is ephemeral," he had said. "It's over. It happens and then it's gone. And so you've got to enjoy it or be bored by it or let it piss you off at that moment. And you may think about it later but the minute you leave the bullring your memory is blurred, whereas you can always go back and see a painting. Bullfighting vanishes. It's the kind of art Leonardo da Vinci warned man not to get involved with."

John was talking about the artistry of bullfighting. I do not think he meant gorings. They seem to stay with you forever if you see a bad enough one, or at least for a long, long time. On the bench in the Plaza de la Encarnación the air is fragrant with the flowers of May and nearby someone is broiling a steak. These are the odors of life, not death—and yet, for months afterward, coming across either one, in a garden or a side street or a backyard grill, I will associate the sensation with Pepe Luis Vázquez and the terrible moment when the bull had him in the air.

I meet friends for a late dinner and drinks. Vázquez is the main topic of conversation, even though I'm the only aficionado at the table. At home I turn on the radio to a local station and listen to the reports. They say that Vázquez is fighting for his life in a local hospital, Sagrado Corazón de Jesús, and that the first night will be the most unpredictable.

Vila, the doctor at the bullring, is on the broadcast. The wound reminds him of the one that killed Paquirri. "Practically identical," he says.

■■■

Vázquez passed a successful night at the clinic, attended by his father and his cuadrilla. His mother reacted badly to the news of the goring and was kept at home. By mid-afternoon, although the prognosis remains very serious, his life appears to be out of danger. I hear this at the train station in Córdoba from someone walking past with a copy of *Toros '92* under his arm; he has heard it on the radio moments earlier. The news seems to travel by word of mouth such as with the assassination of a public figure. And this is for Pepe Luis Vázquez; I can only imagine what it was like for Manolete or Paquirri.

By late afternoon I am back at a bullfight. The bullring in Córdoba is varnished brick, a 1950s suburban look, although this city has a bull-fighting tradition as storied as anywhere save Sevilla, Madrid, Ronda, and one or two other places. On the way here I passed the house where Manolete was born (there is a commemorative plaque), and mounted on the outside of the plaza, near the ticket window, is a shrine to the Four Caliphs of Córdoba: Lagartijo, Guerrita, Machaquito and Manolete. There are bas-relief busts with the names and the dates of their careers.

It is interesting to compare Córdoba's bullfight heritage with Sevilla's, the matadors and the styles that each has produced, but it is all history. Bullfighting has lost its prominence in Córdoba these days. There hasn't been a true *figura* from here in years, not since El Cordobés, which explains the excitement over Finito. Since San Ysidro is going on at the same time, all the most important critics and bull breeders are up there, and the matadors plan their schedule around those cartels. Córdoba gets the second echelon. The seat I have purchased is in the front row of the *gradas* in the shade and costs just two thousand pesetas. It's a steal, because they can no longer fill the bullring if the prices are higher.

There is always the chance of getting something of quality. I see Espartaco cut an ear with a fine left hand and a good kill, and then Emilio Oliva, soporific in Sevilla, gets a wonderful bull and cuts an ear with a faena full of pomp and flash. He wants another ear and doesn't get it, so he takes two vueltas instead. Later Espartaco draws a difficult animal that he finally solves after some difficulty. It is victory enough, and I expect him to set up for the *estocada* and be satisfied with good applause from knowing aficionados. Instead he risks disaster and tries for an ear with a long series of *adornos*. He holds the horn while looking off in the other direction, does three rapid-fire passes from his knees, gazes into the distance for a *manoletina*—anything to please. The *remate* stills the bull and Espartaco kills superbly, almost as well as in Sevilla. The president awards two ears. On his vuelta Espartaco gets a sportcoat, a potted plant and three sweaters, along with the usual flowers and *bota* bags. (The next day there will be an article in the Córdoba newspaper about how the pretty girls always come out to see Espartaco fight and bring all kinds of things to give him. But a potted plant?)

After the corrida I walk with the crowd to a nearby restaurant. There is a porch out front and I find a seat and order some manzanilla wine and watch the commotion. Everyone gets drunk very quickly and soon some teenagers are singing a song that was popular around Spain a few years ago:

> *Yo quiero ser torero, torero yo quiero ser.*
> *Torero, mucho dinero, para gastarlo donde yo quiero.*
> (I want to be a bullfighter, a bullfighter I want to be.
> A bullfighter, much money, to spend where I want.)

John Fusco told me once about a feria in Bilbao and groups of merrymakers that paraded through the streets until dawn singing that song as loud as they could. When he hears it now, it reminds him of that feria, and of having to stay up every night because of the commotion. I smile to myself; my *hostal* is well away from the bullring.

The next day Espartaco, Manili and Fernando Lozano are scheduled in Granada with Torrealtas, but I decide to stay in Córdoba and watch Joselito in his second appearance since his goring. That way I can take the train tonight directly from here. Yesterday Joselito cut three ears in Granada and by all accounts was superb. Today, he's in town with Julio Robles and Rafi Camino—not my favorites, but you never know.

Over breakfast I read in *ABC* that Pepe Luis Vázquez is still under intensive care and his condition is classified as very serious. He will have to undergo another operation because his health has taken a turn for the worse. "His life was in danger from the moment of the *cogida*," says Vila. "It is still in danger, now more than ever." There has been hyperventilation and interabdominal bleeding. The prognosis: very shadowy.

Joselito doesn't seem fearful, a good sign, but he doesn't connect with the crowd, either, and in the end I wish I had gone to Granada. I'll be seeing Joselito soon enough in Madrid and there he'll have everything to prove. Camino is typically terrible, Robles gets cushions thrown at him and Joselito gets silence.

As I've said, this whole business is a gamble. You spend the money and the time and get nothing for it, so the next day you just do it over again. Time flows differently here, a currency to be used to purchase those moments that matter. Packed and ready for the night train to Madrid, where I'll see Ruiz Miguel fight Alonso Moreno bulls tomorrow, I have dinner and carry my bags to the station.

7

THE BLOOMING
OF THE RIVALRY

MADRID is a city formed from
nothing to be the center of all that is Spanish, and it considers itself the
center of bullfighting, too. If you don't believe that Sevilla is where the
most important bullfights in the world take place, you believe they are
in Madrid. There is no third choice.

The bullfight ambience of the two cities is nothing alike and watching
a corrida in Las Ventas is completely distinct from watching one in the
Maestranza. Las Ventas has more than double the seating capacity, and
while some aficionados go each day for the month of San Ysidro and
to all the important corridas before and after, much of the crowd on
any afternoon is there to experience a novelty or a treat or a diversion
and behaves accordingly. At each corrida there are numerous spectators
who will see this fight and no other in that feria and they tend to be
more demanding than in Sevilla, where the plaza is filled with regulars
who will be back the following day and the days after and can wait
with patience for toreo with merit.

If a bull in Las Ventas is recalcitrant or even lame, the matador is
often blamed. If he has the nerve to present himself in Madrid as a
bullfighter, he should be talented enough to turn a difficult bull into a
fighting animal, the sentiment goes.

Madrid's spectators are more like sports fans than devotees of an art.

They want their favorites to succeed and those they have deemed un-
worthy to fail, while in Sevilla the aficionados are pleased to see good
work by anyone. The bigger a *figura* you are, the more difficult it is to
triumph in Madrid. The crowd here enjoys watching an exalted reputation deflated. Aficionados are skeptical of what they have heard and
read; until you prove you can produce great toreo in Las Ventas, they'll
grant you nothing. I have run across Madrileños who freely admit they
have attended a bullfight hoping to be bored, so they can later inform
their provincial friends that the hot bullfighter of the hour, who
triumphed in Valencia or Burgos or Sevilla or wherever, came to the
big time in Madrid and proved a fraud.

A large percentage of the bullfight crowd here loathes Manzanares
because he's erratic and often contrives to torear without putting himself
at risk. Paula is said to hate fighting here. Espartaco has had his troubles
with the public, too, in the past and again this year, and has recently
complained about the atmosphere in the plaza. There are many knowledgeable aficionados at Las Ventas every day, probably just as many as
in Sevilla, but they usually stay silent and applaud only when it is
appropriate. The true aficionados always lose the war to the others, who
like to scream at the toreros.

Because this bullring is so big, there are plenty of cheap seats up high.
On some days these may attract spectators who couldn't afford to buy
a seat in an average plaza, and these are often the worst behaved. On
the other hand, often the most vituperative screaming comes from the
barreras. One section in particular, *tendido* 7, has the reputation as being
the hardest to please in all of bullfighting and the most vulgar and vicious
when aroused.

José Antonio Del Moral and I have talked several times about the
differences between a bullfight in Sevilla and one in Madrid. He's one
of the few experts with a foot in both camps: he learned his toreo in
Las Ventas but lives in Sevilla. He much prefers the ambience of La
Maestranza but agrees that it really isn't a question of better or worse.
There are arguments for both places that make plenty of sense; it all
depends on what you come to a bullfight to see.

Fusco, who also learned his bullfighting here, prefers Madrid because
he says it's closer to the way bullfighting was in the old days. That's
probably true. But I'm in favor of some of the ways in which the spectacle
has evolved. I don't necessarily believe you need huge bulls and absolutely
fearless matadors for a corrida to have validity. Sometimes it seems that

the aficionados here are excessively bloodthirsty. They want to see a bullfighter succeed to the point of apotheosis, and if he can't, the only other noble thing he can do is to die trying.

Wander through the crowd here and you'll find all types of people, at wildly varying levels of *afición*. "Sevilla is, of course, the opposite," says Del Moral. "It's a much smaller plaza and nearly a hundred percent of the people there are good aficionados. There are many *ganaderos* in the plaza, many toreros, many people involved in toreo in one way or another. Therefore they treat the corrida with much more respect."

Does that mean the toreo is more important in the Maestranza? Even Del Moral has to admit it probably doesn't anymore. The *triunfador* of a Sevilla feria would still be something less than a *máxima figura* if he had never succeeded in Madrid, and he'd be paid accordingly. "Success in Madrid carries with it a value that is more transcendent," Del Moral says. "It's worth money. In Sevilla what you earn is prestige. Parada, for example, had great success in his two feria corridas in Sevilla. Now, if he can do the same in Madrid, he'll start commanding some real prices."

■■■

Madrid at seven in the morning is chilly in May. I buy the papers for the short cab ride from the train station to my hotel and learn that the previous day's corrida has been rained out, which is the third time that has happened in a week. This is the rainiest San Ysidro ever, and it is also the most popular: eighteen straight sellouts of the huge bullring.

There's spitting rain and a sky full of heavy clouds as I drag my bags up the steps of my hotel, one of the comfortable and reasonably priced *hostales* on Calle Fuencarral. I have hardly slept on the train from Córdoba so I nap while the rain patters against the roof. By early afternoon the weather is chilly, windy and overcast, but dry. I head to Calle Victoria, where the ticket scalpers in town congregate, to get a *grada* seat.

Not long ago bullfight tickets were easy to obtain at list price all over Spain, and especially in Madrid. Even when interest in the corrida was at its lowest, Sevilla always had ties to the industry, but Madrid fancies itself the most modern city in the country and an up-to-date European capital, and for a time bullfighting didn't fit the image. To an even greater extent than other Spaniards the Madrileños embraced football, rock and roll and modern art and forgot about the bullfight. But the recent surge in its popularity has made San Ysidro the hot ticket in town. Madrileños love to parade up and down the Castellana in the latest fashions or show off new cars, and in the same way they have taken to the bullfight, which is currently *de moda*. This year carteles promoting San Ysidro have been posted in women's clothing stores.

These days a tourist in town during San Ysidro is lucky if he can get a ticket to a good bullfight at three times the printed price. Every cartel in the feria, with the exception of maybe one or two of the novilladas, will be a complete sellout. This renewed interest among the masses is not necessarily good—although in time it may lead to more quality bullfighters—for the aesthetic standard of the corrida has undeniably fallen. The matadors used to play to a smaller but quite knowledgeable audience. Now, newly converted aficionados fill Las Ventas every day and have little idea what they are seeing.

"They almost carried Juan Cuellar out of the Puerta Grande when he didn't deserve an ear on the first bull, and certainly not the second ear they were going to give him," says Fusco when I meet him for lunch. "I was sitting there looking at my *abono*, wondering who I was going to give it to. Because I certainly wasn't going to come back."

Cuellar, a supremely mediocre bullfighter, didn't get that second ear and the honor of what is in Fusco's eyes the greatest bullfight plaza in the world was ultimately saved. But that's one of the few discretions the presidents of Las Ventas have shown of late, according to Fusco. The day before, Espartaco earned what was reportedly an undeserved ear and the ensuing commotion almost caused a riot. That's the danger of increased, and indiscriminate, popularity of the corrida: these people come to the bullring and they want to wave a white handkerchief and see success, just like in the pueblos.

An aficionado in Córdoba once told me: "It's great *ambiente* when Espartaco comes here, because the plaza is always full instead of half-full as usual. But all these pretty young girls come to see him and they have no idea what bullfighting is, and they bring parents or boyfriends or whatever, and this is the one bullfight any of these people are going to see all year. They want to see everything wrapped up into one, and if they don't get it they're disappointed. Well, everything wrapped up into one just doesn't happen in bullfighting."

Tickets on Calle Victoria are reasonable today: only double the list price. The threat of rain has made potential customers wary. If you buy a ticket from a scalper and the fight is called off, you'll only be able to get the printed value of the ticket back from the window at Las Ventas.

And if the bullfight as much as begins, if one bull leaves the toril and is disposed of by a matador and then the rains come, you're out the full price.

Today is cold and windy but it doesn't look as though there will be more rain, so I invest a thousand pesetas in the corrida. Then again, I'm no weatherman. At quarter to six I'm in a bar called Las Clarines up the street from Las Ventas when a downpour begins. It's a hard rain that lasts forty-five minutes. Just when it appears that San Ysidro is about to lose its fourth corrida in a week, the storm disappears as swiftly as it had come.

Las Ventas is a large brick building done in reddish-brown with Arabesque touches. There are Moorish windows and doorways throughout in identical pattern, as if someone had repeatedly forced his way inside with a giant cookie cutter. The plaza is set on a busy corner, but there is a row of greenery along the western edge, hedges and trees, that isolates it from some of the traffic. There are kiosks for newspapers and candy along the street in front, and vendors selling nuts from carts. To the north is the bullfight museum. Las Ventas is a magnificent structure, but not necessarily attractive, and to me its splendor and bulk represent Madrid as aptly as the Maestranza does Sevilla.

Once inside, those with *grada* tickets must walk up several flights of stairs. The plaza has a barrel-tile roof and concrete seating. It is so large that it is forced to use modern amenities not found in most bullrings. There is a public address system here and speakers mounted throughout the plaza. The signboards announcing the name and weight of each bull are the most detailed I have seen. They include the logo of the *ganadería* and the month of birth of the animal.

The sand is wet as the corrida begins. Ruiz Miguel gets a smallish bull with horns wide apart. Through the years he has earned his popularity with *tendido* 7, and he nods to the aficionados there as he begins his faena. His bull is wonderful and the soft sand doesn't seem to bother him at all. He is toreando very truthfully, with no tricks or shortcuts, passing the bull close and *cargando la suerte,* not deviating from the classic repertoire of passes, taking just what the animal will give. There is no music during the faenas at Las Ventas but if there were Ruiz Miguel would have it playing. He seems to kill well but I'm up too high to tell. There is some petition for an ear but not enough; he takes a vuelta.

There have been continued differences of opinion this year between the crowd here and the officials serving as presidents of the bullring.

When Ruiz Miguel doesn't get an ear the president is jeered, most vocally by *tendido* 7. The aficionados realize that there wasn't enough support for one, but the message is: How could you give Espartaco an ear the other day and almost give two to Juan Cuellar and not reward true, unadorned toreo such as this maestro has given us?

Someone near me flashes the horns signal, which is like showing the middle finger only more literal and worse. What it means is that you have the horns of a cuckold; your wife or girlfriend has been sleeping with somebody else. It is easy to do this unknowingly and find yourself in trouble. Similarly, you may emerge from a bullfight with the urge to torear and begin by trying your luck by making phantom passes at cars in the parking lot. Strangely enough, there you are implying the same. If you are a torero, the driver of the vehicle is a bull and therefore wears the horns. The symbolism sounds obscure, but it is a serious matter to many Spaniards.

Rain begins falling again during Tomás Campuzano's faena, and by the time Rafael de la Viña greets his first bull he is forced to fight it in a virtual monsoon. The wind has kicked in and has pink travel-agency handbills sailing high above the sand, caught in a jet stream. The stadium lights come on and de la Viña's suit of lights glistens and then there is a bolt of lightning near enough to elicit a gasp from the crowd. The bull spills the picador and leaves the horse lying in a puddle of mud and it can't be righted. The sand is a sheet of water and de la Viña takes his *zapatillas* off and works the bull in his pink socks, as the traction is better that way. He loses the muleta in the muck and after three *pinchazos* he kills with a *descabello*. There is a delay of fifteen minutes to see what happens to the weather and then the corrida is suspended and we all go home.

Tickets are more expensive the next day for the Torrestrellas with Manzanares, Manili and Joselito. The news of the morning is that Pepe Luis Vázquez appears to be improving. Yesterday he was alert enough to ask for some football information. "How's Betis doing?" he wanted to know—the inquiry of a true Sevillano. The beloved if inept local football club is on the verge of falling into the Second Division of the Spanish League for the first time in years, and it lost again over the weekend. "Betis is a lot worse off than you are," Vázquez's brother told him.

I pay twenty-five hundred pesetas to a scalper, and when I emerge from the Metro I immediately regret my extravagance. Threatening skies loom above: gray opaque clouds all the way west to the horizon. To the east are blue skies and scattered sunshine, but we have already had that weather. The rain is coming.

Manzanares doesn't like his first bull and kills it quickly. *Tendidio* 7 chants "to–re–ro" with sarcasm. Manili begins his capework to a clap of thunder. He's a favorite here for his magnificent faena of a year ago, the finest of that feria, and because he always gives his best effort. He ends a series of verónicas with a lovely stunted little *media,* slapping the cape against his side. Joselito takes a *quite* to good applause and when he takes a bow of acknowledgment the elements punctuate it with a flash of lightning.

Manili has trouble creating a true faena and instead fights the bull fitfully with groups of two and three passes interspersed with inactivity. The thunder and lightning are giving an ominous performance, trading boom and flash every few minutes. Manili takes a long time to profile and kill, and finishes the job after innumerable *descabellos.* Everyone seems somewhat distracted and eager to not be caught with a bull to kill when the rain comes.

It starts moments before Joselito's faena. He shows an isolated good pass in the middle of his first series, and then the bull cuts in on him and he backs away. The jeering starts—for the bull, for the torero, for the weather—and the rain begins to come harder. Joselito lands his sword on his first try in what looks like a good spot and then stands watching, the downpour flattening the hair on his head. The bull strolls toward the barrera as the rain rolls down its flanks, washing the blood away. Finally the bull dies and Joselito runs for shelter.

The corrida resumes after a brief delay, and immediately there is a tremendous thunderclap. Manzanares starts his capework, the rain gets harder, the faena is nonexistent, the kill unmemorable—and after another twenty minutes the corrida is finally suspended. Fusco and I reconvene at Las Clarines and watch Charles Patrick and some Englishmen slowly get drunk as the rain pelts the sidewalk.

■■■

They tell me San Ysidro has never been like this. So much rain is unexpected. To break the soggy monotony I venture to Aranjuez for the corrida there on Tuesday: Curro, Espartaco, and Juan Cuellar, substituting for Litri; but my luck there is no better. There is a huge thunderstorm that lasts half an hour in late afternoon, and although the rain has stopped in plenty of time, the corrida is canceled because the sand is too wet. We later learn that Curro refused to fight; as the senior matador he has the power to make that decision until the corrida starts. "We came here to torear, not to swim," he said, and that was that. A notice is posted rescheduling the cartel for another date, and we wait more than half an hour for refunds while someone is dispatched to open a local bank.

(That corrida was held with the same cartel on a beautiful Thursday afternoon a couple of weeks later. I wasn't there. Espartaco cut three ears and Cuellar two and both of them left on shoulders. That wasn't the big story, though. For the first time since 1981, Curro Romero was seriously gored. It happened on his second bull, a goring in the inner thigh just centimeters from his testicles. The operation at the bullring lasted an hour and a half. After that he was moved to Madrid for further observation. He returned to fight in Badajoz two weeks later, his reputation enhanced.)

Because there hasn't been any good bullfighting to talk about, everyone is still debating the Espartaco controversy of a week ago. In a peculiar way it is helping to fuel a rivalry with Joselito. The corrida they have together on Thursday with Ortega Cano has started to take on epic importance. With each unfulfilling day that passes, the interest in that one increases. If it, too, is rained out, we're all just going to give up and head for sun somewhere.

The details of the feud between Espartaco and much of Madrid's bullfighting public have quickly become known all over Spain. The rest of the country is happy to condemn the capital for alienating the one true *figura* of the day, but here in Madrid the anti-Espartaco sentiment has taken on the proportions of a civic crusade. In truth the controversy is silly and could only have mushroomed into a major incident in the context of something so passionately illogical as bullfighting, fueled by boredom.

Perhaps the faena in question was meritorious and perhaps it wasn't. There is no disputing that a clear majority of the crowd waved white to signify that an ear should be awarded. I have read somewhere that Espartaco actually fell to his knees to plead for an ear and if that's true it's regrettable—but understandable. For Espartaco, pleasing the crowd is a triumph.

Fusco hates that attitude because he believes catering to the masses will eventually bring about clowning matadors and bulls with sawed-off horns and bullfighting that is a parody of the way we know it. This is the influence of Joaquín Vidal of *El País*. A war has started between *Toros '92* and Vidal, insults tossed back and forth between the publications, and Fusco refuses to read *Toros '92* anymore. He says that the critics who write for it don't care if horns are shaved or bulls are drugged or whatever, just as long as Manzanares and Paco Ojeda, if he ever comes back, can do their artwork with the bulls they're given. I tell him that *tendido* 7 starts waving hankies for a change of bull two seconds after it enters the arena if it doesn't weigh six hundred kilos and have horns the size of a mastodon's. This is the type of thing we talk about these days, day and night, over drinks and meals in various parts of the city, there being nothing else of note happening in bullfighting at the moment.

When Espartaco received an ear after what I'll admit sounds like an average faena, *tendido* 7 flipped out. Espartaco held his silence for a day or two but eventually responded in the newspapers, saying that when a torero is playing with his life in order to arouse a crowd it is ignoble to jeer his efforts. "It's not fair," he said in *ABC*. "You can enjoy or not enjoy a torero . . . but he deserves at least minimal respect and consideration." He called for a stop to the loutish behavior of the Las Ventas crowds before their intimidation causes ill-advised risks and serious injury. "If not," he said "they're going to eat us."

Espartaco went so far as to say that he's through fighting in Madrid after this year. But he still has the one cartel on Thursday, and fortuitously it's with Joselito. The two of them were pictured together on the cover of a recent issue of the *ABC* Sunday magazine *Blanco y Negro* with the headline "Espartaco and Joselito: Duel in the Sun." The seven-page article inside, entitled "Bonfire of the Rivalries," all but ignores what happened in Sevilla and does its best to incite yet another competition between the two.

If the Madrileños are predisposed to act kindly toward any torero, it is Joselito. In his first appearance here two years ago he was gored by the biggest bull anyone could remember, nearly seven hundred kilos, which is probably the best thing that could happen to a bullfighter in Las Ventas in terms of future success. Last year he returned to see a banderillero of his caught and killed. He has the Madrid aesthetic and undeniable courage and the local connection and he's a good story: He was raised in abject poverty and spent time in an orphanage, then attended the bullfighting school here on what amounts to a scholarship because he showed so much promise. He became a matador at age sixteen, one of the youngest of the century.

So, suddenly, without any tangible reason why it should have happened, we have all the elements necessary for a classic bullfighting confrontation—except that Joselito still hasn't proved with his toreo that he's worthy of it.

The expectation for his corrida, coupled with the rain and the frustration that it has produced, has driven ticket prices into the realm of the absurd. I discover this on Thursday morning when I visit the three-block-long farmer's market of *reventas* and scalpers along Calle Victoria. As usual, there are groups of men, mostly older and shabbily dressed, standing on the sidewalk among the parked cars. When you pass they mumble at you with various degrees of discretion, asking if you want tickets. Like selling hashish, scalping tickets is illegal in Madrid, but only nominally so.

There are legitimate 20 percent *reventas* on the street but they have been out of tickets for days. Signs are posted in the windows saying that only football tickets and out-of-town bullfights are available. I visit four scalpers and eventually manage to talk one of them down from six thousand pesetas to thirty-five hundred, which is still nearly thirty dollars for a two-dollar ticket.

The weather holds through lunch and into the afternoon, but as I'm walking to the Metro to head for Las Ventas at six o'clock, the sky rumbles. There is a flash of lightning and a thunderstorm starts. This time it isn't rain but hail, and everyone in sight ducks for cover.

8

TRANSCENDENCE

IN THE END THE HAIL is only a meteorological prelude to the storm. This bullfight won't change the course of taurine history, no matter what the outcome. Yet we regard it with the utmost gravity. I can sense the anticipation from the moment I come up the steps of the Metro stop at Las Ventas and discover what I had hoped for: the sky has cleared.

The atmosphere goes beyond the usual sense of excitement for an important corrida. For the first time I have some sense of what Ordóñez and Dominguín must have been like, day after day of this, all over Spain, two of eternity's matadors spurred to ever greater risk by a public that wouldn't accept less.

Compared to that, this is imitation stuff. I'm under no illusion that it is otherwise. Even in the context of today's bullfighting it is certain that there will be other, greater confrontations soon. Perhaps someone will emerge next season, or the one after that, to truly challenge Espartaco. Perhaps it will be Joselito.

For now, however, he remains a neophyte, twenty years of age, lacking some the profundity of a truly mature torero. One corrida cannot change that, no matter what he can accomplish. And while Espartaco is the *máxima figura* of the hour, even his admirers admit he will never rank with the masters. "When the history of toreo is ultimately written," Pepe

Sánchez, the collector of bullfight memorabilia, is fond of saying, "Espartaco won't even be mentioned. Not one line."

But on this forboding second day of June 1989, Joselito against Espartaco is the matter of the moment. We have come to see them compete, a man against a man, one style of bullfighting against another, each matador now representing far more than his own artistry. Chances are the result will be inconclusive, because bullfighting never promises wins and losses. What we should care about is merely that this so-called duel will lead to better toreo. Compared to what we have seen here so far, it's hard to imagine that it won't.

In the end, only two of the afternoon's bulls matter: one called Cordobano, 525 kilos, from the Aguirre Fernández Cobaleda ranch; the other, Macarito, 591 kilos, from the same breeder. Ortega Cano, the third matador of the day, working with one Cobaleda and one Torrealta, has a mediocre afternoon, with the exception of a fine second *estocada*. "I received two bulls that were completely the opposite of my style," he would say later, caught in an emotional vacuum amidst the uproar.

Espartaco's first bull hardly lends itself to artistry, and his fractured faena has much of the crowd whistling. Joselito's first bull is impossibly tiny and built of rags and bones. As soon as it emerges there is a groan from the crowd. *Tendido* 7 calls for its removal—and, amazingly, the bull is removed: lack of good physical condition is the judgment, announced on the public address. In four years of alternativa, this is the best stroke of luck Joselito has had. The substitute, Cordobano, is a superior animal: aggressive, predictable, and with a great capacity to transmit emotion.

It isn't perfect. It doesn't want to begin each series and several times it steps backward to avoid the initial charge. But once Joselito can get it charging each series, he can do what he chooses with it. His celebrated capework is nearly nonexistent in the beginning, but while the picadors are out he makes four smooth passes: feet wondrously still, graceful, sweeping the cape in an arc as though he had time held in abeyance, almost unaware of the bull's existence. It is a first taste of what the public has been yearning for, the first true tug of emotion we've felt here all week.

The faena starts with the left hand, four passes, short and quick and perfect. The bull lingers following the break but then Joselito has a great series, *cargando la suerte,* linking his passes so that it is difficult to tell where one ends and the next begins. The third series starts with the bull even more uncertain, gingerly stepping backward, pawing the dirt. Joselito finally passes it *por bajo* and at once the crowd becomes fevered, aware that something special is taking place. After the rain and the *aplombado* bulls and the *pinchazos,* here is what the aficionados of Madrid have paid their money and come out every day for the past three and a half weeks to see.

The bull is flowing around Joselito's body and every pass brings Olé! Olé! He links four more in the fourth series and then the bull backs up again. The hesitancy of the bull adds just the right amount of grit to the faena, a constant reminder of the work Joselito must do to construct his art.

To start series five he has to pull the bull out of a *querencia* it has made directly below me. And, again, once he has the bull going, it is as if he is fighting it in a dream. He finishes the series by pulling it through a *pase de pecho* to huge applause, showing his valor by staying immobile. He kills *bajo y caída,* low and falling toward the flank, but good enough. There is just about unanimous petition for an ear and just about a unanimous petition for a second, which is awarded. Whatever happens with his second bull, he'll be exiting out the Puerta Grande.

Tomorrow, with everyone distanced from the emotion, chronicles will be written and opinions expressed about the actual merit of the faena, the capework and the kill. The aficionados I talk to, including Fusco, will to a man seem embarrassed that Las Ventas had allowed itself to get carried away in such fashion. The unanimous verdict will be that Joselito probably deserved only a single ear, had the faena been seen dispassionately, as if on film. But on this afternoon, with the sun showing yellow and red from behind the clouds and Joselito taking his vuelta with an ear in each hand, scorekeeping isn't important. Joselito has been given two ears for creating the emotion that is now in the plaza, two ears for finally rising up to fulfill his part of the challenge. What all of us want to see is how Espartaco will respond.

Ortega Cano works his second faena, and then Espartaco steps on the sand to await his bull. As he does, a peculiar sensation overtakes me. I find myself fearful—not for Espartaco, but of another valid faena and the emotion that will be generated by it. Distracted by the rivalry, I hadn't prepared myself for the raw emotion toreo can create. This is how bullfighting is supposed to work—how different from the bloodthirsty exultation many of the uninitiated associate with the spectacle!— yet, what I find myself longing for now is the safety of mediocrity. It is so much easier on the psyche to see an average faena and then, emotionlessly, with a glass of *fino* in hand, dissect the flaws.

Even better, even easier: to fortify yourself in advance with theories and beliefs on how the passes can't be valid—even if they are. *Shaved horns. Pico with the muleta. Not* cargando la suerte. These impediments serve well the emotionally timid, provide protection and distance, for you can't watch a magnificent faena out of the corner of your eye. Valid toreo can often be discomforting, for the truest passes, the most *correct,* not only flip your stomach and dry your mouth but scrape away some of the cynicism hardening around your heart.

Espartaco gets his bull, the weighty Macarito. There is no sign of rain now. There is plenty of sun shining even at 8:30 in the evening.

The bull has huge horns. It spills the horse and then almost spills it again. Joselito takes a *quite* that ends with a good *revolera,* as if to remind Espartaco of the stakes at hand.

When Espartaco starts his faena it's evident even from the *gradas* that he is desperate to succeed. His every step seems impeccable, fortified with an intensity of purpose I have rarely seen. Yet he doesn't succeed at first because his bull is presenting problems. It has a severe buck in its charge and veers dangerously to the left. It also has arrived at the faena far weaker than Joselito's bull had. But none of that matters anymore. Nobody cares about the possible, least of all Espartaco. He merely knows what must be done.

Halfway through the second series the bull stumbles through a *natural* and Espartaco doesn't move a muscle. It chops its horns with nearly every pass and catches the muleta regularly. But Espartaco is linking superbly and gets strong applause after the third series. The fourth is very good. His feet are parallel, not in position to *cargar la suerte,* and yet he manages to pull the bull around his body. By the fifth there are Olés for every pass. The bull is tiring and Espartaco is working very close to it. It charges only a few steps in each direction and he is standing over it, holding his ground. With each pass now there is a tremendous uproar, Espartaco showing his dominion to a plaza full of aficionados, some of whom don't want to see it. But he is making them see it. The clash of wills is palpable, a psychic battle as real as the physical presence of the bull and the man on the sand. It has not been the most artistic of faenas but Espartaco has taken a difficult bull, a dangerous bull, and worked it closely and with an intensity that is communicating itself to the crowd. There can be no mistaking this faena for bullfighting that relies on tricks or adornments. This is pure *lidiar,* solving a bull in the style of Madrid.

He goes in for the kill and pinches, the sword falling off to the left, and sets up again. Time moves slowly. There is absolute clarity in the plaza. Espartaco goes in over the horns and for an instant, a tick of the clock, he and the bull are fused. He is trying for the perfect kill, even though a simple *bajonazo* will assuredly get him an ear and a second mis-thrust will cost him everything.

He pulls his hand away and it is awash in red. He doubles over in pain. He has been gored in the hand and just below the armpit but refuses help until the bull dies. He stands motionless, bleeding, waiting: the bull won't go down. The foot-stamping and yelling resound through the bullring; they threaten to bring down the structure. Two men beside me are hugging each other—for the triumph of Espartaco, the triumph of Joselito, the triumph of emotion over the chill and posture of daily life.

The bull dies and Espartaco exults. Around me is a sea of white, everywhere except in *tendido* 7, where there are only scattered hand-kerchiefs. That section of the bullring was determined not to reward him no matter what he did, and now it refuses to do so—to its detriment. Espartaco gets the ear and then a spontaneous chant begins around the bullring: *"Fuera Siete! Fuera Siete!"* Get out of here. *"Enhorabuena a los aficionados, mis condolencias al 7,"* Fernando Carrasco Moreno would write in *Toros '92* about the faena. "Congratulations to the aficionados, my condolences to 7."

Espartaco has his hand wrapped in gauze as he receives the ear and he walks off under his own power. He will miss ten days, returning for his triumph in Aranjuez. Joselito still has his final bull to fight. He does so with precise capework and then a perfectly good faena, but there is no emotion left to give him. There is silence in the ring as he kills *atravesado.* Joselito is carried out the big door in triumph, while Espartaco has already departed—to the infirmary. The bullring empties its captives out into the sunset.

■■■

Once in Sevilla I had the occasion to have lunch with Robert Vavra, the photographer and writer who for years shared a house with John Fulton and now divides the year between southern California and his Andalusian *finca.* We were talking of bullfighting and the emotions it produces when he described to me a telephone call he had received recently from an old high school classmate.

"It was the prince of our class," Vavra said. "King of the prom, football star, all of that." The man lamented to Vavra that the two of them would never again have it so good as those glorious days back at Hoover High. "That was the apex of his life, those high school days," Vavra told me. "My first impulse after I hung up the phone was to laugh, and then when I thought about it some more I felt bad for him. But now I believe you can't feel bad for a guy like that because he's probably had more highs in his lifetime than most people ever will—being named king of the prom, his football heroics, all that. It just happened that they were all crammed into a small amount of time early in his life, but so what? It wasn't proportional, but it was happiness."

Vavra himself seemed to have once been happier. He said his life has been nearly perfect, but the words came as if he was standing outside them looking at himself. "When I think back at what I did," he said, "sat at a table with Juan Belmonte, went to the beach with Hemingway, it was truly amazing. But now, I don't know." He sighed. "Maybe I'm jaded."

Moments later Vavra paid for the meal and left with alacrity to catch a taxi out on Calle Mateus Gago. I haven't seen him since. But as I sit with Fusco and his friends in the lobby of a Madrid hotel in the evening after Espartaco's triumph, watching the panel discussion about the bullfight that is held there every day of San Ysidro, I remember the conversation. Watching Espartaco land his *estocada* and draw back his blood-covered hand was a reminder that emotion is disproportionate and can't be made to balance on a scale. In the end we will remember the extremes, the highs and the lows. If we're smart, we learn to use the remainder of the time we have as currency to obtain those transcendent moments.

John Fulton is right: the details will soon be forgotten. But the emotion won't be. And that is why I go to bullfights.

That evening I pack my bags for home.

■■■

When I arrive in Sevilla I call John. "Bruce, you didn't hear," he says. He is as happy as a child. "I'm going to be *sobresaliente* again, for Roberto Domínguez in Málaga. He's killing six bulls in the Red Cross benefit. It'll be televised."

The next day, our friend Antonio Vázquez has a novillada in the

Maestranza and John, Judy and I go to watch him. It is a fiasco. The picador manages to lose his pic in the hide of the first bull and needs ten minutes to remove it. By then the fight has degenerated into a comic opera. Antonio's second bull lies flat on the sand and refuses to participate. That night several of us get drunk at the Bar Santa Cruz on the edge of the Barrio and wander up and down the streets, singing songs. "*Yo quiero ser torero . . .*"

On my last afternoon in Sevilla I see Borbujos, the old newspaperman, standing outside the Bar Cairo on Calle Reyes Católicos, holding a glass of water and talking to someone who is nodding furiously. When I approach I can hear the voice: those same lingual contortions that hypnotized me months ago in Utrera.

At a break in the conversation I approach and shake his hand. I tell him I have profited much from the intervening months, increasing my understanding of Spain and the corrida. He looks at me dully, not comprehending, but I don't care. I tell him I expect to see him next year here at the Feria de Abril, with better bulls than ever and the best toreo in the world.

Next year in Sevilla! It happens, never exactly the way we want, but year after year we return to get what we can, the spirituality of a serious thing amidst the insubstantiality of much of life. Sevilla, Lorca's Sevilla, "A city lying in ambush for long rhythms, and it coils them up like labyrinths" . . . and today's Sevilla, not so different: the hard yellow sand of the Maestranza, the history and profundity of the tragedy every day for two weeks and more, and the strange and mysterious and profound effect it has on all of us, seeing Espartaco walking that rocking walk or Curro with the cape folded the size of a napkin or whatever each particular feria has to offer. But always this: A human psyche laid bare, and the courage you need, in a plaza filled with thousands of people, to stand alone with yourself and the truest reality of all, the ubiquitous presence of death.